SO-ASY-597

"SPIRIT AND GOSPEL" IN MARK

"SPIRIT AND GOSPEL" IN MARK

by

M. Robert Mansfield, Ph.D.

HENDRICKSON
PUBLISHERS
PEABODY, MASSACHUSETTS 01961-3473

Copyright © 1987
Hendrickson Publishers, Inc.
P.O. Box 3473
Peabody, MA 01961-3473
All rights reserved.
Printed in the United States of America.

ISBN 0-913573-43-4

276.306
M3/7s

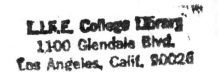
L.I.F.E. College Library
1100 Glendale Blvd.
Los Angeles, Calif. 90026

CONTENTS

035396

ABBREVIATIONS

AUS   *Australian Biblical Review*

CBQ   *Catholic Biblical Quarterly*

ET   *Expository Times*

HTR   *Harvard Theological Review*

Int   *Interpretation*

JBL   *Journal of Biblical Literature*

JBR   *Journal of Bible and Religion*

JR   *Journal of Religion*

JTS   *Journal of Theological Studies*

NovT   *Novum Testamentum*

NTD   Das Neue Testament Deutsch

NTS   *New Testament Studies*

SBL   Society of Biblical Literature

SBLDS   Society of Biblical Literature Dissertation Series

SJT   *Scottish Journal of Theology*

TDNT   *Theological Dictionary of the New Testament*

THNT   Theologischer Handkommentar zum Neuen Testament

ZNW   *Zeitschrift für die neutestamentliche Wissenschaft*

ZTK   *Zeitschrift für Theologie und Kirche*

PREFACE

This work has its ἀρχὴ in NT seminars and my doctoral dissertation in Markan studies supervised by Dr. Leander Keck at Vanderbilt University in the sixties. There I first became aware of the astuteness and adeptness of Mark as a redactor-theologian who composed a new genre called εὐαγγέλιον. At that time numerous scholars were advancing diverse theses, each claiming to provide the key to Mark's theology and Gospel. I too joined the throng and championed the thesis in my budding dissertation that Mark's major purpose was to fashion a soteriology that combined in tension the divine Son as the victor over Satan and the Suffering Servant as the victor over sin. But two events occurred that altered my perspective. First, Professor Eduard Schweizer came as a visiting lecturer and opened new insights into the richness of the form "Gospel" and its role and meaning in Mark's work. Second, Professor James Robinson visited the university and in a private interview performed the painful (to me) service of pointing out the inadequacy of my soteriological thesis in disclosing the major interest of Mark. Subsequently, I began to focus on the concept of "Gospel" itself, and portions of this work are a revised account of material contained in that unpublished manuscript.

My interest in the role of the Spirit in Mark has been engendered in large part by my experiences as a ,professor at Oral Roberts School of Theology. Focus on the presence, power, and gifts of the Holy Spirit is indigenous to the purpose and ethos of the university. This emphasis, combined with my earlier interest in Markan studies, stimulated me to inquire concerning the role of the Spirit in Mark from the perspective of the author and reader. Participation in the Marcan Seminars at the Annual Meetings of the SBL through the years had assisted me in keeping abreast of the newer methodologies of literary, rhetorical, and reader-response criticisms that provided fresh insights into the structure and meaning of the Gospel. Application of these methods as specialized supplements to form and redaction criticisms enabled me to discern that the role of the Spirit in Mark's Gospel is more extensive and prominent than has been recognized previously.

Opportunity to perform diligent research on the topic was provided by the ORU Board of Regents, who granted me a sabbatical leave to study at New College, Edinburgh, Scotland, during the summer-fall of 1984. A first draft of the burden of the manuscript was composed during this period. Professor Hugh Anderson, my former mentor at Duke Divinity School and now professor emeritus at New College, provided many helpful suggestions and encouraging comments in discussions concerning the work, although prior commitments prevented him from reading the completed manuscript. Professor John Drane at Stirling University performed a similar service on my behalf.

As everyone knows, the roles of the Spirit in Luke and John have attracted extensive scholarly attention, but little has been published concerning pneumatology in Mark. It is hoped that this volume will constitute a positive contribution in filling that void and will provoke and produce additional fruitful discussion concerning pneumatology in Mark's Gospel.

To all the above mentioned persons who have assisted me directly and indirectly in the preparation of this manuscript—and to my dear wife Jane who assumed dual parental responsibilities while I was immersed in the project—I give especial thanks.

Oral Roberts School of Theology
May 2, 1986

—1—

INTRODUCTION TO MARK'S GOSPEL

Survey of Past Approaches to Mark

Marxsen's epoch-opening *redaktionsgeschichtliche* analysis[1] of Mark's Gospel surpassed the perspective of the purely *formgeschichtliche* approach and, in the manner of John the Baptist, prepared the way for a stronger approach and appreciation of Mark as a theological work. Marxsen demonstrated conclusively that the evangelist Mark was worthy of the appellation "Author" and was not simply a collector of traditions as Dibelius and Bultmann had assumed. By focusing on permeating themes emphasized by Mark in the Gospel, Marxsen showed that merely tracing the development of originally independent units in the tradition did not suffice to explain the Gospel as a literary whole.

The succeeding decades have brought forth a flood of works in search of the elusive key to the outline and theology of Mark as a literary unit. With respect to the Gospel's outline and form, an incredibly wide variety of models supposedly fashioned or adapted by Mark has been advanced: Numerical symbolism derived from the twelve tribes of Israel (A. Farrar[2]); Lectionary based on the festivals of the Jewish Calendar (P. Carrington[3]); Passover Haggadah (J. Bowman[4]); Jewish-Christian Calendar from New Year (Beginning) to Easter (Passion) (M. D. Goulder[5]); Catechism (G. Schille[6]); Greek tragedy (G. G. Bilezikian[7]); Comedy or Tragicomedy (D. O. Via[8]); Aretalogy (M. Hadas and M. Smith;[9] G. Theissen,[10] with regard to the miracle stories); Biography (C. W. Votaw,[11] C. H. Talbert[12]); Pre-Christian, apocalyptic Jewish writings (H. C. Kee[13]); Canons of rhetorical or dramatic criticism (N. Petersen;[14] D. Rhodes and D. Michie[15]); Parable (J. D. Crossan, J. R. Donahue, W. H. Kelber[16]).

Closely related to the issue of the Gospel's outline and form is the perplexing matter of Mark's purpose and major theological motif. Among the array of leading themes suggested are the following: Awaiting the parousia (W. Marxsen;[17] W. H. Kelber and J. R. Donahue—Jesus is absent until the parousia[18]); Apocalyptic eschatology (H. C. Kee[19]); Soteriology (Conflict with Satan motif: J. M. Robinson;[20] Suffering for forgiveness of sin: E. Best;[21] "Wilderness" as a symbol of God's saving act: U. W. Mauser[22]); Christology (Secret Messiahship: R. H. Lightfoot,[23] T. A. Burkill,[24] M. D. Hooker;[25] Son of God-*Theios Anēr* Motif: P. Vielhauer,[26] H. D. Betz,[27] J. Schreiber[28]); Opposition to false prophets and heresy (T. J. Weeden,[29] L. E. Keck[30]—in use of miracle stories; W. H. Kelber,[31] M. E. Boring[32]); Discipleship (R. P. Meye,[33] E. Schweizer,[34] K. G. Reploh,[35] E. Best[36]); Jesus the Teacher (V. K. Robbins[37]). Finally, H. Räisänen[38] finds no consistent theological perspective and views Mark as a collection of contradictory traditions.

Each contribution has broadened and deepened our understanding of the Second Gospel, but no one theme and thesis has proved adequate to encompass and to explain the fullness of Mark's material and motifs. This is the Achilles' heel of all works that purport to reveal the secret of Mark's major motif and purpose. Gradually a consensus of scholarly opinion has emerged that Mark did not write with one single theological theme in mind. Instead he utilized multiple motifs in both traditional and redactional passages to portray the richness of "Gospel" (Good News) to the hearers and readers in his community (church). His primary purpose was probably more practical than theoretical: to encourage and to build up the faith of the community[39] by utilizing stories and themes stemming from and about the historical Jesus. Through these accounts the Risen Christ in the form of the Spirit still guided and supported his disciples. Although the themes of discipleship, Christology, soteriology, eschatology and parousia, teaching, opposition to heresy, etc., have been rightly recognized by Markan commentators as vital interests of the author, strong disagreement still persists concerning Mark's understanding and prioritizing of these matters in his community context. In one strand of recent studies, the sociological approach and description of Mark's community has provided the point of reference for interpreting and ordering Mark's concerns and themes. A leading example is Kee's[40] analysis and conclusion that Mark was the spokesman for an apocalyptically oriented Christian community on the fringes of society. This sect was influenced by the Qumran community in stressing renunciation and faithful discipleship in expectation of an imminent parousia. Kee's study has not proved persuasive in defining either Mark's situation or major theological interests. The Markan references to context are too meager and general to establish his case. Nor is it clear that Mark is as apocalyptically oriented as Kee suspects. Despite extensive probing, our knowledge of Mark's *Sitz* remains limited and uncertain.

Another strand of contemporary studies[41] has virtually ignored the external context of the author and has focused on the internal narrative world created by the author in telling his story. The internal connections, cues, and clues provided by the narrative itself disclose to the reader the major motifs of the Gospel and the author (although the narrative may take on a life and point of its own independent of the author). Though providing helpful supplementary insights into the nature of the Second Gospel as a literary work, this approach alone is inadequate. Mark did not write in a vacuum divorced from the pressing concerns of fellow Christians in the harsh real world of the first century.

Vernon Robbin's recent work is to be commended for its attempt to utilize both sociological and rhetorical approaches for understanding Mark's structure and theology in a social, cultural, and literary milieu. Less persuasive is his contention that Mark interrelated repetitive, progressive, and conventional forms drawn from biblical-Jewish and Greco-Roman literature and society in comprising a new genre that emphasized discipleship and a teaching-learning cycle.[42] His identification of the literary works from which the forms emanate is not convincing. Robbin's work is suggestive in highlighting from a new perspective motifs that are definitely present; however, he has not established that Mark relied extensively on these particular forms to compose his Gospel and to stress these motifs. For example, the terms and phrases selected in Mark to illustrate the repetitive forms in 1:14–20; 3:7–19; 6:1–13; 8:27–9:1; 10:46–11:11; and 13:1–37 appear to be somewhat arbitrary and do not always constitute true parallels. In addition, it is unwarranted to conclude on the basis of these suspect forms that "the members of this group did not have prestigious social status in major urban centers (but) . . . performed a respected role among people throughout towns and villages in eastern Asia-Minor, Syria, and Palestine."[43] The internal and external evidence is more varied and complex than Robbin's conclusion allows.

The Present Approach to Mark: Methodology and Thesis

A multimethodological approach that coordinates the results of historical, sociological, form and redaction, literary-narrative, and rhetorical reader-response critical methods into a coherent unity seems to us to offer the most promising avenue to understanding Mark's Gospel correctly. Viewed as compatible, not competitive, these methods afford an interlocking chain of insights into Mark's purpose and theology in writing "Gospel" in his community.

The topic or area of investigation of this present work is the concept, role and interrelationship of "Spirit and Gospel" in Mark's drama of Good News. First, we shall consider Mark's concept of "Gospel." We maintain that Mark's major purpose was the proclamation of "Gospel" according to his unique theological understanding of the term.[44] "Gospel" provides the overarching framework and motif within which other themes and concerns are introduced and elucidated. All past efforts to identify the central theological motif of Mark have failed because Mark does not advocate any one specific theological motif per se. He utilizes various themes fraught with theological significance in his portrayal of "Gospel." Mark is not interested in writing a systematic theology or Christology or soteriology. At most he advocates a soteriological understanding of "Gospel" as the past authoritative preaching of Jesus through which the Risen Christ continues to address and to minister to the contemporary readers and community.[45]

C. H. Dodd's contention that the framework of Mark belonged to a form of the primitive kerygma similar to the account in Acts 10:37–41 still has merit. To this skeletal outline Mark inserted a considerable number of isolated pericopes or small units by adopting the procedure of "a compromise between a chronological and a topical order."[46] Although Mark probably adopted and adapted this outline and procedure, he did not do so out of a strong concern about chronological accuracy. Rather, he was interested in representing the kerygma correctly in his community, and this necessitated telling the story of the ministry of Jesus from the perspective of Easter faith. Actually, by the time Mark received the material in the tradition, it had already been heavily "kerygmatized" from the perspective of resurrection faith. Mark made no distinction between material from the historical Jesus and from the early church. It was all simply authoritative "Jesus material" that Mark wove together into a new form of literature called "Gospel," a unique genre.[47]

The above insights lead to a consideration of the role of the Spirit in Mark's Gospel. How does the Risen Christ draw near to the reader of the Gospel? In what form is he present and experienced in and through the Gospel? Certainly for Mark and his readers, the Risen Christ was no longer visible in the form of the historical Jesus nor in a "spiritual body" (cf. 1 Cor 15:44), for Mark is reluctant to include resurrection appearances of the Risen Christ. We maintain that Mark intends the reader to view Jesus as present in the form of the Holy Spirit. Mark, we maintain, wrote in the late 60s after extensive theological reflection on the nature and work of the Holy Spirit had already taken place in Hellenistic Christianity, as evidenced by Paul's letters (e.g. Rom 8:9, 1 Cor 6:11; 15:45)[48] and tradition included later in Luke-Acts. In light of this development Mark presents the Holy Spirit as the divine authority who empowered the preaching (word and act) of the historical Jesus and now gives efficacy to the contemporary preaching of the Risen Christ through the same gospel material attributed to the earthly Jesus. Likewise, the Holy Spirit inspires the reader-disciple's preaching, which should follow the model established by the outline and content of Mark's Gospel. Contrary to the exaggerated, erroneous claims of pneumatic-prophetic ecstatics, who rely upon immediate revelation or signs and wonders from the Spirit for authority, Mark appeals to the Spirit as the guarantor of Gospel which is anchored in traditions preserved from the historical Jesus. Gospel, rightly understood, is the norm of the church's belief and practice.[49]

We contend that "Spirit and Gospel" is a permeating, interlocking concept and theme in Mark in which the function of neither component is fully intelligible apart from the other. Gospel demands the inspiration of the Spirit, past and present; the Spirit guides the Christian community through the medium of Gospel into true discipleship and guards against aberration and heresy.

While the dual nature and orientation of Gospel has been recognized by previous scholars,[50] the concomitant role of the (Holy) Spirit has largely escaped notice. Attention has been focused on Christology and corresponding christological titles in establishing the identity of the Markan Jesus, while the references to Jesus and the Spirit have received only scant passing notice by most redaction critics. C. K. Barrett stated two decades ago, "The fact plainly is that the (Synoptic) Evangelists were not particularly interested in general references to the Spirit, either to emphasize them or to suppress them."[51] This judgment has been modified and corrected with respect to Luke,[52] but it remains the dominant opinion in regard to Mark. Martin Hengel comments in a recent publication, "Nor does the 'Spirit of God' play any decisive part in the Synoptics in relation to Jesus' activities, and when it does appear, the traditions are mostly secondary...."[53] Of course, it is these so-called secondary traditions with which redaction critics are primarily interested in assessing the theology of Mark. Yet in his recent redaction study Ernest Best dismisses the motif with the terse statement, "... the Holy Spirit hardly features in the Gospel."[54]

Contrary to the prevailing perspective, we hold that Mark presupposes and evidences a developed pneumatology which functions as the inseparable correlate and authority for his unique concept of Gospel. His references to the Holy Spirit occur in both redactional passages and in the tradition, and they are both explicit and implicit. Although Mark does not ascribe as extensive a role to the Spirit as Luke does in his *heilsgeschichtliche* portrayal of the life of Jesus (or John in the Paraclete sayings), the rudiments of a "Salvation History" driven by the Holy Spirit are undeniably present in his Gospel. We propose to demonstrate that Mark's pneumatology is more extensive and important in his understanding and proclamation of Gospel than has generally been recognized by Markan scholars.[55]

Procedure

Our *procedure* will be as follows:

(1) We shall identify the references to "Spirit and Gospel" in each major section of Mark according to the divisions determined largely by previous form and redaction critical studies. The overall scope and role of the dual theme in Mark's structure and theology will also be delineated.

(2) Exegesis of explicit redactional additions and activity (e.g., omissions, structuring and ordering of materials) will further clarify the evangelist's use of the motif. This task will occupy a central place in our investigation.

(3) We shall assess the references to "Spirit and Gospel" in the traditions incorporated by the evangelist in his work (e.g., "the Spirit is willing," 14:38). The importance of such references to the evangelist are often difficult to determine precisely; however, it is a legitimate assumption that Mark was in general agreement with his material unless he gives indication to the contrary.

(4) Implicit references to "Spirit and Gospel" in both traditional and redactional passages will be noted and explicated. Mark sometimes uses alternate phraseology and related events to address this same theme; e.g., "The Holy One of God" (1:24) is reminiscent of the One endued with the Holy Spirit (1:8, 10); the feedings are "types" of the Eucharist in which the Spirit is present.

(5) The literary structure and impact of the narrative upon the reader will be considered, particularly in relationship to our theme and thesis. For example, Mark intends the reader to be aware of the present power of the Spirit who supersedes the past story-world of the narrative (16:7).

(6) Correlation between the problems and issues reflected in the Gospel (e.g., false prophets, the time of the parousia-eschaton, lagging discipleship, threat of persecution) and the probable *Sitz im Leben* of Mark will be demonstrated. We shall show how these vital issues in Mark's community affected his understanding of "Spirit and Gospel."

(7) Closely related to the matter of Mark's *Sitz* is the relationship between his Gospel and the theology of Paul, the church at Rome, and Hellenistic Christianity. A concluding chapter will be devoted to this thorny problem in order to buttress our position concerning Mark's view of "Spirit and Gospel" as central, correlated concepts in his theology. We maintain that Mark opposed false prophets and teachings similar to Paul's opponents in Corinth, Thessalonica, and Rome and was familiar with central tenets of Hellenistic Christianity used by Paul in countering erroneous teaching, although his method was different. We contend further that Mark, in accord with Paul and consensus Hellenistic Christianity in the 60s AD, assumed that the Risen Christ and the Holy Spirit were inseparable, if not identical, and that the Spirit legitimized the kerygma. Mark's contribution was to develop a new genre called "Gospel" in which the Risen Christ, through the Holy Spirit, authorized and applied the Jesus traditions to the readers and church in a relevant, direct manner.

(8) A summary of our findings and their implications for related issues in the contemporary church will conclude the study.

Presuppositions

All theological studies and positions involve *presuppositions*. The most important assumptions of which the author is aware for this study are shared by the majority of Markan scholars but are described below for the benefit of the reader.

(1) The priority of Mark. Studies by B. C. Butler,[56] P. Parker,[57] L. Vaganay,[58] W. Farmer,[59] and H. H. Stoldt[60] have reopened the discussion concerning the Synoptic problem and have revived the Griesbach Hypothesis as a possible solution. However, these analyses have succeeded better in identifying weakness in the Four Source Documentary Hypothesis than in constructing a superior alternative position. Until a more convincing positive case is presented, the Lachmann-Streeter[61] citadel of Markan priority still stands intact.

(2) That Mark used sources in a manner analogous to Matthew and Luke is no longer seriously contested by literary-historical critics. The identification of his sources remains uncertain, although many scholars would accept Grant's categories: Reminiscences of Peter, a "Q" collection, a Passion Narrative, a Jewish "Little Apocalypse," a

series of controversy stories, a miracle collection, and a collection of parables of the kingdom.[62] Kelber, Donahue, and others[63] of like mind claim that Mark composed almost freehand the passion narrative *en toto*, but support for their position depends largely upon a speculative, controversial interpretation of Mark's Christology and eschatology. They succeed in drawing attention to Markan redactions and theological motifs in the Passion Narrative but exceed the evidence in denying that a pre-Markan passion narrative existed. Boring has posited that Mark was aware of Q sayings and deliberately omitted them from his Gospel because he was opposed to sayings of the Risen Jesus propounded by Christian prophets.[64] While we applaud Boring's attempts to relate Mark's composition to a plausible *Sitz im Leben*, he is unable to demonstrate that Mark actually did know Q and intentionally omitted logia in the source from his Gospel. Arguments from silence are always tenuous.

(3) The hypothesis of an *Urmarkus* has generally been discredited for three main reasons: (1) Attestation that the Gospel was originally written in Greek,[65] not Aramaic (or Syriac) as most *Urmarkus* theories demand. (2) The insights provided by form and redaction criticism into the growth and development of traditions diminish the possibility or need for an *Urmarkus* to explain the process by which the Gospel came into being. (3) The Q source provides a more convincing solution to the Synoptic problem than an *Urmarkus*, which becomes superfluous. Hence, the originality of Mark's Gospel in essentially its present Greek form is assured.

(4) Mark wrote his Gospel in the mid to late 60s AD, possibly as early as the Neronian persecution, but more likely after the beginning of the Jewish revolt in AD 66 and the siege of Jerusalem in AD 68. The testimonies of Irenaeus and the Anti-Marcionite Prologue, which indicate that Mark wrote after the deaths of Peter and Paul, render a date earlier than AD 64 (Neronian persecution) unlikely. Appeals to internal evidence for dating Mark have focused on references to the destruction of the temple and Mark's eschatology in chapter 13 (Little Apocalypse), and on 14:28, 16:7 ("Galilee"). Brandon claims that the anti-Jewish motif in Mark can best be accounted for by the fall of Jerusalem and the embarrassing situation of Gentile Christians who sought to disentangle Christianity from its Jewish origins.[66] Kelber stresses that the references to "Galilee" depict a Markan community struggling to begin anew by understanding the causes of the "calamity of Jerusalem Christianity" and the destruction of the city.[67]

However, we maintain that the anti-Jewish and "Galilee" motifs, though present, cannot bear the weight placed upon them as determinative for a specific date. They are not dominant interests of Mark that illumine the thrust of Mark's theology in his particular setting.[68] Moreover, it undoubtedly became expedient for Gentile Christians to disassociate themselves from Jewish political aspirations before the actual destruction of Jerusalem. And a new beginning was sought as early as AD 66 by Christians who fled from Jerusalem to Pella.

The years AD 65–72 were characterized by political upheaval in Palestine, threatened persecution of the church, and theological diversity and friction within the church. Mark's Gospel reflects these contextual traits, but we do not possess sufficient evidence to determine a more precise date within this general period. Since, in our opinion the destruction of the temple, while imminent, had not yet occurred, we favor a date shortly before AD 70.

(5) That the author of the Second Gospel was named Mark, the attendant of Peter, is the unbroken testimony of earliest opinion from Papias onward. Was he the same John Mark of Acts and the companion of Barnabas and Paul (Acts 15:37)? Adherents of this view[69] point out that his mother was a resident of Jerusalem and that her house was a rendezvous for Christians in the city (Acts 12:12). Colossians 4:10 implies that he had family connections with the Jews of the Dispersion. Moreover, the Gospel contains material which, it is claimed, could only have been obtained by someone personally acquainted with Peter or other disciples (e.g., call of the disciples 1:16–20; Gethsemane, 14:32–50; Peter's denial, 14:66–72). John Mark qualifies.

Objectors[70] to this position retort that John Mark would not have been as unfamiliar with the geography, customs, and legal procedure of Palestine as the Second Gospel exhibits. Moreover, the editorial parts of the Gospel indicate no close contact with Palestine or Judaism. Mark (Marcus) was a common name among first-century Gentiles; indeed, the Mark of the Second Gospel was not linked with John Mark until the time of Jerome (Hieronymus), and then somewhat tentatively.

In view of incomplete, conflicting evidence it is not possible to identify with certainty the Mark of the Second Gospel. However, his identity is not a crucial concern for our study, though admittedly greater knowledge of his setting and community would assist our understanding of his Gospel. Recent sociological studies indicate that appreciable differences in religious beliefs and customs existed between Galileans and Judeans.[71] Perhaps this accounts for the author's unfamiliarity with Galilean customs and geography. He had no reason or occasion to visit Galilee personally. In the absence of other strong contenders, we consider John Mark of Jerusalem to be the leading candidate for the authorship of the Second Gospel.

(6) We maintain that Rome has the strongest support for the provenance of the Gospel. The traditional arguments in favor of Rome include the following:

A. *External evidence*:[72] Papias' association of Peter and Mark with 1 Peter and Rome; the testimony of other church fathers (e.g., Irenaeus, Clement of Alexandria) who follow Papias and refer to Rome as the place of composition; the inclusion of a non-apostolic gospel in the canon due to the association with Rome.

B. *Internal evidence*:[73] The author's inclusion of Latinisms (e.g., Mk 6:27; 7:4; 15:39, 44, 45), his explanations of Jewish terms (e.g., 7:3–4; 14:36), and his extensive use of the Septuagint rather than the Hebrew text indicate a Gentile provenance; the motifs of complete renunciation and faithful discipleship amid suffering suggest the context of threatened persecution and martyrdom facing Christians in Rome in the 60s AD; the anti-Jewish motif indicates the Gentile bias and provenance of the Gospel; the datings of Mark correspond to Rome's (anti-quartodecimal) observance of the Passion.

In addition to these arguments, we believe that Martin[74] is correct in stressing the Pauline character of Mark. We shall suggest new lines of correspondence between Paul's letters (notably Romans) and Mark based on their compatible concepts of "Spirit and Gospel" in resisting false teaching. (See ch. 5)

(7) As indicated above we believe that prior redaction, literary and reader-response critical studies have demonstrated that Mark is primarily a theological presentation and that the aforementioned methods are the most appropriate and effective for understanding the Gospel correctly as a unified drama of "Good News" addressed to a beleaguered church.

ENDNOTES

CHAPTER 1: INTRODUCTION TO MARK'S GOSPEL

1. W. Marxsen, *Mark the Evangelist* (Nashville: Abingdon Press, 1969), who refined and redirected the methodology of Martin Dibelius, *From Tradition to Gospel* (New York: Charles Scribner's Sons, 1934) and Rudolf Bultmann, *The History of the Synoptic Tradition* (New York: Harper & Row, 1963).
2. A. Farrar, *St. Matthew and St. Mark* (Westminster: Dacre Press, 1954).

3. P. Carrington, *The Primitive Christian Calendar: A Study in the Making of the Marcan Gospel* (London: Cambridge University Press, 1952).
4. J. Bowman, *The Gospel of Mark* (Leiden: E. J. Brill, 1965).
5. M. D. Goulder, *The Evangelist's Calendar* (London: S.P.C.K., 1978).
6. G. Schille, "Bemerkungen zur Formgeschichte des Evangeliums. Rahmen und Aufbau des Markus-Evangelium," *NTS* 4 (1957–58): 1–24.
7. G. G. Bilezikian, *The Liberated Gospel: A Comparison of the Gospel of Mark and Greek Tragedy* (Grand Rapids: Baker Book House, 1977).
8. D. O. Via, *Kerygma and Comedy in the New Testament: A Structuralist Approach to Hermeneutics* (Philadelphia: Fortress Press, 1975).
9. M. L. Hadas and M. Smith, *Heroes and Gods: Spiritual Biographies in Antiquity* (New York: Harper & Row, 1965).
10. G. Theissen, *The First Followers of Jesus: A Sociological Analysis of the Earliest Christianity* (London: SCM Press, 1978), pp. 110–111.
11. C. W. Votaw, *The Gospels and Contemporary Biographies in the Greco-Roman World* (Philadelphia: Fortress Press, 1970).
12. C. H. Talbert, *What Is A Gospel? The Genre of the Canonical Gospels* (Philadelphia: Fortress Press, 1977).
13. H. C. Kee, *Community of the New Age: Studies in Mark's Gospel* (Philadelphia: Westminster Press, 1977), especially Ch. 2.
14. N. Petersen, *Literary Criticism for New Testament Critics* (Philadelphia: Fortress Press, 1978).
15. D. Rhoads and D. Michie, *Mark as Story: An Introduction to the Narrative of a Gospel* (Philadelphia: Fortress Press, 1982).
16. See the contributions in W. H. Kelber, ed., *The Passion in Mark: Studies on Mark 14–16* (Philadelphia: Fortress Press, 1976).
17. Marxsen, *Mark the Evangelist*, passim.
18. J. R. Donahue, "Temple, Trial, and Royal Christology (Mark 14:53–65)," *The Passion in Mark*, p. 78; W. H. Kelber, "Conclusion: From Passion Narrative to Gospel," *The Passion in Mark*, p. 164.
19. Kee, *Community of the New Age*, pp. 169–175.
20. J. M. Robinson, *The Problem of History in Mark* (London: SCM Press, 1957), pp. 27–28, passim.
21. E. Best, *The Temptation and the Passion: The Marcan Soteriology* (Cambridge: Cambridge University Press, 1965), pp. 71, 188–189.
22. U. W. Mauser, *Christ in the Wilderness* (Naperville: Alec R. Allenson, Inc., 1963), pp. 141–142.
23. R. H. Lightfoot, *The Gospel Message of St. Mark* (Oxford: University Press, 1950), pp. 31–47.
24. T. A. Burkill, *Mysterious Revelation: An Examination of the Philosophy of St. Mark's Gospel* (Ithaca: Cornell University Press, 1963), pp. 320–322.
25. M. D. Hooker, *The Son of Man in Mark* (Montreal: McGill University Press, 1967), passim.
26. P. Vielhauer, "Erwägungen zur Christologie des Markusevangeliums," *Zeit und Geschichte*, edited by E. Dinkler (Tübingen: J. C. B. Mohr, 1964), pp. 199–214.
27. H. D. Betz, "Jesus as Divine Man," *Jesus and the Historian*, ed. by T. Trotter (Philadelphia: Westminster Press, 1968).
28. J. Schreiber, *Theologie des Vertrauens* (Hamburg: Furche-Verlag, 1967).

29. T. J. Weeden, *Mark—Traditions in Conflict* (Philadelphia: Fortress Press, 1971), especially pp. 159–168.

30. L. E. Keck, "Mark 3:7–12 and Mark's Christology," *JBL* 84 (1965): 341–58.

31. Kelber, "Conclusion: From Passion Narrative to Gospel," *The Passion in Mark*, pp. 167–168.

32. M. E. Boring, *Sayings of the Risen Jesus* (Cambridge: University Press, 1982).

33. R. P. Meye, *Jesus and the Twelve* (Grand Rapids: Eerdmans Publishing Co., 1968). Cf. also S. Freyne, *The Twelve: Disciples and Apostles* (London: Sheed & Ward, 1968).

34. E. Schweizer, "Anmerkungen zur Theologie des Markus," *Neotestamentica et Patristica*, Supplement to *NovT*, Vol. 6 (Zürich: Zwingli Verlag, 1963), pp. 93–104.

35. K. G. Reploh, *Markus-Lehrer der Gemeinde* (Stuttgart: Katholisches Bibelwerk, 1969).

36. E. Best, *Following Jesus: Discipleship in the Gospel of Mark* (Sheffield: JSOT Press, 1981).

37. V. K. Robbins, *Jesus the Teacher: A Socio-Rhetorical Interpretation of Mark* (Philadelphia: Fortress Press, 1984).

38. H. Räisänen, *Das "Messiasgeheimnis" in Markusevangeliums* (Helsinki: Länsi-Suomi, 1976).

39. E. Best, *Mark: The Gospel as Story* (Edinburgh: T. & T. Clark, 1983).

40. Kee, *Community of the New Age*, esp. ch. 4.

41. Petersen, *Literary Criticism for New Testament Critics*; Rhoads and Michie, *Mark as Story*.

42. Robbins, *Jesus the Teacher*, pp. 197–213. The attempt to identify the literary works from which the forms emanated is not convincing.

43. Ibid., p. 212.

44. P. J. Achtemeier, "He Taught Them Many Things: Reflections on Marcan Christology," *CBQ* 42 (1980): 466, states succinctly and rightly:

> Scholarship is past the point . . . where one needs to justify the statement that Mark had more in mind than a 'simple' objective report of things as they had come to him in the tradition. . . . There are enough indications that Mark had his readers in mind to justify the inference that he is not solely involved in archivistic activity.

45. In essential agreement with Marxsen, *Mark the Evangelist*, p. 131, who states: "In and by his gospel, the Risen Lord re-presents his own life on earth and the goal is that he himself become contemporaneous with his readers in the proclamation." See also Reploh, *Markus-Lehrer der Gemeinde*, who holds a similar position.

46. C. H. Dodd, "The Framework of the Gospel Narrative," *ET* (June 1932); reprinted in *New Testament Studies* (Manchester: University Press, 1954) and quoted by D. E. Nineham, "The Order of Events in St. Mark's Gospel—an Examination of Dr. Dodd's Hypothesis," *Studies in the Gospels*, ed. D. E. Nineham (Oxford: Basil Blackwell, 1955), pp. 223–25, who attempts to refute Dodd's hypothesis by contending that the early church never possessed an outline account of Jesus' ministry. But see Lightfoot, *The Gospel Message of St. Mark*, p. 20, who supports Dodd's position.

47. J. D. Kingsbury, *Proclamation Commentaries: Jesus Christ in Matthew, Mark, and Luke* (Philadelphia: Fortress Press, 1981), p. 30.

48. E. Schweizer, "πνεῦμα," *TDNT* (1968), 6:334, 415–37, and E. E. Ellis, "Christ and Spirit in I Corinthians," *Christ and Spirit in the New Testament*, eds. B. Lindars and Stephen S. Smalley (Cambridge: University Press, 1973), pp. 272–73, who view Christ and the Spirit as virtually identical in the passages.

49. Mark's two major meanings and uses of εὐαγγέλιον are distinguished in this study by the following English forms: (1) gospel—the message, content, and act of the earthly Jesus' past preaching; (2) Gospel—the evangelist's present preaching of Jesus the Risen Christ that is conveyed and authorized by the Holy Spirit through traditional Jesus material. Mark's book was the first complete composition and proclamation of Gospel in this unique dual sense.

50. E.g., Marxsen, Lightfoot, Burkill, Keck, Weeden, Kelber, Boring.

51. C. K. Barrett, *The Holy Spirit and the Gospel Tradition* (London: S.P.C.K., 1966), p. 118.

52. See the index references in J. D. G. Dunn, *Baptism in the Holy Spirit* (Philadelphia: Westminster Press, 1970) and *Jesus and the Spirit* (London: SCM Press, 1975).

53. M. Hengel, *The Charismatic Leader and His Followers* (Edinburgh: T. & T. Clark, 1981), p. 63.

54. Best, *Mark: The Gospel as Story*, p. 77.

55. Hence, we take issue with Best, Ibid., p. 134, who states, "In contrast to John who allows for a continual contemporization of Jesus with his doctrine of a Spirit who leads the church into truth Mark hardly speaks at all of the contemporary work of the Spirit in the church." To the contrary, Mark is remarkably similar to John, though more indirect and subdued in his theological expression.

56. B. C. Butler, *The Originality of St. Matthew* (Cambridge: University Press, 1951).

57. P. Parker, *The Gospel Before Mark* (Chicago: University Press, 1953), and "A Second Look at *The Gospel Before Mark*," *JBL* 100 (1981): 389–413.

58. L. Vaganay, *Le problème synoptique; une hypothèse de travail* (Tournai: Desclée, 1954).

59. W. Farmer, *The Synoptic Problem: A Critical Analysis* (New York: Macmillan Co., 1964). J. J. Collins in his critical review of Farmer's work, *New Testament Abstracts*, Vol. 11 (1966), p. 44, concludes, "his arguments are convincing as long as his basic hypothesis is assumed."

60. H. H. Stoldt, *History and Criticism of the Marcan Hypothesis* (Macon: Mercer University Press; Edinburgh: T. & T. Clark, 1980).

61. B. H. Streeter, *The Four Gospels: A Study of Origins* (London: Macmillan and Co., 1956).

62. F. C. Grant, *The Gospels: Their Origin and Their Growth* (New York: Harper & Brothers, 1957), p. 114f.

63. Kelber, ed., *The Passion in Mark*, includes additional articles by V. K. Robbins, N. Perrin, K. Dewey, T. J. Weeden, and J. D. Crossan.

64. Boring, *Sayings of the Risen Jesus*, pp. 196–203.

65. M. Black, *An Aramaic Approach to the Gospels and Acts* (Oxford: Clarendon Press, 1954), pp. 14–15, who concludes, "The Gospels were written in a predominantly hellenistic environment, and they were written in Greek." (Against C. C. Torrey, *Documents of the Primitive Church* [New

York: Harper & Brothers, 1941], pp. xvii, 2, 3–40, who argues for an Aramaic original.)

66. C. F. Brandon, *The Fall of Jerusalem and the Christian Church* (London: S.P.C.K., 1951), pp. 185–205.

67. W. H. Kelber, *The Kingdom in Mark* (Philadelphia: Fortress Press, 1974), p. 147.

68. L. E. Keck, "Major Book Reviews: Mark and the Passion," *Int* 31 (1977): 432–34.

69. For examples, A. E. J. Rawlinson, *St. Mark* (London: Methuen and Co., 1936), pp. xxx–xxxi; B. H. Branscomb, *The Gospel of Mark* (New York: Harper & Brothers, 1937), p. xxxvii; and V. Taylor, *The Gospel According to Mark* (London, Macmillan & Co., 1959), p. 26.

70. S. Johnson, *The Gospel According to St. Mark* (New York: Harper & Brothers, 1960), pp. 18–19, recounts the evidence.

71. See L. E. Elliot-Binns, *Galilean Christianity* (Chicago: Alec R. Allenson, Inc., 1956) and Kee, *Community of the New Age*, pp. 102–105.

72. Summarized by T. Zahn, *Einleitung in das Neue Testament* (Leipzig: Deichert'sche Verlagsbuchh. Nachf., 1899), pp. 19f., 214f; B. W. Bacon, *Is Mark A Roman Gospel?* (Cambridge: Harvard Univ. Press, 1919), pp. 14–15.

73. Summarized by F. C. Grant, *The Interpreter's Bible: The Gospel According to St. Mark*, (Nashville: Abingdon Press, 1951), 7:633 and D. E. Nineham, *The Gospel of St. Mark* (Baltimore: Penguin Books, 1963), pp. 32–33.

74. R. P. Martin, *Mark: Evangelist and Theologian* (Grand Rapids: Zondervan, 1972), pp. 206–226.

—2—

THE PROLOGUE (MARK 1:1–15)

Extent and Purpose

The Prologue to Mark's Gospel functions like the overture to a symphony. Here the author-evangelist introduces the central themes which he will develop and explicate in the major body of the work. It is generally accepted that in the Prologue the author was able to exercise considerable freedom in arranging traditional materials with editorial additions to convey his own interests and concerns. We purport to show that Mark introduced the motifs of "Spirit and Gospel" as dominant themes in his Prologue which comprises vv. 1–15.

The older Westcott and Hort editions of the Greek text contained a division after v. 8, indicating clearly that they regarded the Prologue to comprise the first 8 verses only.[1] However, in recent decades this view has been overturned. The discussion now revolves around the question whether the Prologue extends through v. 13 or v. 15. Lightfoot opts for the former since vv. 9–13 disclose the identity of the greater "Coming One" foretold by John in vv. 1–8. Together these sections comprise a larger Markan unit that presents John as the forerunner and points to Jesus as the Messiah.[2] Seitz, Kuby, and Keck argue that the Prologue extends through v. 15.[3] Keck presents three pertinent points: (1) εὐαγγέλιον appears in v. 1 and vv. 14–15 as the rubric under which Mark wishes to present his material. For Mark, these verses are part of the same unit. (2) The relationship between John and Jesus is not clarified until vv. 14–15. (3) εὐαγγελ– words were used most often in the Hellenistic world to designate victory. Since no outcome is stated in regard to the test in the wilderness (vv. 12–13), the implication is that the word of triumph in vv. 14–15 completes the episode.

We agree basically with this analysis and defense of the Prologue as a unit extending through v. 15. However, we suggest that Mark followed a "Pattern of Descent" in constructing his Prologue. He begins by affirming Jesus' divinity as the "Son of God" (1:1) and then designates him as the successor of the prophets, represented by John the Baptizer. Finally, in this first level, he is proclaimed the "Coming Mighter One" who will baptize with/in (ἐν) the Holy Spirit (vv. 7–8). Though he touches lightly the realm of history, for Mark he is clearly the transcendent One, a figure of superhuman stature[4] who partakes of deity in a unique way. Indeed, the seeds of preexistence and incarnation are ingrained, though Mark is content to depict Jesus as the mediator between eternity and history, old covenant promise-expectation and new covenant fulfillment-revelation. The suprahistorical, eternal status of Jesus is historicized and concretized in preparation for his soteriological mission in the second level of the Prologue (vv. 9–13). For Mark and his readers it was not enough to proclaim the transcendent authority of Jesus. Rather, assurance that Jesus' authority is present in the world and community is vouchsafed for the reader. With consummate literary skill, Mark prepares the reader for acceptance of an authoritative Jesus who can and will do something about the hopeless plight of humanity by identifying completely with the human situation. The modern question of how a divine Son can be present in human form did not arise for Mark; nor the question of why Jesus had to be baptized, though it had been asked by Matthew's time (Mt 3:14–15). Both the christological kerygma and the practical needs of the Markan church, plagued by internal friction and external oppression, demanded a concrete point of identification of the divine Jesus with the world and human situation. The result was Mark's creation of a narrative structure and world for the reader which has the incredible capacity to depict the baptism and test in the desert as real events of past history which still have efficacy in the present and in the implied future. The gnomic aorist (εὐδόκησα), the continuing present (ἐκβάλλει) and imperfects (ἦν, διηκόνουν) help convey the enduring action of the accounts. This narrative structure and world is consistent with Mark's concept of Gospel, which utilizes historical traditions to re-present Jesus as the authoritative One who continues to act on behalf of his followers.

We view verses 14–15 as redactional, transitional verses which constitute a third level in Mark's Prologue and pattern of descent. Morna Hooker states that "in verse 14 we come down to earth with a bump...,"[5] but we do not think the "bump" occurs until v. 16f when Jesus actually inaugurates his ministry by calling disciples.

Verses 14–15 contain the author's summary of Jesus' major message[6] and retain a general timeless context and quality of victorious authority, new opportunity, and invitation to discipleship applicable both to Jesus' original hearers and to readers-hearers in the ongoing present. As a transitional passage, it points both backward and forward in the narrative. On the one hand, it completes the baptism-testing episode and clarifies the continuity and contrast between John and Jesus. On the other hand, it contains the original call to discipleship which is graphically illustrated in the pericope relating the first event in Jesus' ministry (vv. 16–20). Simultaneously, the passage issues the call to the reader to repent and believe in the good news which has the authoritative, Spirit-filled Son (past and present) at its center and to follow him as faithful disciples. Thereby, the verses function as a transitional passage in a dual sense and complete the vertical pattern of descent (heaven to earth) while bridging the linear gap from past to present (Jesus to Mark). They constitute a fitting conclusion to the Prologue, which is presented under the rubric of εὐαγγέλιον, and truly introduce the body of the Gospel.

Spirit and Gospel

Having established the extent of the Prologue and noted the prevalence of Gospel as a primary theme, let us examine more carefully Mark's understanding of Gospel and the role of the Spirit in relationship to Gospel.

The ἀρχή of Mk 1:1 is anarthrous and indefinite because Mark intends a double meaning by the term. In one sense the "beginning" of the Gospel lies with the appearance and preaching of John, the last of the prophets and the forerunner of the Lord (not Messiah). Although we do not accept Rawlinson's ingenious suggestion[7] that vv. 1 and 4 should be read together, with v. 2 regarded as an interpolation and v. 3 as a parenthesis, the idea is not completely wrong. Verses 2–3 have the function of placing John in the schema of Mark's *Heilsgeschichte* as the premier prophet who echoes but alters Isaiah's and Malachi's prophecies in order to apply them to the coming of Jesus as Lord. "Mark has interpreted the events comprising his "Beginning of the Gospel" in light of Isaiah's promise. . . . it gives the reader the evangelist's perspective for interpreting the events as indicative of the eschatological moment promised by Isaiah."[8] Thereby, the Gospel is legitimized as the fulfillment of Scripture and successor to Torah.

In a second sense, the term ἀρχή means "source" and refers to the authoritative origin of the Gospel which lies behind John in the sacred prophetic word of Scripture. Indeed, a subtle reference to Gen. 1:1 may be intended, implying that the Gospel is grounded in the very schema and power of God's creative word.[9] Although the verse could conceivably serve as a title or superscription to the Gospel, we view it as thematically linked with the following material and as an integral part of the Prologue.

The emphasis falls not on ἀρχή but on the beginning and source of εὐαγγέλιον, linked with the preaching of John and ultimately with Scripture and Yahweh. This Gospel which "begins" with John's preaching expands with eschatological intensity in Jesus' preaching (1:14–15) and continues to spread in the preaching of the church (13:10; 14:9). "In this manner he (Mark) designates the entire period beginning with John and continuing in the world-wide church as a special salvation time."[10]

The genitive Ἰησοῦ Χριστοῦ is best classified as a "general genitive"[11] since neither the objective or subjective function can be omitted without neglecting a part of its value. The εὐαγγέλιον is the content of Jesus' preaching (subjective genitive) which Mark presents, but it is also the evangelist's proclamation of Jesus Christ (objective genitive) as the Spirit-filled Son who continues to address his followers through this preaching.

The precise connotation of the objective genitive is disputed. Some scholars (e.g., Reploh, Keck, Weeden) hold that Mark regarded the Gospel and Jesus to be virtually identical but that "the Marcan preaching of the gospel does not make Jesus present in any real sense."[12] Others (e.g., Schiewind, Marxsen, Reumann) maintain that "he who in Galilee proclaimed the gospel is now present in the gospel his disciples preach."[13] The correct interpretation cannot be determined on the basis of linguistic and grammatical factors. Only a consideration of Mark's purpose and major motifs in his setting, as reflected in his work, can establish the fullness of the meaning of "Gospel of Jesus Christ." We believe that Mark's awareness of the presence of the Holy Spirit to empower Jesus (1:9–11) and Mark's own stress on preaching of the Gospel (1:1, 14–15; 13:11) through use of the Jesus material demands the second interpretation. This position is strengthened further by the realization that Mark's concept of Gospel (content and authority) was shaped in part by the challenge of ecstatic pneumatic prophets who appealed directly to the revelation of the Spirit of Christ for truth and authority in the church (cf. 13:10–11, 22).[14] Mark also knows the presence and power of the Risen Christ in the form of the Holy Spirit (1:8, 3:29, 12:36, 13:11, 16:7) but seeks to control the unbridled claims of pneumatic prophets by insisting that revelatory truth is provided by "Gospel" in which the Spirit encounters readers and the church through the traditions stemming from the Spirit-filled Jesus of Nazareth.

Titles of Jesus

Mark presents Jesus in the Prologue as Christ (Messiah), Son of God, Beloved Son, Stronger One, Lord, and possibly Servant of God—a variable array of titles—but he is first and foremost the One endowed with the Holy Spirit. In other words, Mark employs multiple titles to convey various aspects of Jesus' authority and mission (including Son of Man, which has a special prominence, and even Son of David, 10:47), but they are all undergirded and superseded by Mark's and the reader's awareness that Jesus is the Spirit-filled One who is now experienced in the person of the Holy Spirit. Mark and his community were well aware of the presence and role of the Holy Spirit as evidenced by four specific sayings (1:8; 3:29; 12:36; 13:11) referring to the Holy Spirit in his Gospel and by numerous implicit references (e.g., 1:24; 14:28, 38; and 16:7 with 1:8). The Holy Spirit as the continuation of Jesus' activity and authority gave vitality to the church. However, ironically this undisputed authority provided false prophets (13:22) their opportunity to gain a following by their claim to possess immediate superior gifts bestowed by the Risen Christ = Holy Spirit. Mark was faced with a difficulty. He in no way wanted to reject or to diminish the present authority of the Holy Spirit. In fact, he probably functioned as a "charismatic prophet-teacher" himself in the community. Based on his experience of the Spirit and awareness of the fullness of the Gospel, Mark sought to correct erroneous preaching and practices in the church. Mark's approach and solution was to offer an alternative understanding of the role of the Spirit. The Holy Spirit legitimizes the "Gospel" molded from traditions stemming from Jesus. However, Mark had to overcome a limitation. His traditions from and about the historical Jesus contained no references to the Holy Spirit in the developed post-Pauline understanding of Hellenistic Christianity in the late 60s. Mark's inspired solution was as follows: He accepted all the christological titles in the traditional materials as useful in expressing the identity and mission of Jesus,[15] and he subordinated them to his redactional insertion of the "Holy Spirit" as the basis of Jesus' identity and authority. Mark viewed some titles, especially "Son of God" and "Son of Man," to be more helpful than others due to the connotations attached to them by his readers and community. Yet, all were inadequate[16] for conveying the ultimate source of Jesus' authority and his identity in proclaiming the Gospel extending from Nazareth to all nations, from the ἀρχή to the Eschaton. This ultimate authority is directly identified as the Holy Spirit three times (1:8, 10, 12) in the high points in the Prologue and is clearly the authenticating source of power for Jesus' (and Mark's) preaching of Gospel in 1:14–15. Here in the Prologue Mark had the greatest freedom to convey his own theological convictions, and his redactional spotlight focuses on the Holy Spirit as the supreme authority for Jesus and the Gospel.

In Mk 1:1, χριστός is no longer a title but a proper name introduced by Mark. The appellation occurs seven times in the Gospel and seems to be regarded by Mark as either a proper name or as a venerable but nebulous Christian title only vaguely associated with the Hebrew "Messiah" and requiring reinterpretation (e.g., 8:29f, 13:21f).[17] Mark neither denies the title nor embraces it unreservedly. It retains connotations of dignity but in itself tells us little about Mark's Christology. Even if it retains vestiges of the Jewish concept of מָשִׁיחַ (Messiah), Nils Dahl reminds us that "messianic expectations and use of traditional messianic texts . . . were far more fluid than has previously been assumed."[18] This insight suggests that the concept of "messiahship" in Mark is an extremely general notion without specific meaning. It is more a modern scholars' category to designate Jesus' fulfillment of diverse Jewish prophecies or Jewish-Gentile hopes in keeping with the christological-soteriological theses of commentators than a consistent title of importance to Mark. We must look to the Holy Spirit to discover Mark's view of Jesus' identity and authority.

The title Son of God in 1:1, supported by strong manuscript testimony[19] and Mark's fondness for it (or "Son") at structurally and theologically strategic junctures in his Gospel—beginning (1:1, 11), middle (9:7), end (15:39)—may be accepted as part of the original text.

Unquestionably Mark preferred the "Son of God" title to "Messiah." For Gentile Christians the former title expressed a high Christology in which Jesus was invested with divine traits of *Theios Anēr*. Bultmann was convinced that the *Theios Anēr* concept and figure was introduced into Hellenistic Christianity under the title Son of God from the general meaning of the concept in the Hellenistic environment and methodology with support from Psalm 2.[20] And D. Georgi and S. Schulz assert that "Mark to all intent and purposes adopted the Hellenistic divine-man Christology he has received from the tradition. . . ."[21] L. E. Keck, H. D. Betz, M. Smith, and T. J. Weeden reject the idea that Mark himself introduced *Theios Anēr* Christology into his Gospel and maintain that it was already embodied in the material of his tradition. "On the contrary, Mark has corrected and counteracted that christology of glory by his own presentation of the suffering Christ. . . ."[22]

The whole discussion of the status of the *Theios Anēr* concept and its relationship to the "Son of God" title and Christology has been challenged by the studies[23] of the philologist Von Martitz and by O. Betz, D. Tiede and C. Holladay. Von Martitz and Betz question whether the concept of a divine man ever existed in Hellenistic Judaism; or if so, whether we have the sources to reconstruct it. Von Martitz states that *Theios Anēr* in the pre-Christian era never was a "technical term" or "fixed expression." "But if this is the case, it also follows that neither could 'Son of God' have been a title by which the 'divine man' was known."[24] Tiede concludes that the concept of the "divine man" must be understood as a "comprehensive rubric, encompassing occasionally opposing elements . . . a conceptual umbrella," not a fixed concept or established norm.[25] Holladay's studies substantiate this conclusion, terming *Theios Anēr* "a fluid category" to be used with caution.[26]

The import of these insights is plain. Prior efforts to explain the "Son of God" title and hence Mark's theology by examining Hellenistic or Jewish sources which contain references to a *Theios Anēr* have paid meager dividends. The "Son of God" title may have been linked with *Theios Anēr* in a general way that made the title a strong, authoritative term in Mark's Gentile or Jewish-Gentile community. Mark found it a useful title to designate Jesus as a divine figure, but he was likely aware of its limitations and dangers too, due to its association with the fluid, non-Christian *Theios Anēr* category. Hence, he does not permit the title to stand as an adequate basis and explanation of Jesus' and the Gospel's authority. It is supplemented by a reference to the Holy Spirit as the source and bestower of Jesus' sonship and authority.

Apart from association with the *Theios Anēr* concept, the Son of God title had affinities with OT passages such as 2 Sam 7:14 and Ps 2:7. These passages depict a special relationship between Yahweh and his anointed king which the early church probably applied to Jesus in describing his unique filial relationship to God.[27] Matthew Black and Joseph Fitzmyer have examined fragments in the literature of Qumran which indicate "that being 'God's Son' was one of the distinguishing marks of the Messiah in pre-Christian Judaism."[28] The heightening of the "Son of God" title to exceed traits of piousness and obedience and to assume traits of divine endowment had likely already begun in pre-Christian sectarian

Judaism. But it is quite unlikely that this was the major influence on the development and intelligibility of the title in Hellenistic Christianity. For Mark, writing for a primarily Gentile church, the title "Son of God" conveyed the qualities of supernatural power with uncompromising obedience that were in accord with his purposes. But the pagan, mythological residue had to be combatted. The term, along with Jesus, had to be baptized by the Spirit, and this is precisely what Mark accomplishes at 1:9–11.

The Role of John

It has often been assumed that a major intent of Mark in 1:1–8 was to identify John with Elijah as the forerunner of the Messiah.[29] By placing the baptism pericope next in his account, Mark structured the obvious inference: Jesus is the long-awaited Messiah.

This interpretation is based on the popular assumption that Mark was vitally interested in presenting Jesus as the Messiah. To the contrary, we have suggested that "Messiah" was an ambiguous title that Mark did not find fully appropriate for Jesus. By the first century AD it was applied to nationalistic leaders and supernatural deliverers alike. Both usages were subject to misunderstanding and only a step away from heresy (8:27–28; 13:21–22). "Messiah" was not a totally wrong title or objectionable to the extent that Mark felt it necessary to delete it from the traditional material, but he made certain that his readers grasped that Jesus was more than "Messiah" (8:28–32; 12:35–37).

J. H. Hughes has contended that there is no reliable pre-Christian evidence for the belief that Elijah was to be the forerunner of the Messiah.[30] Nor, according to Best, was there any expectation of the Spirit as the gift of the Messiah.[31] Rather, the prevailing belief in the eschatological expectations of the Jewish people was that Yahweh himself would intervene in history to establish his kingdom, and Elijah was regarded as his forerunner (preserved in Lk 1:17). An outpouring of the Spirit was expected to accompany the coming of Yahweh in the last days (Joel 2:28f; Isa 44:3; Ezk 36:26f; T Levi 18). This accounts for the quote in Mk 1:2–3, derived from Mal 3:1 (augmented by Ex 23:20) and Isa 40:3. The attributing of the Mal 3:1 passage to Isaiah is peculiar. Perhaps Mark simply made a blunder, or possibly he was drawing from a collection of church sayings in which a passage from Malachi followed one from Isaiah. Most likely Mark's interest was focused on the theological significance of the passages, and the OT sources were secondary, with the result that the erroneous reference went unnoticed. Or possibly everyone realized the error, knew the correct source, and were not disturbed by a minor discrepancy. In either instance, Mark's or the church's redaction of the original passages[32] had the effect of identifying John with Elijah's role and making him the forerunner of Jesus as κύριος, not a royal Davidic Messiah.[33] In this manner the way was prepared for confessing Jesus as the divine, Spirit-filled Lord who will initiate God's kingly rule. Thus, Mark's interests in the pericope are twofold: (1) The Gospel is part of a divine plan which has its ἀρχή in OT prophecy and in John's role as Elijah. (2) Via the Holy Spirit, Jesus is linked with God in a close, intimate way as the One who will establish the kingdom through his preaching of Gospel. Since for Mark κύριος was a title for the resurrected, exalted Christ, the living Lord as Spirit still addresses his church through Mark's Gospel.

Mark is not interested in John's message, but in his role. Some commentators suggest that the description of John's clothing and habits in v. 6 suffice only to identify him as a prophet—the last of the prophets before the era of the kingdom. But the close parallel between 1:6 and the description of Elijah in 2 Kgs 1:8 is striking. And Mk 6:15 and 9:11–13 appear to link John with Elijah. On the Mount of Transfiguration, Elijah likely represents the prophetic movement, so that the continuity and contrast between John as Elijah and Jesus as the greater One who fulfills prophecy is maintained. The "fulfillment of prophecy" theme is present, but does not exhaust the significance of John depicted as Elijah.

The way has been prepared theologically and dramatically for the focal announcement by John, acting as Elijah, the premier prophet who was expected to announce the advent of God himself to establish his kingdom. Instead, John announces that the Coming Stronger One, identified immediately as Jesus, will baptize with the Holy Spirit, which implies of course, that he possesses the Holy Spirit. For Mark, Jesus' experience of the Holy Spirit was not a temporary inspiration or inrush of power for a specific task such as the prophets experienced. Jesus was permanently endowed with the Spirit, linking him with the divine nature and heilsgeschichtliche plan of God. The Spirit is the source of his authority, undergirding and supplementing every other christological title. The designations Christ, Son of God, and Lord already mentioned in the Prologue, and those to follow in the body of the Gospel, find their legitimation in varying degrees of importance by virtue of the announcement that Jesus is one with the Holy Spirit. Hence, in a sense, the expectations of Yahweh's coming, aroused by John (alias Elijah), have not been disappointed. He has come in the presence of the Spirit upon Jesus, who immediately launches the kingdom through the preaching of gospel. Since Mark has committed himself to a hermeneutic and form which presents the Risen Christ primarily through traditions from or about the earthly Jesus, he is not free to write a treatise (or letter) expounding his view of the Holy Spirit. Doubtless he could assume knowledge on the part of his readers that is obscure to us today. However, the appearance of four logia, in addition to other oblique references which reflect redactional traits in speaking of the Holy Spirit in an obvious post-Easter understanding, is strong testimony to Mark's interest in the motif. Moreover, he spaces and places these sayings skillfully. The climatic character of the logion specifying the identity and nature of Jesus and his authority in the Prologue has already been described. In the pericopes which follow, this authority from the Spirit will be demonstrated in Jesus' conflict with Satan, matching Holy Spirit against demonic spirits.

Exactly what Mark's concept of the Holy Spirit was, we are unable to determine. We cannot extensively rely upon Luke's and John's later material; although, since we must allow time for development of their traditions, we can assume that some of their concepts were familiar to Mark. Paul, of course, is earlier and reflects a developed understanding of the nature and role of the Holy Spirit, though he does not yet posit an ontological trinitarian view. Similarly, we cannot assume direct dependence upon Paul,[34] though indirect influence (through Rome) from a common Hellenistic Christianity is plausible.[35] We can determine with confidence that Mark has an exalted view of the Holy Spirit and gives the concept a prominent place in his work as the bestower of authority to Jesus and the Gospel, past and present. He undoubtedly assumed additional knowledge by readers that was unnecessary to relate in his concept and composition of Gospel.

The Baptist's prophetic declaration at Mk 1:7–8 raises an additional question with respect to Mark's meaning. When is the promise fulfilled? Taylor suggests that Mark's form and meaning has been influenced by the Christian practice of baptism.[36] Does Mark expect the reader to conclude that Christian baptism is the rite that fulfills the Baptist's promise? This appears to have been Paul's (e.g., 1 Cor 12:13) and possibly Luke's view (e.g., Acts 2:38, 19:5–6 although Luke does not restrict the reception of the Holy Spirit to the rite of water baptism—cf. Acts 8:12–17). But we cannot automatically assume that this is Mark's interest also in 1:8. First, he has done nothing by way of redaction to draw attention to this locus. Second, Mk 10:38f refers to baptism, not as a rite, but in a more symbolical way as the acceptance of a role of suffering and death,[37] a major Markan motif. Mark's stress seems to be on the Holy Spirit as the bestower of power for mission, not on baptism as the locus and mode of reception. Thus, we reject the notion that Mark designated the rite of baptism as the fulfillment of the promise.

Does the promise point to Pentecost? Barrett describes this as an "attractive conjecture,"[38] but we cannot be certain that Mark knew of the day of Pentecost described in Acts 2. It is more likely that Mark considers baptism with the Spirit to belong in a general manner to the period after the resurrection. As Hooker states, "Possibly Christian experience of the Spirit was so much a present experience for Mark and his first readers that an account of its origin seemed unnecessary."[39]

The absence of an advent of fulfillment signifies for Donahue that Mark did not think the promise was fulfilled.[40] Donahue adopts the radical position of Weeden and Kelber that for Mark, Jesus was totally absent from the resurrection to the awaited parousia. But as Petersen points out, the fulfillment of so many predictions (e.g., the passion predictions and others in 14:1–16:8) lead the readers to expect the others that have not come to pass in plotted time will be fulfilled in story time.[41] Moreover, the very presence of the Holy Spirit logia in the Gospel is evidence of Mark's awareness that the promise already had been fulfilled in the church. Believers experienced the presence and power of the Holy Spirit following the resurrection. Mark did not wish to focus on a past Pentecost, even if he knew of such an event, or to restrict the Holy Spirit to the rite of water baptism. The Holy Spirit conveyed Christ through the Gospel rightly presented and understood. His residence in the church via its Gospel is Mark's "word . . . still pregnant with promise" to the reader.[42]

Baptism in the Spirit

Mark has prepared so skillfully and thoroughly for the baptism of Jesus by the Spirit that the climatic event is almost anticlimatic for the reader. Yet, Mark regards it as a central event in the story-world of his Gospel which addresses the reader in his world of conflict and confusion. "From baptism and its attendant vision onwards Mark's story regards Jesus as under the continual influence and direction of the divine Spirit, and for his readers τὸ πνεῦμα was already sufficiently definite and intelligible without qualification."[43]

Mark employed traditional material based on a historical event. Bultmann[44] described the narrative as a "Faith-Legend" and

Dibelius[45] classified it a "myth"; however, in view of the difficulty that Jesus' baptism caused the church by implying Jesus' sinfulness and submission to John[46] (cf. Mt 3:14–15), their evaluations should not obscure the essential historicity of the account. Mark's redactional activity is confined primarily to integrating the account into his Prologue in a pivotal manner that discloses his own perspective.

Mark relates that Jesus came from Nazareth of Galilee (1:9). This is the first mention of "Galilee," a term which Marxsen and many others since have viewed as invested with theological significance by Mark. It is likely that Mark includes it here at the initial appearance of Jesus in preparation for the resurrection appearance announced at 14:28 and 16:7. While Marxsen may exaggerate in stating, "Where Jesus worked, there is Galilee,"[47] the parallel is not fortuitous between Jesus from Nazareth in Galilee, baptized in/with (ἐν) the Holy Spirit in 1:9–11, and Jesus who goes before and awaits his disciples in Galilee (16:7) to baptize them with the Holy Spirit in fulfillment of the promise in 1:8. Indeed, it is the continuing activity and empowerment of the Holy Spirit that establishes the parallel and fills "Galilee" with a significance that surpasses geography. Moreover, the disciples referred to in 16:7 are not confined to the Twelve but encompass Mark's readers and community.

It has often been claimed that the message of the heavenly voice (1:11) is based on a combination of Isa 42:1 and Ps 2:7 interpreted messianically.[48] Typically Barrett holds that Jesus was adopted as Son and elevated to the throne of David as the Messiah, corresponding to the pattern of enthronement of an Israelite King. This is inferred by Barrett from the allusion to Ps 2:7. The allusion to Isaiah 42 declares that Jesus the Son is designated the Servant of God, and the gift of the Spirit equips him for the performance of his service.[49]

With respect to the second reference Jeremias has presented several arguments in support of παῖς (LXX, Isa 42:1) standing behind the Markan text and expressing the real intent of the author.[50] Jeremias' case is problematic. Most dubious is Jeremias' contention that although the author wrote υἱός, παῖς was his original intent. If Mark had been interested in emphasizing Jesus as the Servant here, he had an excellent opportunity to make the connection evident. Best's comment is apropos, "Mark . . . has done nothing to ensure an obvious connection with the Servant."[51] Indeed, H. Anderson denies that Mk 1:11 refers to Isa 42:1 at all. The language is not the same, and there are many OT passages in which the gift of the Spirit is not connected with the Servant (e.g., Isa 11:2; 61:1).

It is by no means certain either that "beloved" in Mk 1:11 echoes the "Chosen" recipient of divine favor in Isa 42:1. "Beloved" may denote "only" or "only-begotten" as the key trait that constitutes the uniqueness of Jesus' Sonship.[52] To these remarks may be added the observation that the Servant in Isaiah 42 does not suffer. Not all Servant passages in Isaiah embody a "suffering" Servant concept, a point often overlooked by commentators anxious to link the Suffering Servant with Jesus in the Prologue. We would grant that Mark may have been aware of the Servant of Isaiah 42 and regarded the concept as congenial to his viewpoint; however, no direct dependence upon or heightening of the Servant role is evident in the passage.

The contention that the "beloved Son" in Mk 1:11 refers to the messianic king adopted as "Son" in Ps 2:7 is equally speculative. First, the king in Ps 2:7 is anointed by God for leadership, not elevated to an exalted messianic office. Second, "beloved" (ἀγαπητός) is not strictly identical with "begotten" (Heb., יְלִד; LXX, γεγέννηκα). Third, the common term "Son" is too brief and the meanings between Isaiah's and Mark's cultures too diverse to admit any direct correspondence. We conclude, then, that Mark does not allude specifically to Ps 2:7 and/or Isa 42:1 for his understanding for Jesus' identity. Even if a correspondence lay behind the text in the complex history of the tradition,[53] this no longer illumines Mark's interests. Instead, we suggest that Mark was influenced by general religious and philosophical concepts of Hellenistic culture which allowed him to think of the "objective" reality of the Spirit endowing Jesus with divine power for ministry. Two emphases emerge: one, the descent of the Spirit indicates that the days of Spirit famine (since the time of Malachi) are over. The Spirit is active again to fulfill the prophetic promises and to usher in the eschatological kingdom.[54] Two, Mark regards the episode as a "divine epiphany (which) reveals the dimension in which everything told about Jesus must be viewed."[55] He is the *Spirit-filled* Son, possessing the very nature and authority of God himself for the benefit of the Christian disciple and community. As Hahn recognizes, "the bestower of Spirit is the central point of the entire baptism narrative.... This distinguishes him qualitatively from all others and it is said to be precisely in this way that he is Son of God."[56] In other words, the Son or Son of God was a familiar title used by Mark to give intelligible content to what it means to be baptized with the Holy Spirit. The "Son" can now replace the "Spirit-Baptized One" in the narrative as a traditional term that was more familiar to the reader. Indeed, the "Son" can mean either the Son of God or the Son of Man in Mark's presentation. But the description in 1:11f informs the reader that the

Spirit is the controller of the activity of the Son, the source of his authority and the driving force of Jesus and the proclamation of Gospel. Much discussion has been occasioned by the reference to the heavenly voice in Mk 1:11. It is commonly understood to refer to the *bath qol* (daughter of the voice): "When Haggai, Zechariah and Malachi, the last prophets, died, the Holy Spirit ceased out of Israel; yet He (God) permitted it to hear the bath qol" (T. Sotah 13.2). A late rabbinic source (Targum to Cant. 2:12) compares the voice of the Holy Spirit to "the cooing of a dove," but Billerbeck (I, 125) discounts the reference as too late to exercise any influence on the Synoptic accounts. As appealing as the view is, there is no firm evidence to connect the heavenly voice with the *bath qol* in Mark's view. Others think that the imagery is connected with the picture of the Spirit of God brooding on the face of the waters like a dove (Gen 1:2),[57] but this parallel appears forced. In our opinion, Kazmierski perceptively and correctly evaluates the passage: "Therefore, whatever the case with the original traditions which underlie the rabbinic notion of the *bath qol*, the voice of Mark 1:11 is understood by the evangelist to be that of God himself. The proclamation therefore has the weight of divine authority."[58] Kazmierski also notes that v. 10 contains a reversal of the normal sentence pattern in the Gospels. This has the effect of casting "special emphasis ... on the descent of Spirit and the voice from heaven, while the rending of the heavens itself becomes secondary."[59]

Commentators have noted that the heavenly voice speaks to Jesus in the second person in Mark, whereas the third person is used by Matthew (3:17; Lk 3:22 retains the second person from Mark). This is usually taken as evidence for the private nature of the experience in the more primitive account. Matthew transforms it into a public experience to enhance the objective nature and glory of the event. Mark may see, and would have the reader see, another insight here. The theme of discipleship, introduced at 1:14–15 and illustrated in 1:16–20, is prominent in the Gospel. Related to this theme is the insider-outsider motif presented in the discussion about parables (4:10–12). True recognition of the mystery of Jesus and the Gospel is given to insiders who faithfully follow Jesus. Perhaps Mark implies in the declaration of the heavenly voice in the *second person* that true understanding of Jesus and the Gospel does not come from spectacular signs and wonders (cf. 13:22) or eschatological portents (which are relegated to the indefinite future, cf. 13:7, 10) but depends on the revelation of the Spirit to the disciple. Those who perceive, follow, and proclaim the whole Gospel become the informed insiders, the true church. To relate the whole Gospel is Mark's task.

The Spirit and the Test in the Wilderness

The scene shifts at 1:12–13, but the Spirit is still the dominant force, driving Jesus into the desert to be tested by Satan. The activity of the Spirit is the motif that provides continuity between the originally separate traditions of the baptism and the testing that Mark has joined. The Spirit is the focal force of interest. Kazmierski notes that the same stylistic trait used in v. 10 to give special emphasis to the Spirit is carried over to the testing narrative. "In verse 12 the subject of the clause again stands first, once again emphasizing the action of the Spirit as in the baptism scene."[60]

Failure to recognize Mark's stress upon the Spirit in equipping Jesus for ministry and the preaching of the Gospel has led to misplaced priorities in scholars' assessment of the meaning and role of the testing pericope in Mark's Gospel. Several scholars think Mark intended his readers to envisage Jesus as the New Adam. The mention of the wild beast and the ministration of the angels is viewed as a reference to Adam in the Garden (Gen 1:28f, 2:19–20). "As Adam was once honored by the beasts in Paradise according to the Midrash, so Christ is with the wild beast after overcoming Satan. . . . As Adam enjoyed angel's food according to the Midrash, so angels give the heavenly food to the new man."[61] S. Schulz has developed this approach into an extensive typological interpretation in which the Wilderness episode is viewed as the antitype to the *paradiesischen Urzeit* and an anticipatory type of the *eschatologische Endzeit* which has dawned with the baptism of Jesus.[62]

H.-G. Leder is representative of scholars who oppose the "New Adam" typological interpretation of Mk 1:12–13. He contends that vestiges of the theme may be retained in the tradition, but there is no evidence that the evangelist himself was interested in developing it. Following his comparison of Mk 1:12–13 with Genesis 3 and other related passages from Jewish literature, Leder concludes: "Markus selber hat anscheinend kein Interesse an einer solchen typologischen Beziehung zwischen seiner 'Versuchungsgeschichte' und der Sündenfallerzählung des ATs gehabt. . . ."[63]

U. Mauser argued for the "Wilderness" motif as Mark's key interest. According to Mauser, "Wilderness" is a theological symbol which means the determination of Jesus to live under the judgment of God as the truly repentant one. In vv. 12–13 this theme is initiated in Jesus' acceptance of the confrontation with Satan and his temptations. "The whole Gospel is an explanation of how Jesus was tempted and emerged victorious."[64] Later, however, Mauser modified his position to admit that "the 'Wilderness' motif is not a pattern which extends through the entire Gospel but only one motif germane to some sections."[65]

Twenty years ago J. Robinson and E. Best published influential works advocating conflicting themes, based on Mk 1:12–13, as central in Mark's theology. The motifs they presented are still prominent issues of discussion today.[66] Robinson stated that Mark's purpose in the Prologue is the "inauguration of eschatological history in the baptism and temptation of Jesus who proclaims the new situation and carries through the struggle against Satan in the power of the Spirit."[67] Robinson attempted to demonstrate that the "conflict with Satan" theme permeates the Gospel until the final Crucifixion-Resurrection event in which Satan is finally vanquished. Mark 1:12–13 introduces the motif and records an initial victory, but the battle continues with the forces of nature, the scribes and Pharisees, and even the disciples being used as the instruments of Satan.

Robinson's thesis encounters three major criticisms: First, he does not delineate precisely the relationship between theological meanings and historical events in his exegesis. The reader is not certain whether to interpret the Wilderness and succeeding conflict narratives as *Geschichte, Historie* or both. The primary reason for this ambiguity is Robinson's inadequate understanding of "Gospel" according to Mark, which has simultaneously past and present aspects with promise of a future culmination. Such a unique concept of Gospel requires a developed doctrine or experience of the Holy Spirit as a necessary correlative.

Second, Robinson tends to confuse his priorities with respect to Mark's purposes. He claims that the inauguration and drive of eschatological history in the power of the Spirit is the dominant motif of the evangelist,[68] but his study actually centers on the "conflict with Satan" motif. He assumes that the former is incorporated within or transformed into the latter since Jesus initiates the coming of the Eschaton through successive victories over Satan. However, it is not clear that the two themes are identical or of equal interest to Mark.

This leads to the most severe criticism: By failing to distinguish adequately between tradition and redaction, Robinson exaggerates the role and function of the "conflict with Satan" theme. The motif is prevalent in traditional material but is meager in Mark's redactional material. Its role is too limited and restricted to explain the unity and purpose of Gospel. In short, Robinson claims too much on the basis of too little.

E. Best argues that the "conflict of Satan" theme occupies a minimal place in Mark's Gospel and that "suffering for sin" is Mark's chief motif. Best notes that δήσῃ in 3:27 is an aorist subjunctive, which suggests a completed act of the binding of Satan. He infers that 3:27 announces Jesus' decisive victory over Satan accomplished in the desert:

> The temptation lies within the ministry as its decisive act: Satan is overcome: The demonic exorcisms of the remainder of the ministry represent the making real of a victory already accomplished. . . . The defeat of Satan is thus attached to the temptation rather than to the passion.[69]

In his most recent work[70] Best reaffirms his position and states that the Temptation account contains the announcement of the decisive defeat of Satan. However, he now describes the announcement occurring in the "timelessness of the Prologue" and in the author's "narrative time" instead of past *Historie*. This insight reflects Best's increased perception of the purpose of the Prologue, but obscures the relationship between the Temptation (1:12–13) in the Prologue and the Binding of the Strong Man (3:27) in the body of the Gospel. Are they related in past chronological time? Present narrative time? Or does the author intend no direct relationship but regards both passages as variation on a single theme of overcoming Satan by the power of the Spirit? Is the author telling us something about Jesus' or the reader's situation? In real time or narrative time? Best's revised assessment of the time and role of the Prologue renders his correlation between 1:12–13 and 3:27 arbitrary and uncertain. He has not worked through the questions and issues raised by regarding Mark as story. This, in turn, weakens his interpretation of the Temptation account as constituting Mark's perspective and point.

Petersen is more consistent in relating 3:27 to 1:12–13 within Mark's *narrative world* as the occasion on which Satan was bound.[71] Viewed as narrative relating the past story of Jesus, the Gospel does not proclaim in 1:12–13 that the victory has been won. At most, it is only anticipated here within the story-time. It is still problematic whether 3:27 describes the victory. According to Petersen, the resurrection may be the victorious event or Mark may leave the event unspecified within the story line and time. In response, we question the perspective that Mark writes in narrative time within a narrative world only. We maintain (as does Best) that Mark is also addressing the real world of his readers with this narrative "Gospel." In preaching the Gospel, Mark announces in 1:12–13 that Jesus is the Spirit-endowed One who has triumphed over Satan. Mark knows the outcome. Jesus faces no "temptation" to avoid or to betray his mission. Even the "test" is never in doubt. Jesus is clearly and decisively the victor. Hence, he can enable the reader to triumph also in whatever form the test comes (persecution, lagging faith, heresy). This constituted a strengthening word to Mark's community. By hearing the Gospel as narrative composed on two levels from two perspectives, the readers and hearers were encouraged to persevere. The church was still engaged in conflict, yet the outcome was certain. They could savor the victory although the test persisted.

If the assurance of "Good News" was Mark's major concern in 1:12–13, this means that he was not interested in defining the relationship of the passage to 3:27 or in answering the question, where did the decisive defeat of Satan occur? If pressed, he might have responded, "Wherever Gospel is truly heard and appropriated." The passage functions in accord with Mark's two-dimensional view of Gospel. To be an authentic word of assurance, though, two requirements were necessary: One, that the word stemmed from the historical Jesus; two, that it have continuing relevance by empowerment from the Risen Christ. The Holy Spirit provided the required continuity and energized and validated the Gospel.

Best also has moved away from advocating the "forgiveness of sin" theme as Mark's major motif and now views Mark stressing multiple themes under the broad umbrella of "Jesus cares."[72] This, too, is a positive gain, but the function of "Spirit and Gospel" in binding together these diverse themes has gone largely unnoticed.

All these treatments of Mk 1:12–13 skirt or omit the most obvious motif—the supreme authority and activity of the Spirit dramatically demonstrated by Jesus' subduing of Satan. Why this omission? Perhaps because of a preconceived notion by commentators that Mark was not interested in the role of the Holy Spirit. This evaluation is a holdover from a prior period of scholarship that sought to interpret the Gospels by tracing the traditions back to their origins (*Sitze im Leben*), a period in which perception of the Holy Spirit's activity was admittedly meager. But when the time and context of the *author* takes precedence in the theological task, the central role of the Spirit emerges as a vital theme in the evangelist's Gospel and theology.

In accord with this position, Anderson suggests that the angels in 1:13 may represent the power of God and signify that God himself, not merely human resources, was engaged in the overcoming of

Satan.[73] For Mark no authority other than God's Spirit was sufficient to meet the demonic challenges that Jesus encountered and Mark's community faced. Mark may have seen in the pericope the continuation of the fulfillment of prophecy theme evident in the Elijah-John-Jesus typology and succession. The Wilderness testing is permeated with strong OT imagery depicting the creation of the old Israel. The reader is thereby supplied clues to understand that the Spirit is moving again decisively in Jesus to establish and equip the new people of God for effective ministry. Jesus and the church are heirs of the covenant and the prophetic promises.[74]

Spirit, Gospel, and Kingdom

It is generally accepted that Mk 1:14–15 reflect the terminology of the early church and that Mark either redacted an existing summary of Jesus' message, or more likely, constructed it himself.[75] Placed by Mark at the conclusion of the Prologue, the verses presuppose the units and themes that have preceded. The reader knows now that Jesus is authorized and empowered for ministry by the very Spirit of God who is superior to the power of Satan and all manifestations of evil. He knows that Jesus may be called by many titles (e.g., Christ, Son of God, Lord, Son) but that he is foremost the Spirit-filled One. He knows that Jesus may be depicted in many roles but that all aspects of his ministry are undergirded by the Spirit residing permanently in him. He knows that the prophetic promises are now in the process of fulfillment, for the Spirit that has been absent from Israel for generations has returned with unparalleled power to initiate the Eschaton. He knows that this whole drama of salvation is part of God's plan from the beginning of creation and cannot be foiled by any adversary. He knows that the "Good News" of "God with us" manifested in Jesus is continued in the proclamation of Gospel in the power of the same Spirit that was present in Jesus and remains somehow identical with him. In light of this extensive preparation of the reader, Mark announces the advent of Jesus' ministry and Gospel with a summary of Jesus' message.

Scholars have championed virtually every term in the passage (1:14–15) as the key to Mark's Gospel. W. Popkes' thesis is that the term παραδοθῆναι discloses Mark's interest in the *Dahingabe* as the major motif. Popkes states:

Mk parallelisiert das Los des Täufers und das Jesu, und zwar in der Weise, dass er zugleich eine scharfe heilsgeschichtliche Periodisierung vornimmt: auf die Wirksamkeit des Täufers folgt die Jesu, und beider Ende ist die Dahingabe.[76]

Mark does make this distinction, but the one appearance of the term παραδίδοναι and the two references to John's death (6:17f, 9:13) are hardly convincing evidence for the claim that in 1:14−15 the *Dahingabe* is already presented as the major motif of Mark. Mark's purpose here is simply to remove John from the stage and to prepare for the entrance of Jesus in the new age of the Spirit. John's function is finished. The era of prophets as the period of preparation for the Gospel is over. John preached a baptism of repentance for the forgiveness of sins. Jesus preaches the Gospel of God. The Spirit-filled Son stands in the spotlight, and the dawning of the kingdom is the inevitable, happy consequence. Indeed, for Mark the dawning of the kingdom marks the beginning of the era of the Holy Spirit at work in the church. Thus, the kingdom theme is subsumed into the broader theme of "Spirit and Gospel."

The phrase ἡ βασιλεία τοῦ θεοῦ has attracted strong attestation from adherents as the major concept in Mark's theology. Schweizer states that the presence of the Spirit is interpreted as the presence of the kingdom of God (1:15).[77] Dunn is more explicit:

> The eschatological kingdom was present for Jesus only because the eschatological Spirit was present in and through him: In other words, it was not so much a case of "Where I am there is the kingdom" (Marxsen) as, "Where the Spirit is there is the kingdom." It was the manifestation of the power of God which was the sign of the Kingdom of God.[78]

Aune and Dunn rightly observe that the presence of the Spirit almost axiomatically brings the presence of the kingdom. However, they err in regarding "Spirit and Kingdom" as Mark's primary motif in 1:14−15. Though the advent of the kingdom undoubtedly took precedence in Jesus' teaching, in Mark's understanding it is a secondary motif concomitant with "Spirit and Gospel."[79] The shift in emphasis is due to the change of perception from Jesus to Mark in their different situations. Critical scholarship has long debated the interpretation of ἤγγικεν ἡ βασιλεία τοῦ θεοῦ (1:15) *from Jesus' perspective.* Well known are the views of Dodd (realized eschatology), Schweitzer (consistent eschatology), and a host of scholars (e.g., Jeremias, Cullmann, Marshall) advocating a mediating position: The term βασιλεία denotes both the future realm of God and the present reign of God; ἤγγικεν connotes that the kingdom as present reign has dawned in Jesus, but the consummation of God's realm is future. All that remains is the troublesome matter of determining to which category each saying belongs.

For Jesus' hearers this was a novel concept that staggered the imagination, especially in light of the populace's lack of present eschatological expectations. This bold announcement, declaring that God's future benefits were on the horizon and indeed were already breaking in and available through Jesus to the believer, was the core content of Jesus' message of Good News. Though that assessment is valid for Jesus' preaching, as Lightfoot has stated, "The contention that the chief interest of the evangelist is in the proclamation by Jesus of the kingdom of God cannot be maintained."[80] The expression "the kingdom of God" elsewhere is confined to the tradition and receives no attention as a special interest of the evangelist. This does not necessarily mean that Mark has no interest in the concept; rather, it signifies that the significance of the kingdom has been subsumed into the more comprehensive concept of τὸ εὐαγγέλιον, as Mark indicates in 1:1 and 14–15, at the beginning and end of his Prologue. After all, the church has experienced the eschatological power of the Risen Christ in the Holy Spirit for a generation. It awaits the parousia and the culmination of the kingdom in the Eschaton. The church may need reminding of the reality and promise of the kingdom, but it is no longer a novel idea. These experiences and convictions are now incorporated into the larger concept of "Gospel." The discussion has moved on; the needs and issues and perspectives have changed. Mark is more concerned with such issues as the basis and limits of true Gospel and the mode or medium of the Spirit's presence (bringing God's kingly rule and power) in the community for rebuke, aid, and assurance.

Other redaction critics have centered on "Messiahship and Kingdom" as Mark's primary theme. For example, Lightfoot has noted that "the kingdom" is not Mark's emphasis and thinks that the evangelist is more interested in proclaiming the identity of the herald of the kingdom. "No doubt, the two conceptions, Jesus as Messiah, and the kingdom of God, of which he is the herald, are inseparably connected; but the primary interest of our earliest evangelist is in the significance of the person of Christ."[81] No one doubts that Christology is a concern of the evangelist, but "Jesus the Messiah" is not Mark's favorite title, as we have seen. The title was too vague and carried too many political connotations to be fully acceptable to Mark. Literary-historical critics popularized "Messiah" as a major title in Mark (and the Synoptic Gospels) by claiming that it linked the motif of the Davidic royal kingship with the concept of the Suffering Servant in designating Jesus' identity and mission.[82] But Porter's dictum still stands, "Any cogent proof of a Messiah between the Deutero-Isaianic servant and Jesus Christ whose work was conceived by Judaism in sacrificial terms is still to be sought."[83]

If the term "Messiah" is no longer taken as a reference to definite Jewish messianic expectations, as Vielhauer holds in his assessment of Mark's Christology,[84] then we must determine what the cryptic term now means in contemporary scholarship and if Mark has an equivalent view (divine man, Son of God, Son of Man, etc.). The matter becomes complex; indeed, we may find ourselves in the awkward position of holding a definition foreign to Mark, as Tiede and Holladay have warned us with respect to the concept of the divine-man.

A related position contends that Mark introduces in the Prologue the "Messianic Secret" motif as the controlling motif and "hermeneutical presupposition of the genre, 'gospel.'"[85] Again the precise meaning of "messianic" is left undefined.

Burkill offers a contemporary expression of this position first advanced by W. Wrede. In virtue of his "messianic status" and unique filial relationship to God declared at the baptism, Jesus overcomes the temptation of Satan in the wilderness and enters upon his mission to establish finally the kingdom of God with great power and glory. However, prior to his resurrection Jesus concealed his messiahship from his own people in accord with the saving plan of God. In this way, "by resorting to the concept of the secret, St. Mark is able to maintain the apostolic belief in the Messiahship without denying the plain facts of the historical traditions."[86]

It is not our intention to deny the existence of a "secrecy" motif in Mark but to quarrel about the validity and intelligibility of a secret "messiahship" in Mark. David Aune raises the same objection:

> While modern critics speak of the "messianic secret" of Mark, the evangelist himself was concerned with the "secret of the kingdom of God" (Mark 4:12). . . . T. A. Burkill is certainly wrong in assuming that this mystery is the fact that Jesus is the Messiah, the son of God, for although Jesus stands in the closest connection to the kingdom of God it is nevertheless the kingdom itself which is given primary emphasis.[87]

Aune's comment brings us full circle, back to Dunn's position and the inadequacy of "kingdom" or "kingdom secret" to encompass Mark's purpose and motifs.

Mark stresses that Jesus came preaching τὸ εὐαγγέλιον and summoning hearers to repent and believe in τῷ εὐαγγελίῳ. The message of the inbreaking kingdom accompanies τὸ εὐαγγέλιον as an important component, but the focus falls twice on the more comprehensive term: τὸ εὐαγγέλιον. This is consistent with Mark's introduction of the term in 1:1 as the *leitmotiv* of his work, as we have noted. In preaching Jesus to his church, apparently threatened by persecution from without and racked by internal dissen-

sion within, Mark began his Gospel at v. 1, which stretches back to
the creation and perhaps even to the eternity of God, though the
appearance of John marks the beginning of the new act of God in
Historie. Jesus is proclaimed "Christ, the Son of God," titles which
are undergirded by the surpassing disclosure that he is baptized
with the Holy Spirit. The entire Markan Prologue is structured in
descending suprahistorical levels to witness to Jesus' identity and
authority as the Spirit-endowed Son who issues the call to discipleship to contemporary hearers and readers. Discipleship means foremost to believe in the Gospel which preaches and embodies Jesus
as its core and content. In that sense, for Mark, belief in Jesus
and belief in the Gospel are virtually identical, as Marxsen has
insisted. The qualifier τοῦ θεοῦ (1:15) points to the ultimate origin
of this proclamation on the one hand and to Jesus himself as
the content of the Gospel on the other: "Jesus is the gospel
of God."[88]

At the same time Mark is aware that he is recounting Jesus'
past preaching at 1:14–15. In this sense, the Gospel begins when
Jesus begins preaching. The Gospel, then, has a past referent in
the person of the historical Jesus. Apart from the Spirit's activity in
and through Jesus of Nazareth, there is no Gospel. Gospel is more
than a record of Jesus' past word and deeds. It is the conveying of
the living Spirit of Jesus as the Risen Christ through the medium of
Mark's interpretive presentation of the traditions. Mark does not
attempt to explain exactly how the reader-hearer encounters Christ
through the Gospel. It is simply the experience of the Christian
attributed to and authenticated by the presence and work of the
Holy Spirit. The Holy Spirit empowers Gospel in both aspects of its
dual meaning and provides the connecting link. Mark's use of Jesus'
traditions (or traditions he believed to come from Jesus' contexts)
as the basis and medium for the contemporary preaching of Jesus
(objective genitive) controlled and defined the material and motifs
that were acceptable as true Gospel. Mark 13:22 infers that pneumatic false prophets were bypassing and ignoring the person
and work of the historical Jesus in ecstatic appeal to immediate revelation from the Spirit. For Mark, this was a corruption of Gospel, a
heretical perversion that threatened the welfare and existence of the
community from within as strongly as persecution from without.
What could Mark do about this dangerous situation? He could not
deny outright the present power of the Spirit in gifted individuals,
nor did he wish to do so. They manifested the Spirit in striking,
self-evident ways that Mark could not refute. Besides, to deny the
presence of the Spirit in the church was to deny the very life of the
Gospel and the community and to commit the unforgivable sin

(3:29). What was the alternative? Mark, inspired with a stroke of genius, redefined "Gospel" as the conveying of the presence and power of the Spirit-Christ through the material preserved from the ministry of Jesus. This "Jesus material" was still respected and honored in the church. Paul mentions a group of incipient gnostic radicals who may have denied the relevance of the Jesus of history (1 Cor 12:3), but this view was not typical in the church. Evidently it was not dominant in Mark's church, for he appeals to Jesus and Jesus' traditions in curbing and controlling the claims and influences of false prophets in the community. "Gospel" is not the recitation of present religious experiences, however glorious and victorious. "Gospel" is not the demonstration of spiritual gifts, however spectacular and inspiring. "Gospel" includes the proclamation of the objective reality of Jesus and his sufferings as well as his resurrection and exaltation. Correspondingly, to believe in the Gospel means to follow Jesus in the way of suffering as well as to experience his present aid and gifts in the form of the Spirit.

We have no knowledge of the effectiveness and outcome of Mark's strategy and design of Gospel in his community, but the preservation of his Gospel is an indication that it found acceptance in the church. By redactional activity in structure, syntax, emphasizing of theological motifs, and relating content to context, Mark presents the concept of "Spirit and Gospel" as a leading motif in the Prologue for the understanding of his work.

The objection may arise, if Mark considers the concept of "Spirit and Gospel" to be paramount, why is the motif not more pronounced in passages, especially redactional verses, beyond the Prologue in the body of the work? In reply, we can do no better than quote two scholars who, though separated by sixty years of scholarship, voice remarkably similar responses. E. F. Scott concludes:

> After the episode of the Temptation Mark does not explicitly return to the idea of a control by the Spirit, and in view of the prominence given to the investiture at the baptism, this may appear strange. But his silence does not prove that Mark departs from the theory with which he sets out. . . . He feels, rather, that henceforth it is unnecessary to insist on a fact which may be taken for granted. . . . We are meant to read the whole subsequent history in the light of the solemn incident which marked its beginning.[89]

And M. D. Hooker concurs:

> If references to the Spirit are rare in the rest of the Gospel, this is not because Mark loses interest in the idea, but because these first few verses are a kind of theological commentary on the rest of the

narrative. . . . But though the characters in the story are bewildered, Mark does not intend us to forget the truth which he has uncovered in these opening verses. From time to time in the course of the narrative he will nudge his readers, reminding them of the true significance of what is going on. Like a Greek chorus explaining the meaning of events in a play, he will make sure that we, at least, realize that the story he unfolds is good news about the Son of God in whom God's Spirit is at work.[90]

ENDNOTES

CHAPTER 2: THE PROLOGUE (MARK 1:1–15)

1. See also M. Dibelius, *Die urchristliche Überlieferung von Johannes dem Täufer* (Göttingen: Vandenhoeck & Ruprecht, 1911), p. 47.

2. Lightfoot, *The Gospel Message of St. Mark*, pp. 17, 19. See also G. Hebert, "The Resurrection-Narrative in St. Mark's Gospel," *SJT* 15 (1962): 66–67, who agrees with Lightfoot.

3. O. J. F. Seitz, "Gospel Prologues: A Common Pattern," *JBL* 83: 262–68; Alfred Kuby, "Zur Konzeption des Markus-Evangeliums," *ZNW* 49 (1958): 54; L. E. Keck, "The Introduction to Mark's Gospel," *NTS* 12 (1966): 352–370, who makes the points following.

4. Bilezikian, *The Liberated Gospel*, p. 56.

5. M. D. Hooker, *The Message of Mark* (London: Epworth Press, 1983), p. 16.

6. P. Stuhlmacher, *Das paulinische Evangelium. I. Vorgeschichte* (Göttingen: Vandenhoeck & Ruprecht, 1968), p. 236, states, "Dass wir in beiden Versen ein markinisches Summarium vor uns haben, ist seit langem erkannt."

7. Rawlinson, *St. Mark*, p. 6.

8. R. A. Guelich, "The Beginning of the Gospel, Mark 1:1–15," *Biblical Research* 27 (1982), p. 12.

9. Marxsen, *Mark the Evangelist*, p. 132, refers to Lohmeyer, *Das Evangelium des Markus*, p. 10, who states that Mark traces the "beginning" back to God. He is the author of this event.

10. E. Schweizer, *The Good News According to Mark* (Atlanta: John Knox Press, 1970), pp. 30, 32. See also J. Rohde, *Rediscovering the Teaching of the Evangelists* (London: SCM Press, 1968), p. 114: "The title ἀρχή means that an event is being described which does not end with the resurrection of Jesus. It is continued in the preaching of the Apostles. It has its beginning in the activity and proclamation of Jesus and is legitimized by it. Even the fact that Jesus succeeded the Baptist is not a succession in time but an essential succession in a formal pattern in salvation history."

11. A term given by M. Zerwick, *Biblical Greek: Scripta pontificii intituti biblici 114* (Rome, 1963), p. 36 and noted by C. R. Kazmierski, *Jesus the Son of God* (Würzburg: Echter Verlag, 1979), p. 24.

12. Weeden, *Mark—Traditions in Conflict*, p. 83. See also Reploh, *Markus—Lehrer der Gemeinde*, pp. 18, 19, and Keck, "The Introduction

to Mark's Gospel," p. 357.

13. J. Reumann, "Mark 1:14–20," *Int* 32 (1978): 405–410. See also J. Schniewind, *Das Evangelium nach Markus* (Göttingen: Vandenhoeck & Ruprecht, 1960), p. 1; and Marxsen, *Mark the Evangelist*, p. 131.

14. See Boring, *Sayings of the Risen Jesus*, p. 198, and W. H. Kelber, *The Oral and The Written Gospel* (Philadelphia: Fortress Press, 1983), pp. 99–102, who in our opinion identify rightly the context and opponents of Mark but do not explain satisfactorily his purpose.

15. Perceived also by L. S. Hay, "The Son of God Christology in Mark," *JBR* 32 (1964): 106, and L. E. Keck, "Jesus in New Testament Christology," *Aus* 28 (1980): 14, who also recognizes their limitations.

16. É. Trocmé, "Is There a Marcan Christology?" *Christ and Spirit in the New Testament*, ed. B. Lindars (Cambridge: University Press, 1973), p. 8, recognizes the inadequacy of the titles applied to Jesus in Mark's Gospel to convey the evangelist's theology but does not appreciate fully their positive function.

17. J. Lambrecht, "The Christology of Mark," *Biblical Theology Bulletin* 3–4 (1973–74): 258, 269.

18. N. A. Dahl, "Eschatology and History in the Light of the Dead Sea Scrolls," *The Future of Our Religious Past*, ed. J. M. Robinson (New York: Harper & Row, 1971), pp. 9–28.

19. Taylor, *The Gospel According to Mark*, p. 152; C. H. Turner, "A Textual Commentary on Mark i," *JTS* 28 (1927): 145–58. A. Globe, "The Caesarean Omission of the Phrase 'Son of God' in Mark 1:1," *HTR* 75 (1982): 209–218, offers five sound reasons why the title is original.

20. R. Bultmann, *Theology of the New Testament*, (New York: Charles Scribner's Sons, 1951) 1:50. See also the summary and critique of Bultmann's position in O. Cullmann, *Christology of the New Testament* (Philadelphia: Westminster Press, 1963), pp. 271–281, who thinks "Jesus called himself by this name."

21. Noted by J. D. Kingsbury, "The Divine Man as the Key to Mark's Christology–The End of an Era?" *Int* 35 (1981): 210, 213–216. D. Georgi, *Die Gegner des Paulus im 2. Korintherbrief* (Neukirchen-Vluyn: Neukirchener Verlag, 1964), pp. 210, 213–16, argues that the traditions Mark inherited and adopted were of a "Hellenistic-Jewish stripe," and S. Schulz, *Die Stunde der Botschaft* (Hamburg: Furche Verlag, 1967), pp. 54–79, especially p. 77, concurs, adding that Mark converts the "theology of the cross" into a "theology of glory." Cf. also J. Schreiber, "Die Christologie des Markusevangeliums," *ZTK* 58 (1961): pp. 154–83, who views Mark's Christology being determined indirectly by the gnostic myth of the secret savior.

22. O. Betz, "The So-Called 'Divine Man' in Mark's Christology," *Studies in New Testament and Early Christian Literature*, ed. D. E. Aune (Leiden: E. J. Brill, 1972), p. 230.

23. W. Von Martitz, "υἱός," *TDNT* (1972), 8:338–40; Betz, "The So-Called 'Divine Man' in Mark's Christology," pp. 229–240; D. L. Tiede, *The Charismatic Figure as Miracle Worker*, SBLDS 1 (Missoula: Scholar's Press, 1972), pp. 254–55; C. R. Holladay, *Theios Aner in Hellenistic Judaism*, SBLDS 40 (Missoula: Scholar's Press, 1977), pp. 239–40.

24. Kingsbury, "The Divine Man as the Key to Mark's Christology," p. 248.

25. Tiede, *The Charismatic Figure as Miracle Worker*, pp. 254–55.

26. Holladay, *Theios Aner in Hellenistic Judaism*, p. 240.

27. E. Schweizer, "υἱός, κτλ," *TDNT* (1972), 8:367f, 378f; H. C. Kee, *Jesus in History: An Approach to the Study of the Gospels* (New York: Harcourt Brace Jovanovich, 1977), pp. 150–152.

28. Kingsbury, "The Divine Man as the Key to Mark's Christology," p. 250, citing references from M. Black, "The Christological Use of the Old Testament in the New Testament," *NTS* 18 (1971–72): 2–4, and J. A. Fitzmyer, "The Contribution of Qumran Aramaic to the Study of the New Testament," *NTS* 20 (1973–74): 391–94. However, they do not recognize the fluid nature of the term "messiah."

29. Taylor, *The Gospel According to St. Mark*, p. 156.

30. J. H. Hughes, "John the Baptist: The Forerunner of God Himself," *NovT* 14 (1972): 191–218. Barrett, *The Holy Spirit and the Gospel Tradition*, p. 29, alluding to Strack-Billerbeck, IV, 779–798, maintains that the rabbinic literature indicates that the expectation was present, though it may not have been widespread.

31. E. Best, "Spirit-Baptism," *NovT* 4 (1960): 236–243. J. D. G. Dunn, "Spirit and Fire Baptism," *NovT* 14 (1972): 86–92, suggests that "influenced by the Qumran sect, it is quite possible that it was John the Baptist who finally linked the eschatological outpouring of the Spirit to the Messiah and who first spoke of the Messiah's bestowal of the Holy Spirit under the powerful figure . . . of a baptism in Spirit-and-fire." This is plausible, but Mark shows no special interest in linking the Spirit with the Messiah.

32. See Schweizer, *The Good News According to Mark*, pp. 28, 31, and Taylor, *The Gospel According to St. Mark*, p. 153, for descriptive explanations of the process.

33. Against D. E. Aune, *Prophecy in Early Christianity and the Ancient Mediterranean World* (Grand Rapids: Eerdmans, 1983), pp. 131–132, who states, "John is assigned the role of Elijah *redivivus*, the eschatological prophet who will prepare the way for the Davidic Messiah." This may have been Matthew's emphasis (1:1ff.) but not Mark's. Aune may be right that "historically, however, John was probably referring to the future eschatological judge without specific reference to Jesus." This issue is largely immaterial in assessing Mark's perspective, as is the debate whether John originally spoke of both "Holy Spirit and fire" (Q). However, if Mark knew Q and intentionally omitted "fire," this would indicate that he wished to stress the bestowal of divine authority upon Jesus (and the reader) by the Holy Spirit rather than the theme of eschatological judgment. J. E. Yates, *The Spirit and the Kingdom* (London: S.P.C.K., 1963), p. 13, argues that "Mark 1:8, though less explicit, has much the same meaning as the fuller Q form," but his arguments lack firm evidence.

34. M. Werner, *Der Einfluss paulinischer Theologie im Markusevangelium* (Giessen: Alfred Töpelmann, 1923), p. 209.

35. Grant, *The Gospel According to St. Mark*, p. 632. See Ch. 4 for a fuller discussion.

36. Taylor, *The Gospel According to St. Mark*, p. 157, and Barrett, *The Holy Spirit and the Gospel Tradition*, p. 125.

37. Mauser, *Christ in the Wilderness*, pp. 91–92. Cf. G. Delling, "βαπτισμα βαπτισθηναι," *NovT* 2 (1957): 95–96, and A. Oepke, "βάπτω, κτλ," *TDNT* (1964), 1:538.

38. Barrett, *The Holy Spirit and the Gospel Tradition*, p. 125.
39. Hooker, *The Message of Mark*, p. 10.
40. J. R. Donahue, "Jesus as the Parable of God in the Gospel of Mark," *Int* 32 (1978): 384.
41. Petersen, *Literary Criticism for New Testament Critics*, p. 77.
42. L. Williamson, Jr., "Mark 1:1–8," *Int* 32 (1978): 404.
43. E. W. Winstanley, *Spirit in the New Testament* (Cambridge: University Press, 1908), p. 11.
44. Bultmann, *The History of the Synoptic Tradition*, p. 248.
45. Dibelius, *From Tradition to Gospel*, p. 271.
46. Dunn, *Jesus and the Spirit*, pp. 63–64, who adds, "And the decisive indication that the kingdom was present for Jesus was the presence of the Spirit working in and through him." This is the focal characteristic of the Markan Jesus.
47. Marxsen, *Mark the Evangelist*, pp. 93–94.
48. For examples, Johannes Weiss, *Das älteste Evangelium* (Göttingen: Vandenhoeck & Ruprecht, 1903), pp. 47–48; V. Taylor, *The Names of Jesus* (London: Macmillan & Co., 1954), p. 36; O. Cullmann, *Christology*, pp. 283–284; Schweizer, *The Good News According to Mark*, pp. 38–39; Barrett, *The Holy Spirit and the Gospel Tradition*, p. 44.
49. Barrett, *The Holy Spirit and the Gospel Tradition*, p. 44. W. H. Robinson, *The Christian Experience of the Holy Spirit* (London: Nisbet & Co., 1928), pp. 124–125, expresses the same position, though he attributes the blending of passages and concepts to Jesus and does not consider the evangelist's theology.
50. W. Zimmerli and J. Jeremias, *The Servant of God* (Naperville: Alec R. Allenson, Inc., 1957), p. 80ff; cf. B. M. F. van Iersel, *'Der Sohn' in den synoptischen Jesusworten* (Leiden: E. J. Brill, 1961), pp. 9–10, who also thinks that παῖς was the original reading and was changed later to υἱός due to Hellenistic influence.
51. Best, *The Temptation and the Passion*, p. 149.
52. H. Anderson, *The Gospel of Mark* (Grand Rapids: Eerdmans, 1976), pp. 79–80. I. H. Marshall, "Son of God or Servant of Yahweh," *NTS* 15 (1968–69): 326–336, also rejects Jeremias' position, and instead of Isa 42:1, favors Ps 2:7, Gen 22:2, and Isa 61:1 as background passages for the saying in which υἱός stood originally.
53. See G. S. Shae, "The Question on the Authority of Jesus," *NovT* 16 (1974): 1–29, who uncovers three levels of tradition-history in the passage.
54. Anderson, *The Gospel of Mark*, pp. 79–80.
55. Schweizer, *The Good News According to Mark*, p. 39. E. F. Scott, *The Spirit in the New Testament* (London: Hodder & Stoughton, 1923) p. 67, affirms, "We are meant to read the whole subsequent history in the light of the solemn incident which marked its beginning."
56. F. Hahn, *Christologische Hoheitstitel: Ihre Geschichte im frühen Christentum* (Göttingen: Vandenhoeck & Ruprecht, 1963), pp. 338, 340f.
57. Taylor, *The Gospel According to St. Mark*, p. 161.
58. Kazmierski, *Jesus, the Son of God*, p. 37.
59. Ibid., p. 31.
60. Ibid., p. 64.
61. A. W. Schulze, "Der Heilige und die wilden Tiere," *ZNW* 46 (1955):

282, in dependence upon J. Jeremias, "Αδαμ," *TDNT* 1:141.

62. Schulz, *Die Stunde der Botschaft*, p. 56.

63. H.-G. Leder, "Sündenfallerzählung und Versuchungsgeschichte," *ZNW* 54 (1963): 207–208, 216. However, Leder does think that the passage anticipates the eschaton.

64. Mauser, *Christ in the Wilderness*, pp. 96–100. An important aspect of Mauser's interpretation is the rendering of πειραζομενός to mean "temptation," not "testing."

65. U. Mauser, Personal Letter (August, 1968), addressed to the author.

66. For examples, Kingsbury, *Jesus Christ in Matthew, Mark, and Luke*, p. 42, and W. D. Carroll, "The Jesus of Mark's Gospel," *Bible Today* 103 (1979): 2105–2115, who follows Robinson's cosmic conflict theme.

67. Robinson, *The Problem of History in Mark*, p. 28, 32.

68. Ibid., pp. 28–32.

69. Best, *The Temptation and the Passion*, p. 15.

70. Best, *Mark: The Gospel as Story*, pp. 57–58.

71. Petersen, *Literary Criticism for New Testament Critics*, p. 57.

72. Best, *Mark. The Gospel as Story*, p. 51.

73. Anderson, *The Gospel of Mark*, p. 82.

74. J. A. T. Robinson, "The Temptations," *Twelve New Testament Studies* (London: SCM Press, 1962), pp. 53–60.

75. See Taylor, *The Gospel According to St. Mark*, pp. 90, 165, and Schweizer, *The Good News According to Mark*, p. 45.

76. W. Popkes, *Christus Traditus* (Zurich: Zwingli Verlag, 1967), pp. 143–144.

77. E. Schweizer, "πνεῦμα" *TDNT* (1968), 6:398, who refers specifically to the exorcisms, but for Mark the kingdom is present in all that Jesus says and does in the power of the Spirit.

78. Dunn, *Jesus and the Spirit*, p. 49, who refers to F. Hauck, *Das Evangelium des Markus*, THNT (1931), p. 172, and J. Schniewind, *Das Evangelium nach Marcus*, NTD (1963), p. 190, for support of this understanding.

79. R. H. Lightfoot, *History and Interpretation in the Gospels* (New York: Harper and Brothers, 1934), pp. 60–61, recognized also the secondary role of kingdom for the evangelist but mistakenly viewed Messiahship to be Mark's chief concern.

80. Ibid., pp. 60–61.

81. Ibid., pp. 60–61.

82. V. Taylor, "The Origin of the Marcan Passion Sayings," *NTS* 1 (February, 1955): p. 165, lists J. Jeremias, W. Manson, W. D. Davies, J. Bowman, M. Black, and H. Hegermann as advocates.

83. J. R. Porter, "The Messiah in the Testament of Levi XVIII," *ET* 61 (1949): p. 91. Cf. G. R. Beasley-Murray, "Jesus and the Spirit," *Mélanges Bibliques* (Gembloux: Duculot, 1970), p. 477, who states that "the Messiah in the Old Testament is not the agent through whom the kingdom comes, but the agent of God's rule when the kingdom has come." But this concept is also vague and inconsistent in the OT.

84. P. Vielhauer, "Erwägungen zur Christologie des Markusevangeliums," *Zeit und Geschichte*, ed. E. Dinkler (Tübingen: J. C. B. Mohr, 1964), p. 157.

85. Tiede, *The Charismatic Figure as Miracle Worker*, p. 256, quoting

Conzelmann.

86. Burkill, *Mysterious Revelation*, pp. 1–5, 68–69. Cf. also T. A. Burkill, "Strain on the Secret: An Examination of Mark 11:1–13:37," *ZNW* 51 (1960): 31–46. C. Tuckett, *The Messianic Secret* (Philadelphia: Fortress Press, 1983), offers a helpful history and appraisal of scholarship on the messianic secret motif since W. Wrede, *Das Messiasgeheimnis in den Evangelien* (Göttingen: Vandenhoeck & Ruprecht, 1963).

87. D. Aune, "The Problem of the Messianic Secret," *NovT* 11 (1969): 25.

88. Marxsen, *Mark the Evangelist*, p. 133.

89. Scott, *The Spirit in the New Testament*, p. 67.

90. Hooker, *The Message of Mark*, p. 16.

—3—

THE BODY OF THE GOSPEL
(MARK 1:16–13:37)

Introduction

We contend that Mark structured the Prologue to set forth the related concepts of "Spirit and Gospel" as a primary dual motif in his work. We now purport to confirm this thesis by demonstrating that the evangelist continues this theme in his composition of the body of his Gospel. We intend to show by analyses of the author's redactional phrases, connecting comments, summaries, use of tradition, and narrative development[1] that he regarded "Spirit and Gospel" as an integral, central motif in his work. Since this study is not designed to be a complete commentary on Mark's Gospel, it is not necessary for us to examine every pericope or section. We shall focus on central passages that embody the motif and endeavor to show how it illumines the larger literary context of the Gospel addressed to Mark's community. Some references to the theme are mere passing allusions; in other instances the appeal is direct. To what extent Mark was thoroughly aware of the prevalence of this motif in his composition is uncertain. Some of his references and emphases may have been made with an unconscious acumen. But the theme evidently functioned as an important theological component in his presentation of Gospel.

SECTION 1: MARK 1:16–3:6 (1:14–15)

The Spirit and Discipleship: Mark 1:16–20 (1:14–15)

It is generally recognized that this section has been structured by Mark out of originally independent traditions:[2] A story or stories about the call of the disciples (1:16–20); a series of miracle stories (1:21–39) and a healing story (1:40–45) which Mark linked under the rubric of "Capernaum"; and a collection of conflict stories (2:1–3:6).[3] Editorial summaries are interpolated at 1:32–34 and 3:7–12 (following this section), and redactional, transitional passages are found at 1:21–22, 39, and 3:6.[4] Mark constructed the section to demonstrate the divine authority of Jesus in every realm of life as the Spirit-endowed One whose power is unparalleled. The proper response is unqualified discipleship. Hence, for the reader the blindness of the Jewish authorities is incredible.

We have argued that 1:14–15 is a transitional passage which beckons in two directions in accord with Mark's dual concept of Gospel. It concludes the Prologue and discloses to the reader how to read the Gospel. Verses 14–15 introduce the theme of the call to discipleship which still goes out to the reader. The verses also preserve the tradition of the inauguration of Jesus' earthly ministry and preaching which called persons to believe in the Good News of the dawning of the kingdom. They point ahead to the actualization of this ministry and message in the call of the first disciples at 1:16–20. Thus, the past tradition serves as the basis and medium of the present call of Jesus/Spirit to discipleship.

Yates' suggestion is appealing that "these two sections, Mark 1:14–15, 16–20, complete the introductory sections of the Gospel account."[5] However, the ostensible cosmic quality of the Prologue (vv. 1–15) is only latently present in vv. 16–20. The reader now follows Jesus in his earthly ministry, but discovers surprisingly that he is invited to discipleship with Simon, Andrew, James, and John. Such is the quality of Mark's unique Gospel, fashioned from tradition and quickened by the Spirit.

The response by the four fishermen to Jesus' call is immediate and unreserved. No mention is made of completing previous commitments or making preparations. They left their nets εὐθύς, a prevalent Markan term, and followed him (1:18). Thereby, Mark uses and redacts tradition to establish a positive model and call to discipleship for his readers. The invitation of the Spirit-filled Jesus in 1:15 has found initial fruition—in prior history and in present storytime with an appeal to the reader in present "real" time.

Jesus: The Authoritative Teacher

In 1:21–22 the hand of Mark is evident in the formation καὶ εἰσπορεύονται εἰς Καφαρναούμ and in the inclusion of εὐθύς and ἐδίδασκεν—common editorial additions of the evangelist.[6] The term ἐδίδασκεν, repeated in the redactional vv. 22 and 27, discloses the Markan interest in the pericope: "Teaching with authority." Mark has not yet recorded any of Jesus' teachings. Only his mighty acts have been recounted. Mark connects the two functions under the one heading of "teaching" in v. 27, which he has "bracketed in" to correspond to vv. 21–22.[7] Whereas originally the pericope portrayed Jesus primarily as a thaumaturge, Mark has altered the emphasis to fall upon Jesus' activity as a teacher. This redactional change indicates that "teaching" and especially the portrayal of "Jesus as teacher" is a strong Markan interest.[8]

Although most commentators classify Mark as an action-oriented Gospel, the statistical evidence shows that nearly half of the Gospel is devoted to teaching. The title διδάσκαλος occurs twelve times while "Rabbi" is used three times and "Rabbouni" once (10:51). These accumulative figures are higher than the corresponding ones in Matthew (12 total) and Luke (13 total), although these Gospels are much longer than Mark's and devote extensive sections to Jesus' teaching. The teaching motif is so pervasive and obviously Markan that Achtemeier concludes: "All of this makes it apparent that it was important for Mark to make it clear to his readers that one cannot rightly understand Jesus if one does not take into account his activity as teacher."[9]

Why does Mark wish to draw special attention to Jesus as an authoritative teacher, even in his exorcisms? We suggest that the clues to the answer are found in the "insider-outsider" distinction in chapter 4 and in the challenge of false prophets in chapter 13, passages that afford insight into Mark's context. Mark is disturbed by the claims of fanatical pneumatic prophets that they have an exclusive "inside revelation" from the Risen Christ that is validated by "signs and wonders." Mark counters these excessive, erroneous claims by presenting Jesus as the authoritative Teacher. This characterization carried the following implications: First, it directed attention away from spectacular acts as signs of spiritual superiority by subsuming mighty deeds under the heading of teaching. Second, it directed attention away from immediate revelation as proof of truth by referring to traditions of Jesus' teaching as an alternative authoritative norm. Third, it directed attention to the Teacher and teaching function and gift within the community as a check upon unbridled, irresponsible prophecy. Earlier Paul had proclaimed that both prophecy and teaching were inspired functions in the church at Rome (12:6–7) with priority apparently accorded the former. It is highly probable that the two functions were not totally separate. As Hengel states:

Indeed in the New Testament period if a "prophet" wished to be more than a mere "visionary," he had to be in a position to expound, with some degree of "authority," the demands of the Law and the "secrets" of the prophets, by virtue of divine inspiration and authority. This is true for Daniel in Daniel 9 as well as for the môreh hassedeq; nor are the various Essene, early Pharisaic (!) and Zealot "prophets" any exception here....[10]

Yet, though prophecy and teaching have a common ground in the tradition, their roles can be distinguished: (1) Teaching—to pass on and to interpret the tradition; to give a new insight into an old word from God, i.e., traditions already accepted as authoritative. (2) Prophecy—to bring new revelation, a new word from God consistent with the old revelation. As Dunn notes, from the beginning we find both a conserving function (teaching) and a creating function (prophecy) within the early church.[11] The distinction between the two functions was developing into a cleavage in the Markan church, as Paul had experienced earlier in several churches (cf. 2 Thes 2:2, 1 Corinthians 12–14, Romans 12, 16:17–20). The excitement and stimulus of fresh revelation delivered by prophets tended to diminish the role of teachers and to neglect the tradition of Jesus' teachings and the received Gospel (cf. 1 Cor 11:2, 23; 15:3; 2 Thes 2:15; 3:6). Quite likely tension between the two functions and positions in leadership in the community had existed for some time. The situation was made more difficult by the fact that the same leaders probably exercised both teaching and prophetic functions with no conscious awareness that they were deviating from the tradition. Mark perceived that certain prophets were compromising the fullness of the Gospel by virtually ignoring the call to a discipleship of suffering and service issued and exemplified by the historical Jesus.

The extent of the creative role of prophets in the early church is much debated. Hawthorne[12] and Boring[13] think that the creative impulse was extensive in fashioning dominical sayings of the Risen Christ. Boring states his assessment of the process of development and impact upon Mark in the following summary:

In the earliest Palestinian church, disciples who believed that Jesus had been exalted to the presence of God and that this risen Jesus spoke through them, delivered pronouncements in his name in which he addressed the community as the exalted (and soon-to-appear) Son of Man.... The Palestinian-Syrian Church handed on the tradition of Jesus' words, but made no sharp distinction between them and the new words of the exalted Lord that came into being through the Christian prophets in its midst. This collection of sayings...later crystallized into...Q....One fact in Mark's creation of the Gospel form was

his awareness of the genre of sayings-collections represented by Q, in
which the sayings of Jesus threatened to float free from the Jesus of
history.... Mark created a narrative form, "gospel," in which the risen
Jesus addresses the community only from within the framework of the
pre-Easter life of Jesus.[14]

Hill contends that Hawthorne's and Boring's positions are under-
mined by two telling criticisms:[15] (1) The assertion that the Christian prophet was "a pneumatic and awesome figure within the early
church" is a vastly overdrawn assumption. (2) There is not one
absolutely certain prophetic word which became a part of the tradition of Jesus' utterances. Hill's criticisms constitute a warranted
caveat against identifying too hastily Christian prophecy as the
matrix and source of multiple sayings that exhibit certain formal
prophetic characteristics. But the tide of scholarly opinion in current exegetical and socio-religious studies has given impetus to
Christian prophecy as exercising a more formative influence than
previously recognized. Buttressed by knowledge of Paul's problems
with enthusiasts and awareness of the genre fashioned by the author
of the Fourth Gospel, who combined sayings from the earthly Jesus
and the Risen Christ,[16] contemporary scholarship has established a
convincing case for Christian prophets exercising an extensive role
in creating or modifying sayings within the early Christian church.
This influential role and function of pneumatic prophecy also fits
the references and situation projected by Mark. In light of exalted
claims by prophetic leaders to speak in the name of the Risen
Christ, Mark appealed to the normative role of the Gospel composed of Jesus' words to provide a control upon the excessive, erroneous teachings of charismatic prophets.[17] The likelihood that in
the pre-Markan traditions some prophetic sayings already had been
attributed to the historical Jesus would not weaken or affect Mark's
strategy. He and the community in general believed that all these
sayings were spoken by the earthly Jesus. Hence, Mark ascribed
them to Jesus as Teacher and expanded the scope of the title to
encompass the deeds of Jesus as well. The true Gospel is based
upon the teaching of Jesus, and Jesus as Teacher still instructs the
community through this Gospel inspired by his spiritual presence.
Thereby, Mark's Gospel, rooted in the tradition and quickened by
the power of the Risen Teacher in the presence of the Spirit, was
established as the norm for the church's belief and practice.
Henceforth, all prophetic words are to be measured by the standard
of the Gospel, a unique genre blending Jesus tradition and Risen
Christ revelation into an authoritative standard surpassing mere
human claims to truth. Indeed, Mark himself undoubtedly func-

tioned as a teacher-disciple of Jesus with a stronger claim to leadership in the community than the self-styled prophets.

Ellis[18] points out that "the holy Spirit or holy spirits have a special relation to 'the wise' (מַשְׂכִּילִים), i.e., the teachers at Qumran." These *maskilim* were the recipients and transmitters of mysteries, possessors of wisdom, discerners of spirits, and interpreters of the traditions. We suggest that the functions of the *maskilim* in Jewish circles were paralleled by those of the prophet-teacher in the early church. In the Pauline and Markan churches, buoyed with the exhilaration of a lofty revealed gnosis, the ecstatic prophetic function threatened to gain the ascendency.[19] Paul and Mark, through the use of different genres (Letter and Gospel), both stressed the type of functional leadership similar to the *maskilim* or prophet-teacher in whom the Holy Spirit was present to reinterpret the older traditions in meaningful new ways to meet the needs of communities. In this way the teacher exercised a measure of control over the unbridled claims of pneumatic prophets who brought new gnosis to the community. In creating Gospel, Mark fulfilled the highest aim of the *maskilim*. Henceforth, the Gospel itself would serve as the norm and guide of truth for the community.

Boring has seen rightly the influence of Christian prophets upon the purpose and genre of Mark, but has not perceived the relationship between the theme and role of Jesus as Teacher in the Gospel and the impact of Christian prophecy. Nor does he realize the dual nature of "Gospel" as Mark's alternative norm and solution to the challenge posed by unbalanced, erroneous prophetic proclamations. Boring's approach focuses too heavily on the absence of Q sayings in Mark as indicative of Mark's anti-prophetic purpose. First, the extent of Mark's familiarity with Q sayings is a debated, unresolved issue. Second, if Mark did know Q, while opposition to prophetic sayings in Q offers a possible explanation for their omission, this is at best a speculative, educated guess. Our approach is simpler and less speculative: To relate Mark's obvious emphasis on Jesus as authoritative Teacher to his *Sitz im Leben* in a manner that indicates his purpose and form in composing Gospel as a norm and check upon the extravagances of pneumatic prophets.

So far we have concentrated on the term διδαχή (and cognates) in elucidating Mark's interest in 1:21–28. But Mark is also concerned to present Jesus as teaching κατ᾽ ἐξουσίαν (1:27; cf. 1:22) in his redactional verses. The term ἐξουσία in the NT normally refers to divine power disclosed in miraculous works (e.g., Mk 6:7) and is closely associated with δύναμις (mighty work) which demonstrates ἐξουσία.[20] Jesus' ἐξουσία is displayed in numerous ways: Exorcisms (1:34, 39; 3:11–12, 15; 5:1–20), healing of diseases (1:30–31, 34, 41–42) and infirmities (2:11; 3:5), forgiveness of sins (2:5, 10), supersession of the Law (2:28; 3:4–5; 7:14–23), profound teaching ἐν παραβολαῖς (4:1–34), and control over the forces (storm demons!) of nature (4:35–41). In 1:21–28 Jesus' ἐξουσία is demonstrated by his exorcism of the unclean spirit with a word of rebuke. Although the conflict with Satan motif was ingrained in the tradition and was received favorably by Mark (evidenced by his inclusion of multiple exorcism pericopes), the redactional passages indicate that this motif was not Mark's primary interest. Rather, Jesus' authority is emphasized in contrast to the inferior power of the unclean spirit. Indeed, we suggest that Mark has intensified this contrast and drawn attention to the source of Jesus' authority by inserting the title "the Holy One of God." The title is unusual, neither a known "messianic" title nor a common Christian designation.[21] It is highly probable that Mark has designed the title within his secrecy motif to refer the reader back to the baptism when the Holy Spirit came upon him.[22] Thereby the contrast between the One empowered by the Holy Spirit and the unclean or evil (ἀκάθαρτον) spirit is sharply drawn. As in the Wilderness, there is no contest: The Holy Spirit is superior to any adversary. "The unclean spirits are being destroyed by 'the Holy One of God,' who is armed with the power of the Spirit of God."[23] This authoritative teaching, which includes deeds of power, is communicated and conveyed to the reader through the pericope as a part of Gospel. The same Holy Spirit present in Jesus to exorcize is still available to overcome demonic powers for the Markan community. This is the heart of the "secrecy" motif for Mark. It is a misnomer to refer to a "messianic" secret in Mark which does not become apparent until the cross and resurrection are recounted. Instead, Mark's interest lies in insisting that one must follow and be illumined by the Risen Christ/Holy Spirit to understand the cross and resurrection within the total scope of Gospel. The "secret" consists of the Holy Spirit disclosing the identity and mission of Jesus through the Gospel to disciples, past and present, transforming them into "insiders" who have truly been given the mystery of the kingly rule of God (4:11; cf. 1:14–15). Jesus' authoritative teaching is called καινή (new) in the sense of being unprecedented and previously unknown[24] but now revealed in a unique way in God's good time according to his divine plan.

Jesus' Authority: The Titles and the Spirit

In the pericopes that follow in this section (1:16–20, 1:21–45, 2:1–3:6) Mark continues to emphasize the theme of ἐξουσία. He selects material from the tradition to demonstrate that in all areas and aspects of life Jesus has supreme authority, for he has been endowed with the Holy Spirit. N. Perrin has called attention to the prominence of the ἐξουσία motif in 2:1–3:6, but he has not noted the association with the Spirit as the source of this authority.

> Here we have Jesus calling disciples, healing the sick, and teaching with authority—exercising his authority in every possible kind of way —and here we also have Jesus involved in controversy with his Jewish contemporaries. This section has been carefully composed by Mark in order to exhibit the authority of Jesus. This would be true even if he is using a cycle of traditional controversy stories, because 3:6 is certainly Marcan and the whole section of 2:1 to 3:6 moves carefully to this climax.... It is to Mark that we owe the actual use of *exousia* in connection with the earthly Jesus.[25]

Perrin thinks that the ἐξουσία of the Markan Jesus flows from the author's concept of the "Son of Man" title which he first attributes to Jesus in 2:10. It is widely recognized that there are three classes of Son of Man sayings in Mark: present ministry logia (2:10, 28), passion sayings (8:31; 9:31; 10:33, 45), future apocalyptic sayings (8:38; 13:26; 14:62). Perrin recognizes that the early church tradition contained all three types of Son of Man sayings but believes that Mark developed the ambiguous term into a definite christological title and structured the three categories of sayings. Thereby Mark established "Son of Man" as the dominant title for Jesus that encompasses his entire ministry. He only used "Christ" and "Son of God" to establish rapport with his readers and then reinterpreted and gave conceptual content to these titles by his developed use of the Son of Man designation.[26]

We concur with Perrin's conclusions (or presuppositions) that the "Son of Man" was not a clearly defined designation or title in the pre-Christian sources or in the pre-Markan Christian tradition. G. Lindeskog, G. Vermes, R. Leivestad, and J. Bowker have undertaken depth studies[27] in the history and development of the term and unanimously reject the view that it functioned as a title in pre-Christian Judaism. Vermes considers the "absence of the Book of Parables, the main alleged source of the 'son of man' concept, from the Qumran Aramaic manuscripts of Enoch," to be the decisive factor in his dismissal of the title.[28] Leivestad is impressed by the apparent ignorance of any such concept as a heavenly or apocalyptic Son of Man on the part of the Qumran community. Lindeskog maintains that a suffering and dying Son of Man has no antecedent in Jewish apocalypticism. Bowker goes even further and maintains that "even if the problem of date (of the Parables) were solved, the apocalyptic use is insufficient to establish that there was a widely known figure in Judaism known as 'the son of man.'"[29]

If the origins of the term as a definite title or concept are not to be found in Judaism, how did it develop in the early church? Many scholars are prepared to attribute a wide diversity of traits and uses to the term "Son of Man" in Judaism, but most think Leivestad goes too far in claiming "that the apocalyptic Son of Man title is a modern invention."[30] More conservative scholars such as W. Manson, V. Taylor, and O. Cullmann hold that Jesus, merging diverse Jewish concepts and traditions in awareness of his own messianic self-consciousness, fashioned a new, broader concept of the Son of Man that is expressed in the three categories of authentic sayings.[31] More liberal scholars such as R. Bultmann and M. Dibelius, while acknowledging that Jesus used the term in some sense, attribute the development of the Son of Man sayings, categories, and title to the preaching of the early church.[32] Moderate scholars such as Higgins, Tödt, and Hooker attribute the development partly to Jesus' sayings about the Son of Man (referring to himself or another as a human or heavenly figure) and the impact of the resurrection upon the church.[33] The church developed and combined older sayings and concepts into a comprehensive christological title. Perrin, as we have seen, goes one step further and attributes great creativity to Mark in this last stage of development.

We maintain to the contrary that Mark has no developed, consistent Son of Man Christology. There was no unified concept of "Son of Man" in Judaism or of "the Man" in Hellenistic sources, and the NT writings beyond the Synoptic Gospels show virtually no interest in the title. Hence, we are largely dependent upon Mark and Q for our assessment of the development of the "Son of Man" concept in the church. Here we find the moderate position, which recognizes both the creative ingenuity of Jesus and the influence of his resurrection upon the church, to be the most convincing. While admitting that we do not have the sources and tools to describe the precise development, we agree basically with Higgin's description:

> It is to his (Jesus') use of the title and concept that all Son of Man sayings in the four gospels ultimately owe their existence. Through its understanding that Jesus was himself the Son of Man, the early church, by increasing the use of the term in future references and by extending it to Jesus' earthly ministry, passion and resurrection,

restored to it a personal content, which in Jesus' usage, although referring to his future status, it did not possess.[34]

Mark accepts the term in the tradition as an authoritative title
applicable to Jesus but has done nothing to coordinate the diverse
nature of the Son of Man sayings and categories into a unified,
coherent christological title. Jesus' climatic confession before the
high priest (14:62) at best supplements the "Christ" and "Son of
the Blessed" (Son of God) titles with the "Son of Man" designation;
however, it does not usurp them, for the centurion at the point of
highest drama confesses Jesus as "Son of God," harking back to
the voice at the Transfiguration (9:7), Baptism (1:11), and the ἀρχή
(1:1). The "Son of Man" sayings are employed by Mark because
they have already been attributed to Jesus in the tradition. They
expressed diverse functions of Jesus that Mark considered part of
his mission, and they presented him under an authoritative title particularly appealing to Jewish Christians in the church. The "Son of
God" title likely was preferred by Gentile Christians. Hence, the brief
mediating title "Son" (1:11; 9:7), which could refer to both concepts and cultures, may be the title that comes closest to expressing Mark's Christology intelligibly and relevantly to his readers in a
mixed Jewish-Gentile community.

When we examine the full scope of Mark's titles for Jesus, we see
that he has taken no initiative in redactional phrases or structure to
integrate the titles into a systematic Christology. He allows each to
stand with its own content and authority as a contribution to the
overall paradoxical portrayal of Jesus as both human and divine,
suffering and exalted, rejected and followed. Mark's real interest is
not in the titles per se but in the authority (ἐξουσία) of Jesus that
they convey in diverse aspects and context of his ministry that
Mark's readers regard applicable to their own situation. As Martin
remarks, "The underlying sense is *Jesus' tacit claim to authority* on
the strength of which he does these things in his ministry which
only God can do (Mark 2:1–12; 2:23–28; 8:38; 13:26; 14:62)."[35]
Hence, to return to Mark 2:1–12, Mark inserts the term ἐξουσία
into the respected Son of Man saying (2:10) as the climax to the
incident in order to stress his main point: Forgiveness of sin, in
addition to exorcisms and healings, demonstrates Jesus' authority
in another sphere of God's kingdom. Mark is not concerned with
the precise connection between sickness and sin, a matter Best
examines meticulously in contending that Jesus' healings involved
the forgiveness of sin.[36] Rather R. Mead perceives correctly that
"the premise that sickness connects with sin is neither affirmed or

denied; it is *used*. It provides a convenient basis upon which the healing of vs. 11 'proves' the claim of authority set out in verse 10."[37] The source of this authority is well stated by Dunn, though we would extend to Mark the understanding he ascribes to Jesus: "Jesus' experience of God embraced non-rational as well as rational elements—*dunamis* to heal as well as *exousia* to proclaim —and he regarded both as valid and important manifestations of the Spirit."[38] Mark has already impressed upon the reader that all the authoritative teaching (word and deed) of Jesus proclaimed in association with manifold honorific titles are undergirded by and testify to the power of the Holy Spirit. Mark's inclusion of the title "the Holy One of God" in the secrecy motif at 1:24 is a not so subtle reminder to the reader of the source of Jesus' authority. In the last analysis, then, Mark's christological concerns are based on his pneumatology.

Finally, we note that the Son of Man sayings and other demonstrations of Jesus' ἐξουσία are used in the service of Mark's dual concept of Gospel: These authoritative events tell the past story of Jesus but in a unique way that anticipates the Spirit of Jesus ministering in power to the receptive reader. This "preaching" interest of Mark is apparent in the redactional transition at 1:39 (cf. 3:14–15; 6:12–13) in which ἐκβάλλειν is connected with κηρύσσειν as a demonstration of Jesus' sovereign power in both word and deed; indeed, the act is the concrete evidence of the power of the word. Mark has already linked the two terms under the heading of "teaching," a function of Jesus he views himself and the Gospel continuing in opposition to extremist prophetic activity. In 2:2 he narrates that Jesus preached the word (λόγος) to them (cf. also 1:45). As U. Luz, J. Schreiber, T. A. Burkill, and J. Jeremias have shown from different perspectives, ὁ λόγος is tantamount to the word "Gospel" in Mark.[39] Also Kee comments, "Obviously, by the time Mark is writing his gospel, the term λόγος includes the fuller Christian message of both kingdom and passion."[40] The passion motif, introduced by Mark in the redactional statement at 3:6, receives stronger emphasis in the latter half of the Gospel. First Mark seeks to convey to the reader the transcendent authority of Jesus in his "teaching," which can be described as "preaching the word." Mark and his readers understand this phrase as a reference to the Gospel. Jesus' past preaching, preserved and re-presented by Mark, continues to instruct the community through the empowerment, past and present, of the Holy Spirit.

Spirit, Authority, and Gospel

Within the section 1:21–3:6 we propose now to treat additional references in the tradition that implicitly refer to the presence and authority of the Holy Spirit as the guarantor of Gospel. These references serve as literary cues to the reader for following perceptively the plot of the story with a sense of personal involvement.

The incident in 2:5b–10, "a secondary interpolation" by either the early church or the evangelist,[41] heightens the divine authority of Jesus. Jesus, in claiming the right to forgive sins, infringes on the prerogatives of God. Only God had the authority to forgive sins —not even the Messiah was ever credited with such authority in Jewish thought.[42] The audacious authority of Jesus is thrown further into relief by the scribes' characterization of his claim as "blasphemy," a term and motif in which Mark shows a key interest by its recurrence at 3:28–29, 14:64, and 15:29. The term implies more than the misuse of the ineffable name; rather, it denotes a denial of the sovereignty of God and monotheism.[43] The reader knows that the charge is false because Jesus' unique relationship to God has already been established by his baptism with the Holy Spirit. Moreover, in 2:8, immediately before Jesus' double act of forgiveness and healing, the reader is told that Jesus perceives "in his spirit" ($\pi\nu\epsilon\tilde{\upsilon}\mu\alpha$) the scribes' *inner* objections[44] and does so "immediately" ($\epsilon\dot{\upsilon}\theta\dot{\upsilon}\varsigma$), a typical Markan term of emphasis. Gently the reader is reminded of the source of Jesus' authority in the Holy Spirit and shares in the author's omniscient narrator perspective over against the blindness of the scribes. This is confirmed by Mark's reference to the Holy Spirit as a developed Christian concept in the redactional passage at 3:28ff. The reader identifies acutely with Jesus in the hearing of Gospel. He reads in recognition that the Holy Spirit is at work in the community in the post-resurrection era in even greater measure for the forgiveness of sins, the deterring of heresy, and instruction in the Gospel.

The authority of Jesus as the Son of Man abrogating the Law (2:23–28) is understood similarly to his authority as the Son of Man who forgives sins. Hooker writes with the eye of Mark:

> for if the Son of Man is Lord of Sabbath—and is therefore entitled to abrogate the regulations concerning it if he wishes—then he possesses an authority which is at least equal to that of the Mosaic Law, a law which was not of human origin, but was given by God himself.[45]

The readers' recall is immediate. This authority was bestowed by the Holy Spirit who resides permanently within him (1:10–11) as the Son of Man (2:10).

There is no evidence that Mark stresses prayer as a permeating motif as does Luke, but he is not oblivious to its role and function (1:35; 6:46; 9:29; 11:17; 11:24–25; 12:40; 13:18; 14:35, 38, 39). Jesus withdraws for prayer at 1:35 in a passage (vv. 35–39) which Bultmann terms "an editorial section." We maintain that Mark has reworked an older tradition,[46] possibly a preserved Petrine pericope, but the present form of the passage is due to the evangelist. For Mark, Jesus' praying was consistent with his unique sonship due to the Spirit's indwelling. Jesus prays in order that he may go and preach under the impetus of the Spirit. Mark and his readers know that effective praying and preaching of the Gospel still require the presence and empowerment of the Holy Spirit. The summary passage (vv. 35–39) connecting the two functions in Jesus' ministry would be read with realization of the vital role played by the Spirit in the church. Thereby, Mark relates prayer, Spirit, and Gospel in his understanding of the passage.

After the pericope of the forgiveness and healing of the paralytic, Mark narrates the tradition of the call of Levi (2:13–14). The account is reminiscent of the call of Simon and Andrew (1:16–20). In both instances Jesus says "Follow me," and instantly the hearers obey. The similarity of form and content indicates that Mark in 2:13–16 expected the reader to recall 1:16–20 and the empowerment of the Spirit that immediately preceded and prepared for Jesus' authoritative call to discipleship. That same empowerment of the Spirit underlies the call to Levi with the identical immediate response. The temporal-spacial gap between Andrew/Peter and Levi in past history and in present narrative-time, and between Gospel and reader in Mark's community, is bridged by the Spirit who enables Jesus to issue the compelling invitation to all hearers of the Gospel: Follow me. The discipleship theme is unquestionably of major importance to Mark, but it functions in Mark's Gospel under the auspices of the power of the Holy Spirit who is the controlling force in the drama.

SECTION 2: MARK 3:7–6:6a

The Authoritative Son and Discipleship

This section begins with a redactional, transitional passage (3:7–12) that links the preceding section with the following materials and discloses the perspective of the evangelist. L. E. Keck thinks that 3:7–12 is the conclusion to the prior section and that the new section begins at 3:13 with the call of the Twelve. He posits three points:[47] (1) 3:7–12 does not introduce any new themes; (2) 3:7–12 stands as a good summary of the preceding section; (3) 3:7–12 is composed largely of traditional material which belongs to a cycle of pre-Markan pericopes (4:35–5:43; 6:31–52, 53–56) reflecting the Hellenistic concept of the *Theios Anēr*. It does not function as an introductory summary.

In response we grant the second point, but challenge the other two. In a detailed critique of Keck's position, Burkill[48] analyzed the syntax and vocabulary of 3:7–12 and concluded that the pre-Markan element is not as extensive as Keck maintained. The geographical sites (v. 8), the Son of God title (v. 11), and the secrecy motif (v. 12) are likely editorial additions designed to enhance the fame and followers of Jesus. The passage is primarily Markan, and the mention of the boat at 3:9, pointing ahead to its recurrence at 4:1, is an indication that it serves as an introductory summary. The reference to the unclean spirits prepares for the climactic clash in 3:22–30 (complete with editorial interpretation). The more plausible view is that 3:7–12 functions in the same manner as 1:14–15— as a transitional passage which links smoothly the two sections stylistically and thematically in the development of the narrative story.

The dominant Markan motif(s) that emerges from the passage is as follows: (a) The growing response of discipleship (b) to the authority of Jesus (c) as the "secret" Son of God. Mark composes 3:7–12 as a transitional passage which looks back to 3:6 as the culmination of a collection of five conflict stories received in the tradition and points ahead to the teaching on the Holy Spirit (3:28–29) and parables (4:10–12). Thereby he expresses the paradox of human culpability and divine illumination that characterizes his Gospel. On the one hand the Jewish leaders can not respond to Jesus because of their own obstinacy and refusal to acknowledge the divine authority of the Holy Spirit in him; on the other hand, the secret of the kingdom of God has not been given to them. In contrast, the common people flock to him and acknowledge his divine authority and power to heal and to subdue demons. The force of this contrast was not lost upon a church fraught with friction within and persecution from without.

Mark is not interested in resolving the theological paradox. His interest is in explaining practically how one may become an "insider" and receive divine aid—by acknowledging that Jesus' authority is from the Holy Spirit, who still brings Jesus to the community to act on their behalf, and by following Jesus (discipleship), which involves suffering service as well as divine benefits. Both conditions are vitally important. Not to see the former leads to spiritual blindness, the state of the Jewish and Roman leaders in both Jesus' and Mark's eras. To miss the latter leads to distortion of the Gospel, represented by Peter and the Twelve (see 8:31–38) initially and continued by radical pneumatic prophets in Mark's church. The corrective is to perceive and to follow the fullness of the true Gospel sanctioned and illumined by the Holy Spirit. To present this kind of unique Gospel was Mark's primary purpose as a teacher following Jesus and using his gospel as his model.

The note of universality is struck by the mention of a great multitude coming from everywhere (3:7), virtually the whole known world in Jesus' time. For Mark the geographical locales signify that both Jews and Gentiles responded to Jesus, and this may well describe the constituency of the Markan community.

Appropriately the pericope of the calling and authorizing of the Twelve follows the editorial summary passage. Consistent with the function of Jesus in 1:14 and 1:39, the primary mission of the Twelve also is to preach (κηρύσσειν). For Mark, κηρύσσειν is virtually synonymous with εὐαγγέλιον. The Twelve are "sent," i.e., divinely commissioned, to proclaim the Gospel. This remains Mark's commission and task and that of his readers who are called by the same authorizing Spirit through the medium of Gospel.

Holy Spirit and Beelzebul

The Beelzebul pericope (3:20–30) elucidates the second aspect of the theme in the summary (3:7–12): the source of Jesus' authority and identity perceived only by committed disciples. The pericope in its present form reflects the hand of the evangelist in bringing together originally separate traditions with redactional connectives into a larger unit. Verse 20 is an introductory comment beckoning back to the multitude at 3:8. The "crowd" and the "scribes" (v. 22a) are readily available whenever Mark summons them to form a context for Jesus' teaching. Verse 21 may have been originally attached to vv. 31ff and inserted here or composed by Mark to prepare for the incident in vv. 31–35.[49] Verses 22b–30, with the exception of the editorial edition in v. 23a which prepares for chapter 4 by the catchword ἐν παραβολαῖς, comprise a unit that was composed originally from independent sayings (vv. 24–26, 27, 28–29) but came to Mark already joined[50] in controversy form by vv. 22b, 23b. The simpler, earlier Q form (Mt 12:22–30; Lk 11:15–23) parallels, with modifications, the Markan structure through Mk 3:27, but Luke's Q logion on blasphemy against the Holy Spirit is placed in another context (12:10). R. Holst argues persuasively that Matthew has inserted a Q saying into a Markan saying in Mt 12:32.[51] H. Anderson contends that Mark reworked the Q logion into the form of Mk 3:29,[52] but it cannot be shown conclusively that Mark knew Q.[53] It appears more likely to us that Mark's and Q's versions developed independently from an earlier saying in the tradition.[54]

The difference between the two versions is striking. Whereas the Q form contains a reference to blasphemy against the Son of Man, which is pronounced forgivable, the Markan form has "sons of men." Schweizer holds that Mark's more general version is later, reflecting a time in the early church when Christians equated Son of Man with the Risen Christ and would no longer pardon any blasphemy against him.[55] Crossan has gone the next step and argued that Mark himself altered the earlier saying because, in the redactor's mind, the earthly Jesus already possessed the Spirit of God.[56] No forgiveness was possible for blasphemy against either the Son of Man or the Holy Spirit since they are virtually identical. The earlier stage of the tradition, closer to the Q form, contained the phrase "speak a word against" (Q: Mt 12:32; Lk 12:10a) instead of the expression "blaspheme against" (Mk 3:28–29; Mt 12:31; Lk 12:10b). The phrase is still visible in Mt 12:32 and less so in Lk 12:10. Mark removed any reference to Jesus as Son of Man by the insertion πάντα ... βλασφημήσωσιν (3:28) and then added ἀλλὰ ... ἁμαρτήματος in 3:29b. The result was that the disjunction between Son of Man and Holy Spirit in the traditional logion (similar to the Q saying) was overcome.[57]

We find this position persuasive and in accord with Mark's perspective concerning Gospel. Mark uses the tradition to convey the Risen Christ/Holy Spirit. Jesus acts in the power of the Holy Spirit in his earthly ministry and in his risen state. There is no significant difference in the evangelist's view. The Holy Spirit is operative in Jesus in both times and forms (earthly and resurrected) for the benefit of his followers. Only the medium of disclosure of the Spirit's "teaching" has changed.

Formerly, the person and gospel of Jesus were the agent and means of revelation; now the Markan Gospel serves the same functions. Since Mark accepts the Son of Man sayings and title as authentic, authoritative designations for Jesus, though qualified by the Holy Spirit, forgiveness of blasphemy against Jesus the Son of Man is as absurd as "Satan casting out Satan." It is highly probable, then, that Mark changed "Son of Man" to "sons of men" to bring the logion into conformity with his theological perspective and concept of Gospel. The objection may be raised that Mark, given his respect for the tradition and the honorific title, would not have deliberately negated a Son of Man saying. Admittedly, Mark has high respect for the tradition: he has committed himself to portray the foundation of the church's life through the tradition. But he is genuinely an author who redacts the tradition extensively, though not arbitrarily, to disclose his consistent theological understanding of the full meaning and significance of the tradition. In view of his emphasis on the role of the Spirit in the Jesus tradition and awareness of the Holy Spirit in the church, he undoubtedly believed he was guided by the Spirit as Teacher to interpret the tradition correctly. In this instance (3:28-29) redaction was necessary to preserve the consistency of the tradition's portrayal of Jesus as the Son of Man baptized with the Holy Spirit.

Verse 30 is generally classified an editorial addition of the evangelist, clarifying to the reader that v. 29 is Jesus' reply to the charge of the scribes in v. 22.[58] This clarification became necessary when Mark altered "Son of Man" to "sons of men," for this removed in the saying the direct reference of Jesus to himself as the Son of Man. The redaction in v. 30 restores that reference and emphasizes that the Holy Spirit in Jesus is the refutation of the scribes' charges. Mark could hardly have drawn attention more forcefully to the authority and role of the Holy Spirit in his Gospel if he had been permitted to compose freehand. Verse 30 marks his stamp of approval on the Holy Spirit as the source of Jesus' authority and the vital norm of judgment and salvation for his own church.

Mark 3:31-34 is traditional material to which Mark has already prepared an introduction in v. 21. Verse 35 is either Markan redaction or a logion rephrased by Mark to include Jesus' entire family in the warning directed to the scribes in the Beelzebul pericope.[59] Crossan sides with Trocmé and more recently Kelber in arguing that the Markan polemic here "is not only a conflict within the Markan community over doctrine (Weeden) but also a manifesto from the Markan church, in whole or in part, against the jurisdictional and doctrinal hegemony of the Jerusalem church."[60] More pointedly, Trocmé, after noting that Jesus' severe condemnation in vv. 28-29 of blasphemy against the Spirit is directed at his family as well as the scribes of v. 22 (ἐξέστη means βεελζεβοὺλ ἔχει), states dogmatically: "What more could he have done to destroy the claims of James and his party? We must therefore consider the author of Mark . . . as the avowed enemy of James, the Lord's brother, sole head of the church of Jerusalem for many years, until his martyrdom in the year 62."[61]

We shall defer detailed discussion of this position since it is obviously connected with the issue of the provenance and purpose of Mark. Suffice it to say at this point that we do not find Jesus' family and disciples portrayed throughout the Gospel in the totally negative manner as this perspective demands. We consider Lambrecht's and Best's evaluations more balanced. They maintain that Mark cast Jesus' family and disciples in a contentious light in this instance, not to completely discredit them, but to show by contrast what true kinship and obedience (v. 35) really mean.[62]

Having made these source and redaction distinctions, we are now in a position to perceive Mark's understanding of this complex. The transitional passage (3:7–12) focuses on the authority of Jesus which is already bestowed on the disciples in 3:14–15. What is the nature and source of this authority? Mark summons the crowd and the scribes again to heighten the drama (vv. 20, 22). On the one side stand the followers of Jesus who seek instruction, and on the other side are gathered the antagonists who seek to discredit and to destroy him. They represent respectively the reader and adherents of Mark's Gospel and the opponents of Mark in the community. The stage is set; the issue of authority is raised; what is the resolution? Mark uses the tradition (vv. 22–29) to stress irrefutably that Jesus' authority is not from Satan, but to the absolute contrary, it is from God in the form of the Holy Spirit. The editorial phrase in v. 30 sharpens the conflict and contrast: unclean/evil spirit versus Holy Spirit. It is the same antithesis that has pervaded the conflict with Satan and exorcism accounts. At this strategic juncture, at the conclusion of the conflict episodes and before the teaching in parables section, Mark reminds and clarifies for his reader the source of Jesus' unparalleled power and authority: the Holy Spirit. The terrible condemnation uttered by Jesus upon blasphemers against the Holy Spirit takes the reader back to the baptism when the Holy Spirit came upon him. Jesus' deeds and words (teaching) are bracketed by these specific interrelated references to the Holy Spirit (1:10; 3:10–29) with the result that all the intervening events, the total ministry and Gospel of Jesus (subjective and objective genitive) is seen as authorized by the very Spirit of God. Mark is not interested foremost in the conflict with Satan theme per se. The earlier debate between Robinson and Best about whether Mk 3:27 declares the complete binding of Satan (Best) or another advance in the continuing conflict (Robinson) is seen to be a secondary issue. Rather, in an age in which Satan was viewed as the source of the evil and calamities that afflict mankind, if Jesus was to be regarded as the Savior, he had to demonstrate authority over Satan. That was the condition *sine qua non* of commitment in discipleship. It is not surprising, then, that the early church interpreted and preserved stories which declared Jesus' divine authority over Satan and his subordinates. In fact, this trend became so popular that the danger arose in some quarters of turning Jesus exclusively into a miracleworker or thaumaturge.[63] Mark had to "tone down" the tradition and balance a miracle ministry with a suffering ministry while presenting both aspects as part of Jesus' mission in accordance with the saving plan of God. The motif of "victor over Satan" was strongly ingrained in the tradition that Mark received. He used the motif, partly because the defeat of Satan still spoke persuasively to his own community, but primarily because it was the best material he possessed for demonstrating Jesus' absolute authority, which he attributes unreservedly to the Holy Spirit. The saying in 3:28–29 attests to the certainty that the Markan community possessed the Holy Spirit.[64] The Spirit maintained continuity between the early Jesus and the Risen Christ for continuing ministry to the community through an efficacious Gospel proclaiming truth and acts of power. It is impossible to read the saying simply as Jesus' past declaration that "the power behind his miracles is that of the Spirit"[65] or that "the drought of the Spirit has ended" and the powers of the age are here,[66] or more specifically, "that all sins shall be forgiven to men, however much they may blaspheme"—an extension of the Son of Man saying in Mk 2:10.[67] Although the Markan logion is likely derived from a saying of Jesus which may well have expressed such convictions, the present literary form and narrative context of the logion reflects foremost Mark's theology and *Sitz*. The Holy Spirit is vividly present through the Gospel to continue the salvific ministry of Jesus.

Is it possible to determine more specifically the function and significance of the passage for the evangelist? We suggest that Mark uses the pericope to address and to correct the topics and meanings of Gospel and discipleship in a community in which both were misunderstood.

The warning to the scribes and the relatives of Jesus is surprisingly short and absolute—condemnation without possibility of forgiveness on this one point. We would not expect Mark to retain excessive hostility toward the Jewish leaders over the original conflict which occurred a generation ago. The intensity of the dialogue (monologue?) and the inclusion of Jesus' relatives within the ranks of those who misunderstand and oppose Jesus alerts the reader to look for an immediate concern of Mark expressed in the narrative. What contemporary conflict and issue is Mark addressing? A polemic against the Jerusalem church and leaders? We have already expressed objection to this position, rendered even less likely if Mark is writing from Rome, removed from these tensions, as we maintain. We suggest that the opposition by first the scribes and then the relatives, according to the redaction by Mark, represents for the evangelist the dual opposition to the church and the Gospel in the Markan community. The scribes who "come down from Jerusalem" typify the continuing blindness of the synagogue to the truth of the Gospel. The Christian community in Rome was flanked by Jewish synagogues in the city that likely openly opposed the fledgling church in its midst. We know precious little about the relationship that existed, but evidently extensive conflict of some kind precipitated the edict of Claudius in AD 49–50, expelling the Jews from Rome. According to Suetonius (*Life of Claudius* 25.4), the ones responsible for the expulsion were "Jews who persisted in rioting at the instigation of Chrestus" (see Acts 18:2) generally understood as a reference to "Christ." John Drane reconstructs the situation as follows:

> So as Christian missionaries came into this situation, the scene was set not only for a confrontation between Christians and Jews, but between one Jewish synagogue and another, as the Jews themselves gave different answers to the new questions introduced by the Christian claims. So serious did these debates become that they seemed even to threaten the stability of the population, and so Claudius decided to ban the Jews from Rome altogether.[68]

Although this depicts a time and situation earlier than Mark's Gospel, the tension and conflict here among synagogues and between synagogue and church in Rome likely continued unabated into Mark's time. There is no need to resort to Jerusalem to find a context accounting for Mark's opposition to Judaism. Mark and his church had challenge aplenty from the Jews in Rome. Quite plausibly the Jewish opposition included attributing to the church "satanic powers," the same charge issued against Jesus by the scribes. In response to this charge, Mark appeals to a word of Jesus as a guarantee that the church is carrying out its ministry by the power of God against those who so slander God's Spirit.[69]

Simultaneously, Mark may intend the warning and rebuke to extend to the wider audience of the Gentile imperial leaders. The scribes who come down from Jerusalem may also typify Roman officials who assault the church in a time of actual or imminent persecution. Let them beware, and let the Christian reader take heart. In denying the Gospel and in opposing the church, they are blaspheming against the Holy Spirit and shall not go unpunished. The sentence of holy law, fueled by the Holy Spirit, applies to Jewish and Gentile opponents alike—to all who oppose the church of Jesus Christ.

Jesus' Family and Blasphemy Against the Holy Spirit

The pericope describing the attitude of Jesus' family brings the challenge even closer to home, right within the Christian community. The history of Markan exegesis evidences many noble attempts to save the reputation of Jesus' relatives, the most ingenious being the suggestion that the phrase οἱ παρ' αὐτοῦ (3: 21) does not refer to Jesus' family but to others who were saying that "he has lost his senses" (ἐξέστη).[70] The apologetic intent of such "exegesis" is obvious, and the interpretations rendered are not supported by solid grammatical and syntactical evidence.

Consistent with our prior depiction of Mark's *Sitz* and purpose in the Prologue (1:1–15) and first section (1:16–3:6), we consider the relatives of Jesus to represent for Mark pneumatic prophets in the community who misunderstood and opposed (unknowingly?) the true Gospel of Jesus. We note anew how awkward and anticlimatic the relatives pericope seems as the conclusion to this unit. We have seen how Mark chose to bend the pericope into the Beelzebul incident instead of deleting it or using it as a separate incident to enjoin obedience, either in the present context or elsewhere in the Gospel. It appears Mark has gone to great pains to preserve the pericope in this particular context. Why? Perhaps Mark was struck by the parallel between the misunderstanding by Jesus' family and the misunderstanding of a contingent in the family of the church. G. Theissen considers Mk 3:28–29 and the Q logion to represent the views of wandering charismatics who identified themselves with the prophetic Holy Spirit to which they gave expression. They set themselves over all other leaders and functions in the church and even claimed "that anyone who has failed to recognize the Son of Man at work on earth has a further chance to arrive at the truth through their preaching."[71] Had such a group become attached to the Markan church?

Earlier, Barrett anticipated that the context of church prophecy provided the clue to interpreting the logion (3:28–29) rightly. The supreme authority ascribed to the Holy Spirit in the saying directed him to situations described by Paul and the Didache in which the gifts of prophecy, allied with tongues, were the chief manifestations of the Holy Spirit in the church. It was even possible for an inspired prophet to declare ἀνάθεμα Ἰησοῦ, accursed be Jesus! (1 Cor 12:3, cf. 1 Jn 4:1–6) in his exaltation of the Risen Lord over against the human Jesus known as the Son of Man. The author of the Didache held prophecy in such high esteem that at one point he boldly equated the testing or examining of any prophet who is speaking in (the) Spirit with committing the unforgivable sin (11:7). Barrett included Mk 3:28–29 within the category of "blasphemy against the Spirit" sayings and implied that the logion condemned critics of prophecy, for the rejection of prophecy "denies the root and spring of the church's life."[72]

Unfortunately, Barrett did not pursue further this avenue of understanding. Instead he focused primarily on the origin and meaning of Mk 3:28–29 in light of OT parallels. He identified Isa 63:10 ("they grieved his Holy Spirit") as "the closest, and perhaps the only, Old Testament parallel to blasphemy against the Holy Spirit." Based upon the Isaiah context, he perceived Jesus as a second Moses whose mission of delivering his people was rejected in a manner analogous to the people's resistance to Moses' efforts long ago. In both instances, the people grieved (blasphemed, LXX) God's Holy Spirit; but since God's final, eschatological act of salvation has occurred in Jesus, those who utterly reject it can no longer find salvation.[73]

Whatever be the merits of Barrett's linguistic-historical analysis (the parallel is forced!), he did not show how this understanding of the passage in Jesus' ministry relates to his tentative suggestions concerning the meaning of the saying in the church. M. E. Boring has sought to correct this deficiency in his exegesis of the passage. His solution is to show that the logion (3:28–29) has always been associated with Christian prophecy from its origin in the early church to its uses in diverse forms in the Synoptic Gospels. His seven-point program[74] may be summarized as follows:

(1) The introductory formula ἀμὴν λέγω ὑμῖν is an indication of prophetic speech.
(2) The saying is a chiasmus in the "sentence of holy law" form used by Christian prophets.
(3) The eschatology in the saying relates it to Christian prophets, who anticipated the Last Judgment and pronounced the divine verdict in advance.
(4) The absolute authority claimed in the logion is such that it could have been claimed only by a charismatic.
(5) The saying was formed as a pesher on Isa 63:3–11 (as Barrett suggested) by Christian prophets who saw in the Isaiah passage the advent and suffering of Jesus by virtue of which the church, empowered by the Spirit, announced forgiveness and judgment.

(6) The saying's concern with the Spirit, which would mean Spirit of prophecy in Palestinian Judaism, indicates that it likely derives from a circle of charismatic prophets who protested against those Jews who claimed that the Spirit (of prophecy) had ceased since Malachi.

(7) The Didache (11:7, 11) confirms that the saying was associated with Christian prophecy by the church.

Boring concludes, "The earliest form of the unforgivable-sin logion is to be interpreted in terms of Christian prophecy and is, in fact, its product."[75]

D. Hill has examined Boring's criteria for establishing the saying as a post-Easter prophetic logion and rejects them as biased in favor of a presupposed position. Based upon other criteria not clearly formulated, he draws two central conclusions:[76] (1) The saying originated with Jesus who also interpreted the OT in a pesher-type way with reference to himself and his mission; (2) The evidence for the logion coming from Christian prophets is peripheral and exaggerated; indeed, ". . . to say that the whole tradition of Son of Man sayings depends on an early prophetic speech event smacks of irresponsibility."[77]

D. E. Aune has also subjected Boring's criteria to careful scrutiny and rejects all but the last point as based upon inconclusive evidence and traits too general to claim any firm connection with early Christian prophetic speech. Aune grants that Did 11:7 does associate a late version of the Unforgivable Sin saying with Christian prophets but questions whether this tells us anything about the original setting. He parts company with Boring's position in this concluding critique:

> When Boring limits the concept of blasphemy against the Spirit to blasphemy against the Spirit of *prophecy,* he has moved illegitimately from the general to the particular. Although the Spirit was primarily associated with prophecy in *rabbinic* literature, the same association does not hold for early Judaism generally or early Christianity, where prophecy is but one of many manifestations of the presence and activity of the Spirit.[78]

Indeed, Aune suggests that the phenomenon of prophecy in the early church was too fluid and varied to define and to categorize adequately. Whereas Boring views the logion as representative of prophetic pronouncement at the Last Judgment, Aune links the Unforgivable Sin saying and the entire Beelzebul pericope with Mark's antimagic polemic. In Greco-Roman paganism, magical procedures were used to acquire divine revelations and to perform miraculous feats. Jews and pagans termed these manifestations acts of magic. In response Christians branded this characterization of practices within the church as blasphemy against the Spirit of God. "The Unforgivable Sin saying appears to fit well in just such an apologetic context in which the Christian community's confidence that the Spirit, and not demonic powers, is at work in their midst is expressed."[79]

The criticisms of Aune against Boring's prophecy thesis may aptly be applied to his own antimagic motif. It offers a possible context and explanation, but the evidence is inconclusive. However, Boring and Aune are not as far apart in their understandings as might appear at first reading. In the ancient world, as in certain cultures and sects today, prophetic activity and magic have traits in common, and no doubt magical procedures were sometimes baptized into Christ as channels of the Spirit (cf. Acts 19:12). In a peculiar turn, Aune's alternative position partially supports the practice and position he sought to abolish: the saying pertains to magical-prophetic activity. However, we maintain that the saying has a more specific function. Mark recognized the danger of uncontrolled magical-prophetic activity in the church and employed the logion in 3:28–29 to bring it under the control of a full, balanced Gospel inspired by the Holy Spirit. Neither Hill, Boring, nor Aune reckon seriously enough with the Markan form and redaction of the logion. If the Unforgivable Sin saying originally was linked with magic-prophecy and the Q form was expounded by prophets, this provides circumstantial evidence that Mark used the logion in regard to magical-prophetic activity also. But sufficient attention has not been given to the fact that in Mark the logion is *not* a Son of Man saying. Neither is it a pronouncement from a prophet but from Jesus. This signifies to the reader that the saying has a positive orientation and content. It does not represent primarily the prophet's views but Mark's rejoinder. We have argued with Crossan that Mark purposely altered the saying from a Q-like saying (though probably independent of Q) in order to eliminate discontinuity and conflict between the earthly Jesus as Son of Man and the Risen Christ. For Mark, they are virtually identical due to the endowment of the Holy Spirit in Jesus who was resurrected. Mark's intentional change in the logion means that in his Gospel it functions, not as an expression of Christian prophets, but as a response to prophets in the church. Mark reshaped 3:28–29 in order to repudiate or to correct a radical expression of pneumatic prophecy that was departing from the true Gospel. Mark adroitly turned the prophets' appeal to the authority of the Spirit against them, and so to speak, fought fire with fire. He found in the material drawn from the tradition the fuel supply for his explosive countercase. Do not the kerygma and tradition testify to the Spirit of God, whom the church knows as the Holy Spirit, endowing Jesus with God's authority? Did not Jesus teach and call disciples to a suffering, serviceful discipleship as the Spirit-baptized Son of God? Did he not die as the Son of Man on behalf of many? Are not these aspects of Jesus' mission, empowered by the Spirit, still a part of the Gospel as the past basis and a present medium of the Holy Spirit's work in the church? Who would deny the revered tradition and the validity of Jesus' earthly ministry under the impetus of the Spirit as the cornerstone of the church's existence and the model for its present life? In this reconstruction of Mark's scenario, making intelligible his alteration and use of the Unforgivable Sin saying, we notice that Mark does not deny the validity of the prophets' manifestations and role. He does not state here or elsewhere that they do not have the Spirit. They are false prophets, not because they are unable to perform "signs and wonders" (13:22), but because they use these spiritual powers illegitimately, for wrong purposes, "to lead astray, if possible, the elect" (13:22b), i.e. to promulgate their own abridged gospel and exalted status in the community. Mark does not attack these narrow pneumatic prophets directly in a manner that would create a complete schism. Perhaps the tension between Mark and the prophets had not yet escalated to the point where communication had become severed and distinct polarities formed. Or perhaps the prophets were so highly esteemed in the community that Mark astutely realized a direct attack would be futile and self-defeating. We do not know exactly what kind of atmosphere and attitudes prevailed. We simply note that Mark's approach appears to be pastoral.[80] He firmly presents his own understanding and content of the full, true Gospel authorized by the Holy Spirit without denying that the prophets demonstrate manifestations of the Spirit. Thereby, the door is left open for a possible reconciliation and reception of the total community to the truth of the Gospel and additional empowerment of the Spirit. Upon these twin pillars stand the future of the church.

To return to 3:31–35, Mark either places or retains with redactions the pericope as the fitting conclusion to the episode in order to dramatize the family or household context of the issue. As serious as the oppression of the external leaders (Jews, Romans) is, the internal challenge is an even greater threat to the survival of the community. Yet, Mark's approach is reserved and pastoral.

Jesus' rebuke of his relatives comes as a shock to the reader. It stimulates the reader's attention readily. How extraordinary! Yet the rebuke does not extend to exclusion of the relatives from the family of Jesus. Kinship is now lifted to a new plane and put on a new basis: obedience to God, as exemplified by the total ministry of Jesus. Likewise, the pneumatic prophets, symbolized by the relatives of Jesus, are invited to participate in this new family of God by becoming the disciples and kinsmen of Jesus, who has the Spirit of God. They are not beyond the pale of redemption and reconciliation. They misunderstand and need correction and instruction. What will be their response? Mark seeks to make their response and each reader's response to Jesus and the Gospel a positive one by supplying further teaching about discipleship and Gospel, undergirded by the Spirit.

In preparation for the upcoming teaching on "insiders" and "outsiders" as part of the Markan "secrecy" motif, the evangelist draws a similar contrast in vv. 31–35 between those who are "outside" and those who are "around Jesus."[81] Those who purport to be closest to him are the ones from whom he has the most to fear. They (the relatives) are "outside." Will they turn to Jesus anew and become "insiders?" What will the disciples do, who are caught in the middle and understand him so imperfectly? How does one move from "outsider" to "insider"? Is it not clear that, contrary to blaspheming the Spirit, one must embrace the Spirit? How does this come about? By doing the will of God exemplified by Jesus. How does one learn about Jesus? By reading and hearing the Gospel. Here is the ἀρχή (beginning and foundation) of the reader's spiritual journey. The Spirit of Jesus is still active. There is hope for illumination and reconciliation within the community.

The Purpose of Parables

The scene shifts with the editorial verse at Mk 4:1, but the redactional references to the crowd (ὄχλος) and the teaching (διδάσκειν) of Jesus continue a theme becoming increasingly familiar: Jesus as the Teacher about discipleship. The evangelist has his own convictions about how hearers come to understand Jesus' teachings, conveyed in this section in the form of parables. Not just anyone can comprehend; only to disciples is it given, that is, revealed, the true meaning of Jesus' parables. This "revelation to disciples" motif is a distinctive Markan contribution in vv. 10–12 to the traditional parabolic material. Mark has inserted these verses between the parable (vv. 3–9) and its interpretation (vv. 13–20) to convey his own understanding of the purpose of parables.[82] He has also composed

v. 13 as an introduction to the interpretation, which may be second-ary but pre-Markan, linking it with the hardening/revelation concept of vv. 10–12.[83] Mark has retained and stressed two OT concepts in the tradition to support his own view. First, he draws upon the concept of par-able as "riddle." The Hebrew equivalent (מָשָׁל, mashal) for parable (παραβολή) is a comprehensive term for many forms of compari-sons, including proverbs, similitudes, stories, and allegories. Mark regards parables as riddles or allegories which cannot be under-stood without divine disclosure. Second, he is influenced by the concept of hardening contained in Isa 6:9ff. The debate over which version (Hebrew or Aramaic) of Isaiah that Jesus and the church used and why Jesus taught in parables has a lively history and continues unabated. However, these matters are tangential to our purpose in determining Mark's understanding. Evans sums up the critical point:

> it would appear that the best understanding of the ἵνα/ μήποτε con-struction in Mark 4:12 is that it is telic, or final, in meaning. According to the logion, Jesus tells his disciples that all things are given in par-ables to those outside *in order that* they may not understand, not repent, and not be forgiven.[84]

In concurrence, we affirm that Mark reflects the harsh view that parables are designed to obscure the secret meaning and are intelli-gible only by divine revelation given to disciples of Jesus. A sharp contrast is drawn between "the ones about him with the Twelve" to whom the secret is given (revealed) and "those outside" for whom everything is in parables (hidden). To whom is Mark referring in these redactional references to "insiders" and "outsiders"? The pre-ceding Beelzebul incident and the interpretation to the parable of the Sower following vv. 10–12 provide clues. Mark 4:17 speaks of "tribulation or persecution" arising "on account of the word" (λόγος, cf. vv. 14–20), a Markan synonym for "Gospel." Coupled with the opposition of the scribes in 3:22, Mark depicts a situation of imminent or actual persecution against the church, probably from both Jews and Gentiles. These antagonists are deaf to the Gospel (4:15) because it is conveyed as a riddle and they do not possess the key to unlock its secret meaning. What is the key? Obvi-ously within the narrative structure and plot, Jesus himself is the key. He provides the hidden interpretation to the Sower parable and instructs the disciples privately concerning the others (v. 34). But this is not the whole story—there is a further development. "Those who hear the word and accept it" (4:20, tradition that fit Mark's purpose perfectly), that is, those who are enlightened and become insiders and disciples have constant access to revelation and the meaning of subsequent parables. Following Jesus as his disciple is the prerequisite for understanding the parables, the word, the Gospel. Discipleship, then, is the ultimate intention of teaching in parables. Within Mark's "secrecy" motif, the "divine hardening" aspect is temporary and subservient to the "divine revelation" that comes through following Jesus.

Mark's situation, though, is much different from that of the Twelve. Jesus is no longer present in human form to explain the parables to the disciples in the church. How does Mark bridge the time gap? He does so by alluding to his dual concept of "Spirit and Gospel" that guarantees the contemporaneousness of Jesus to instruct the church. We have already noted the Markan significance of the "word" ($\lambda \acute{o}\gamma o \varsigma$) in 4:14–20. The term appears again in the concluding editorial passage at 4:33–34, confirming the importance of the "word" for the evangelist. Schweizer comments, "When used without qualification, the concept "word" (TEV: "message") means the preaching which is an ongoing process. Today Jesus' message, of which the parable was speaking, encounters the church in that preaching."[85] Or as E. Linnemann expresses it, the Word for Mark means simply "das Evangelium von Jesus Christus."[86] Through the Gospel which Mark supplies, the Risen Jesus continues "to explain everything privately to his own disciples" (v. 34). In what manner and by what authority? In 3:23, Mark prepared the reader for the ensuing teaching in parables (chapter 4). Then in the logion on the Holy Spirit and the Unforgivable Sin (3:28–29), he provided the hermeneutical key for understanding the $\lambda \acute{o}\gamma o \varsigma$ expressed $\grave{\epsilon} \nu$ $\pi a \rho a$-$\beta o \lambda a \tilde{\iota} \varsigma$. The message is clear: only the possession of the Holy Spirit, permanently linked with Jesus (v. 30), makes one an "insider" and grants entree into the true family of God (vv. 31–35). The section on teaching in parables constitutes in part an expansive commentary on these themes. It is by the revelation of the same Jesus, now present to the reader and church in the form of the Holy Spirit, that understanding of the Gospel and membership in the household of God (church) is achieved. Since Mark was writing foremost to church members, he could assume an initial response of discipleship and access to the Holy Spirit in the church. As a result, he did not work out clearly the relationship between the work of the Holy Spirit and the response of discipleship. On the one hand, discipleship is the prerequisite for revelation by Jesus/Holy Spirit (4:34); on the other hand, revelation by Jesus/Holy Spirit makes discipleship possible (4:11). Mark is content with the paradox, for both truths are acknowledged in the church, though it may be noted that Spirit and Gospel precede discipleship and the church (1:1–15) in temporal sequence and in theological priority.

Calming of the Storm

The pericope of the Calming of the Storm (4:35–41) follows the section on parables and confirms Mark's emphasis upon the Spirit as the manifestation of Jesus to the church for instruction. Given Mark's twofold view of "teaching," it is appropriate that he should select a story depicting the divine power and authority of Jesus in "deed" to undergird further the force and validity of his "word." The story is especially appropriate at this juncture because it is so transparently applicable to the Markan church. As Martin remarks:

> [Mark's church needed] the assurance of Jesus' living presence with them. This is perhaps the chief value of the miracle-stories as they passed through Mark's hands. He is the Lord of the waves, conqueror of death, controller of evil powers, restorer of human dignity and dispenser of true bread.[87]

One of the earliest symbols for the church was the boat or ship. Whether or not Mark knew the symbol, the power of Jesus' acting in ways similar to Yahweh in times of oppression to bring salvation or to re-create the harmony of the universe[88] is readily apparent. Van Iersel sees in the exclamation of the disciples in v. 38 an indication of persecution that was on the verge of sweeping over the church.[89] This is uncertain but is consistent with the reference to persecution in the interpretation to the parable of the Sower (4:17). At any rate, it is clear that Mark has "sandwiched" the teaching of Jesus in parables between references to the authority of Jesus as the Teacher (4:1–2, 38) who is endowed with and still comes in the Spirit to instruct, strengthen and protect the church in time of adversity. Through the very word (i.e., Gospel; cf. 2:2; 4:14–20; 4:33) that Mark proclaims, the Spirit of Jesus is available to the reader and community with unfathomable power.

Our analysis indicates that the specific contents and themes of the parables and miracles were not Mark's foremost concerns. Whether he intended the rebuke (ἐπετίμησεν) and muzzling (πεφίμωσο) of the storm to be a form of exorcism story (cf. 1:25) in an ongoing cosmic conflict, as Robinson and Burkill contend,[90] is uncertain. Possibly this theme was part of Mark's plan to dramatize Jesus' incontestable divine authority. But it was not his primary interest or reason for composing Gospel. Similarly, the parables are vitally concerned with the kingdom of God, but the kingdom per se is not Mark's major concern. The "kingdom of God" is the key theme of Jesus' preaching in the introductory summary by the evangelist at 1:15. Yet, even there it is overshadowed by the dominant concept of "Gospel." The "kingdom of God" was Jesus' major theme, but for Mark, Jesus as the proclaimer of the kingdom has coalesced into the Gospel as the conveyor of Jesus and the kingdom through the agency of the Holy Spirit. The explication of the kingdom and the content of kingdom ethics may be a chief Matthean concern, e.g. in the Sermon on the Mount, but this is not Mark's leading concern. The parables function first and foremost as the background against which Mark explicates his "secrecy" motif of "divine hardening," which characterizes "outsiders," and "divine revelation" given to "insiders." Jesus proclaims his parables and performs his miracles before "outsiders" and "insiders" alike. The content is the same, but the responses are radically different. Why? Because Jesus is present in the Spirit to teach through the parables and miracles, i.e., the Word, the Gospel, and to assure believers that they are indeed "insiders." To provide this basis, means, and assurance of true discipleship is Mark's overarching concern and purpose.

An accompanying theme is the call to faithful discipleship in order that one may have this confidence continually. Instruction in the specific content of the parables on the kingdom, while helpful, did not meet the immediate needs of a church facing persecution. The church must realize that persecution is inevitable, due to human blindness and divine hardening; but comfort and confidence are found in the assurance that she is a privileged community endowed, illumined, and protected by the Spirit/Jesus/God.

Conflict within the Community: Critique of Weeden's Reconstruction

Persecution was not the only problem that the Markan church faced. It is likely that the "insider-outsider" dichotomy of 4:10–12 pertains to a conflict, if not schism, within the community. Best states pertinently:

> If Mark's purpose was pastoral, he was not writing a tract for the community to use outside itself.... The gospel is not something to be proclaimed to outsiders alone... the gospel as it is proclaimed still speaks to the community and should change the way in which its members live.[91]

Weeden claims that "the focus on a secret and exclusive kerygma, concealed from all except those who belong to the narrow circle of the elect (4:10–12, 33–34) is in complete harmony with the *theios aner* attitude."[92] According to Weeden, the disciples represent this heresy in the Markan community. The evangelist opposes the disciples by showing the ludicrousness of their claim—to the contrary, outsiders do see while the disciples remain blind to the truth about Jesus and the Gospel.

We are not convinced by Weeden's totally negative characterization of the disciples. Although they undeniably misunderstand and fail Jesus on numerous occasions, they are still accepted and instructed by Jesus as his disciples. Even after Peter denies him and they all flee, leaving him to die, the resurrected Jesus tells the women to convey the message of a reunion and reconciliation to Peter and the disciples. Best's threefold critique[93] of Weeden's position merits mention:

(1) If the disciples were being represented as heretics, then we should expect a contrasting good or "orthodox" group, but no such group surfaces. We are left with the disciples, warts and all, as the followers of Jesus.
(2) If the disciples were being represented as heretics, we should expect their heresy to be made clear. But their failures are too wide ranging to form any coherent pattern.
(3) Mark depends on the reliability of the disciples in handing on the tradition. His community cannot be expected to accept an attack on the ones to whom they are indebted for their knowledge of the Gospel.

In addition, Tannehill has noted that in the narrative development, the reader tends to identify with the disciples as central characters.[94] Their positive role surpasses the negative features.

In 4:10–12, 33–34 Mark depicts the disciples in a positive, almost idealistic way as "insiders" to whom revelation is given. Mark justifies this portrayal by emphasizing that their understanding is not due to their own merits, but it has been "given." Moreover, their understanding is not based on a secret, esoteric knowledge or gospel divorced from the teaching of Jesus. Instead, the disciples' understanding comes through perceiving the full scope and meaning of the (Markan) Gospel of Jesus Christ. Mark communicates a perspective consistent with the earliest church's view toward independent traditions and collections of parables (4:1–34) and miracle stories (Mark 4:35ff): each pericope or section was heard and understood in light of the whole Gospel, or expressed differently, each pericope conveyed the Gospel of Jesus Christ.[95]

We suggest that this holistic perspective was being ignored by radical pneumatic prophets in the Markan community. They were appealing to a direct secret revelation that was largely divorced from the earthly Jesus and the preserved traditions. They claimed immediate, independent revelation from the Holy Spirit as a special gift. Though personal spiritual pride probably played a part, their claim may also be attributed to the fact that no extended Gospel of Jesus Christ existed. In a community in which only disconnected sayings, stories and catena of pericopes were available, it was inevitable that the comprehensive understanding of Jesus' mission should become obscure or lost as time passed. It is completely intelligible that in some circles the entire ministry of Jesus would have been relegated to the mystic past and the present experience of the Holy Spirit been regarded as the touchstone of truth. This had already occurred in Corinth, Thessalonica, and possibly Rome, and likely in other places from which no records have survived. As the apostles died out during second generation Christianity, the time of Mark, the anchorage of the faith in eyewitness remembrances and accounts of the historical Jesus became unsteady and unsubstantiated. No adequate authoritative norm was available to serve as a check upon subjective formulations of the Gospel and verifying manifestations of the Spirit. The pneumatic prophets filled the void and offered the excitement and verification of personal revelation replete with signs and wonders.

Mark confronted this misunderstanding and perversion of the Gospel by appealing first to the prestige and model of the disciples in idealistic terms and by placing the ultimate source of authority in revelation from Jesus/Holy Spirit. Though the disciples did not completely and consistently appropriate the revelation given, they had that opportunity, and potentially that privilege is still offered to disciples in Mark's church. The reader-disciple is at no disadvantage; indeed, he has the advantage of going beyond identification with the disciples and learning from the disciples' failure in order to demonstrate superior obedience and faith.

Second, Mark emphasized that this revelation and true understanding comes through the Word, that is, the Gospel. The Gospel is firmly tied to the tradition stemming from the historical Jesus, and apart from the preaching of Jesus preserved and proclaimed by Mark, there is no Gospel (literally and figuratively). Boring's comment, in light of these developments, takes on new importance beyond his purview: "The achievement of Mark, in creating the gospel form and thereby binding the word of the Lord to the pre-Easter Jesus, has not been sufficiently appreciated."[96] Truly, in redefining

Gospel by this new form and establishing Gospel based on tradition but alive with the Spirit of Jesus as the norm of Christian teaching (word and act), Mark performed an ingenious (inspired) feat. His achievement was particularly remarkable as the first work of its kind and as a unique solution to a life-threatening situation in the church.

Conflict within the Community: Critique of Kelber's Reconstruction

Boring's observation (quoted above) is also shared by Werner Kelber, who, in essential agreement with Boring, formulates a new perspective on Mark's purpose in composing his Gospel in a written text. Kelber, too, views Mark as a polemical work combating false prophets who stressed the authority of the "orally effected presence of Jesus.... Utilizing the prophetic *egō eimi* style of speech, these prophets spoke as representatives of Jesus and embodied in this manner his very authority."[97] According to Kelber, Mark responded to this challenge by use of the written medium in composing a Gospel text. "The very form of gospel came into existence as a radical alternative to a tradition dominated by an oral ontology of language."[98] By composing a written text with a pre-resurrection, christological framework, the authority of the living Lord, which in the same genre of the prophets continued to address hearers, was stilled and transferred back to the earthly Jesus. Kelber agrees with Boring that "Mark has so few sayings of Jesus because he is suspicious of Christian prophecy as it is present in his community and experienced in his sayings tradition."[99] Indeed, Kelber views, not only the text and framework of Gospel but also its content, to reflect the aim of Mark in combating a living oral tradition with emphasis on the Risen Christ.

> The textually facilitated return to the past, the reconstruction of Jesus' past authority, Mark's distancing himself from the immediacy of the crises, the deflation of aspects of realized eschatology, the absence of a resurrection appearance story, Mark's reservation toward *logoi*, the de-eschatologizing function of the two speech complexes, Mark's dismissal of the disciples and the prophets, the personal and charismatic heirs of Jesus, as legitimate representatives of oral transmission—these and other features combine to offset the dilemma created by Jesus' oral over-representation and the ensuing crises in confidence.[100]

According to Kelber, the result of Mark's work is that Jesus is proclaimed to be absent from the present time of the community until the parousia. The only presence reconstructed by Mark is "a written re-presentation of Jesus' past...an alternative to the presence of the living Jesus in oral proclamation."[101]

We concur basically with Kelber's assessment of the tension and dilemma confronting Mark in his conflict with the false prophets, although we do not find evidence of the exacerbated polarities he posits. Instead of harsh condemnation, Mark warns (3:28–29), corrects, and instructs about revelation and discipleship (4:10–12, 13–20, 33–34) and encourages hearers to become obedient relatives of Jesus and members of the family of God (3:31–35). We read the first Gospel as Mark's reply to the pneumatic prophets in a different way from Kelber. First, Kelber has been misled, possibly by modern obsession with the printed word as the guarantor of validity, into viewing the contrast between text and orality as the decisive issue for Mark. Our examination indicates that the clash and contrast is not between text and orality, but between private revelation and public Gospel as the norm of truth and life for the church. Kelber has mistaken the form of expression of the opposing positions for their substance and intent. It is true that the "false prophets" relied heavily upon immediate revelations voiced in sayings accompanied by "signs and wonders." It is true that Mark writes a Gospel text as an alternative corrective, but it is a false assumption that "text versus orality" is the principal issue; rather, subjective revelation versus public Gospel based on tradition is the issue in contention. Given the emphasis on oral expression in the ancient world, it is highly probable that Mark told and retold the Gospel many times before he wrote it down.[102] Even after he committed it to writing, it is doubtful that his church thought of the Gospel as a text. There were few readers in the community (an anachronism of which modern critics are still guilty!); rather, the Gospel was heard as a preached message, a sermon, by the vast majority of members. It was an oral event similar in mode of delivery to the prophets' orations. The Gospel was written down, likely to aid disciples in relating to others the fullness of the Word so critical to Mark's interest, lest further misunderstanding and perversion occur, and to preserve the Gospel (the only "Gospel" in Mark's unique sense) for posterity in the church.

Second, Kelber has failed to recognize the twofold focus of Mark's Gospel. Kelber sees correctly that Mark attributes authority to the earthly Jesus and the Jesus tradition over against an unbalanced obsession with esoteric revelation from the Risen Christ. However, he does not see that Mark views Jesus as still present in and through the medium of the Gospel. He rejects this insight first popularized by Marxsen because, third (with Marxsen), he does not apprehend the role of the Holy Spirit in the Gospel and community to re-present Jesus and his entire ministry from his baptism in the Holy Spirit to his resurrection and presence in the Holy Spirit until the arrival of the promised parousia. It is Mark's concept and awareness of the Holy Spirit in the Gospel and in the community that renders completely unconvincing Kelber's concept of the absent Christ in Mark's Gospel.[103] We defer to a later section the examination and rebuttal of his exegesis at 14:28 and 16:7, preferring at this point to demonstrate the methodological fallacy in his approach to the Gospel. His artificial contrast between "orality and text" obscures the dominant issue of whether esoteric revelation or Gospel was to function as the medium and content of Jesus'/Holy Spirit's authoritative word to the Markan community.

The Markan "Secrecy" Motif

The Markan meaning of "the secret" (τὸ μυστήριον) is now evident. Among Jewish apocalypticists at Qumran and in the mystery religions, μυστήριον denoted mysterious, secret knowledge or rites which were communicated to initiates. In the NT, and especially in Paul's letters, the term means "open secret" made known by God and may designate "the Gospel."[104] Mark reflects familiarity with both of these connotations. "The kingdom of God" for Mark is virtually identical with Jesus. Jesus proclaimed that the kingdom was being mediated in part through his words and deeds; for Mark, the kingdom and Jesus, now merged and known as the Risen Christ, are virtually identical. As we have seen, he has already inseparably linked Jesus with the Gospel (1:1, 14–15) in his theology. Mark drew upon these insights to present "the secret of the kingdom of God" as the revelation of Jesus through the Gospel. The Gospel is proclaimed to hearers in general, but, as the larger context discloses, in the Markan community only those disciples who are illumined by the Holy Spirit/Risen Jesus can penetrate the meaning and understand the Gospel. What they understand is not foremost cognitive information but the Good News that the Risen Jesus in the form of the Holy Spirit still comes in and through the Gospel to guide the hearer and the church. The "secret" then is removed from the "messianic secret" motif in the editorial sense represented by Wrede or Dibelius in his popular characterization of Mark as "a book of secret epiphanies."[105] The "secret" in the passage is neither messianic nor apologetic, i.e., neither a reply to the question why Jesus was not universally recognized as the Messiah nor a veiling of the fact that faith in his messiahship presupposes belief in his resurrection.[106]

Nor is it accurate to state that while modern critics speak of the "messianic secret" of Mark, the evangelist himself was concerned with the secret of the kingdom of God[107] in the same way that Jesus gave primary emphasis to the kingdom. As we have seen, the proclamation of the kingdom has been largely subsumed into the proclamation of Jesus himself by Mark. John's Gospel shows the culmination of this development in the church.

Against the trend of most contemporary scholarship, we contend that "secret messiahship" and "kingdom" were not Mark's primary concerns in 4:10–12. Rather, the "secret" in the parables serves a polemical and pastoral function. The secret is disclosed, not to all who claim charismatic powers, but to disciples and readers who hear the Gospel. They understand that Jesus, empowered by the Spirit to initiate the kingdom, continues to impact the church with God's kingly rule by the same Spirit. Those who substitute "Spirit and Prophecy" for "Spirit and Gospel of Jesus" (objective and subjective genitive) jeopardize the church's survival. They do not understand the secret rightly and must be corrected and instructed in the full scope of the Gospel that calls readers to mature discipleship. To become faithful disciples who adopt the model of the Gospel's portrayal of Jesus and are equipped by this same Jesus/Holy Spirit for service—this is Mark's pastoral aim toward the community.

Miracles in Mark's Gospel

There is general agreement among scholars that Mark received from the tradition a catenae of miracle stories[108] (4:35–5:43) that he worked into his narrative with minor redactions. As we suggested above, Mark included these stories in order to dramatize Jesus as the "doer of beneficent and wondrous deeds" following accounts that established the authority of Jesus' word. Moreover, each pericope proclaims the call or necessity of faith and/or discipleship as the expected response (see 4:40, disciples; 5:20, Gerasene demoniac; 5:34, restored woman; 5:36, Jairus). Thus, the stories in the complex reiterate four times a dual Markan motif: the authority of Jesus—over nature, over demons, over sickness, over death—as the basis and stimulus for the call and benefits of discipleship (past and present). It was not necessary for Mark to make any radical alterations in the material to accomplish his aim. The nature and content of the complex served well this purpose.

Many scholars consider these stories in their pre-Markan form to have presented Jesus in the mold of the Hellenistic *Theios Anēr.* Mark, it is claimed, "tried to play down the importance of miracles by subordinating them to the picture of Jesus who had to suffer."[109] This claim has merit, but it is badly expressed. First, as we have seen, one can no longer speak with confidence of a well-defined *Theios Anēr* figure in the Hellenistic world. Second, as Achtemeier recognizes, Mark does not "play down" the miracles but balances them with the equally important picture of Jesus as the one who is under divine necessity to suffer and to die."[110] Third, Mark encompasses both these roles of Jesus in his understanding of "Gospel" as his overarching category and purpose. Gospel embodies traditions that express the charismatic miracles of Jesus and the redemptive death of Jesus. Through these traditions the Markan community looks to Jesus for healing and for salvation, which are closely related and encompassed in the term σῴζω (5:23, 28, 34; cf. 8:35, 10:26, 13:13, 20).

Again, the pastoral approach of Mark is apparent. If he had wanted to invalidate and to reject the charismatic prophets in his church who stressed "signs and wonders," he would have omitted or severely restricted the element of the miraculous in the Gospel. Instead, he emphasizes Jesus as healer and exorcist and restorer. He considers these activities to be legitimate functions of Jesus that members of his own community should affirm. To "play down" the miraculous is not Mark's intent. Rather, his insistence is that the current charismatic activities of the church be validated by historical traditions in the Gospel and be balanced and checked by awareness of the sufferings and death of Jesus. Both are equally valid emphases of the church's activity. Correction, instruction, and reconciliation in a divided but not polarized church are Mark's aims.

Mark repeatedly reminds his readers that the Holy Spirit is the divine force in Jesus and is currently available through the medium of Gospel. The reader knows that Jesus has the authority (ἐξουσία) and power (δύναμις) to perform miracles because the Holy Spirit resides within him. The unclean/evil spirits have confronted Jesus/Holy Spirit and attempted to subdue him by invoking knowledge of divine names: "The Holy One of God" (1:24) and "the Son of God" (3:11). In 5:7, a verse Best characterizes "a peculiarly Markan factor,"[111] a similar title is introduced: "Son of the Most High God." By associating this title with the previous names and the event of the baptism of the Son by the Holy Spirit, Mark directs the reader's gaze to the source of Jesus' authority: the Holy Spirit of God. The use of "Lord" in the redactional vv. 5:18–20[112] reflects also Mark's knowledge of the Risen Christ who dwells in the Spirit with his church. The restored man is told to tell how much the Lord has done for him (v. 19). This is the privilege and responsibility of each disciple in the church who has been cleansed by Jesus/Lord/ Holy Spirit, titles Mark frequently interchanges from his post-resurrection perspective. Indeed, conceivably the reference to "the Decapolis" contained a veiled reference to the mission of a predominantly Gentile church such as Rome.

In the pericope of the healing of the woman with the flow of blood (5:25–34), Jesus perceives in himself that power (δύναμις) has gone forth from him. The belief that thaumaturges possessed special powers is ancient; hence, it is likely that 5:30a belonged to the pre-Markan tradition. However, it is also likely, in light of the evangelist's fondness for ἐξουσία and δύναμις in expressing Jesus' divine authority, that he understood the δύναμις to be a manifestation of the Holy Spirit. The Holy Spirit heals! To deny him and to attribute this power to any other source constitutes blasphemy (3:28–29), a subtle reminder to prominent pneumatic leaders in the church concerning the source of their "signs and wonders." In no way does Mark diminish the miraculous healing power of Jesus. But he is careful to make clear to the reader that the healing power comes from Jesus via the Holy Spirit and is verified by venerable tradition incorporated in Gospel, not by subjective experience and exalted claims alone.

Mark concludes this second major section by stressing again the themes of teaching, authority, and discipleship as prerequisites for receiving the benefits of Jesus' power. The pericope (6:1–6a) has been reworked by the evangelist, evidencing editorial editions in vv. 1, 2a, 5b, 6a[113] in order to stress these themes forcefully.

Under the heading of teaching (διδάσκειν) Mark includes both wisdom (σοφία) and mighty works (δυνάμεις). They both manifest Jesus' authority as "teacher" consistent with Mark's emphasis at 1:22, 27. Ellis suggests that "wisdom" in Mk 6:2 should be understood "as a gift of the Spirit or one expression of the Spirit's work, i.e., in prophetic perception (1Cor 12,8; cf. Col 1,9) or teaching"[114] similar to the meaning of the hendiadys in Acts 6:8, 10. Mark may have assumed this knowledge by the reader. Certainly it is in agreement with his own theology, but admittedly he has done little to stress this point in the pericope. He was more concerned with establishing the specific authority of Jesus as the Teacher issuing the call to faithful discipleship.[115] Where a positive response is lacking because of unbelief (ἀπιστίαν) no (or few) mighty works are possible (6:5–6). What constitutes unbelief? As the context indicates, failure to perceive that Jesus is the divine Teacher. His teaching includes the whole of the Gospel, i.e., Mark's entire composition based, so he believed, on authentic reports concerning the words and deeds of the earthly Jesus. Mark intended for the reader to grasp two leading ideas:

(1) The Gospel is founded on Jesus' teaching and conveys Jesus' teaching in the present situation. The perceiving, faithful disciples (insiders) receive the benefits of Jesus' authority; for the unfaithful (outsiders) there is catastrophic loss.

(2) Jesus is foremost the divine Teacher and secondarily a Prophet. Mark acknowledges the prophetic role as a valid one, but it is subsumed under the teaching function and receives no special attention in the Gospel as a function of Jesus. This treatment is in accord with Mark's *Sitz* in which he occupies the role of the Pastor-Teacher in correcting an unbalanced prophetic contingent and motif in his church through his unique concept and composition of Gospel.

SECTION THREE: MARK 6:6b–8:21

Teaching and Discipleship: Mark 6:6b, 7–13

Mark 6:6b appears to be another editorial, transitional verse. Though brief, it expresses the evangelist's interest in the comprehensive teaching ministry of Jesus. The verse serves to conclude the previous section and to introduce a new section in a manner similar to 1:14–15 and 3:7–12. Although some critics have maintained that the verse is too brief to serve as a summarizing passage,[116] the rubric of Jesus as Teacher has been well established by Mark. He teaches by word and deed, proclaiming the Gospel past and present, endued with the Holy Spirit. Hence, the brevity of the passage constitutes no sound objection to its function as a summarizing, transitional verse.

As in Mk 1:14–15 and 3:7–12, 6:6b is followed by the call to discipleship (6:7–13). The response of discipleship is consistently stressed as the appropriate response to the preaching, teaching mission of Jesus, that is, to hearing the Gospel. The exercise of authority by the disciples in the redactional verses (6:12–13)[117] is a significant accompanying point of importance to Mark. He believed that as Jesus bestowed authority upon the "Twelve" in the past, the Risen Christ in the Spirit still gives authority to persons who hear the Gospel and become his followers. Other Markan motifs in the passage, such as the significance of the "Twelve," the "conflict with Satan" and the "forgiveness of sins," are secondary to the major theme. The evangelist depicts the disciples proclaiming (to the reader) the distinctively Christian Gospel.[118]

John and Jesus

The lengthy account of John's death serves to disassociate completely John's ministry of preparation from Jesus' ministry of fulfillment, a contrast first introduced at 1:2–8, 9–15. In the confession at Caesarea Philippi (8:28–29), the distinction in authority between John and Jesus is again drawn. In 11:27–33 the authority of John as a prophet is upheld, but the greater authority of Jesus is evident to the readers (insiders), though not to the chief priests, scribes, and elders (outsiders). No further references to John appear in the Gospel. From this point on, Mark alludes only to Elijah (15:35), whose function John assumed. Mark's treatment of John is intriguing. It may be that he regards John (Elijah) as a type or model of the pneumatic prophets in his church. Elijah was possessed and empowered by the Spirit for miraculous deeds and passed on the mantel of the Spirit to his disciple Elisha (2 Kings 2). Similarly, the prophets in the Markan community admittedly performed extraordinary feats by the endowment of the Spirit. Nevertheless, although John has a significant role in announcing the eschatological inbreaking of the Lord (χύριος), participating even in the crucial event of Jesus' baptism in the Holy Spirit, John was only preparatory to the mission and Gospel of Jesus, the Spirit-endowed Son of God. In Mark, John does not announce the kingdom of God as in Matthew's account (3:2). He does not preach the Gospel. Likewise, the prophets in the Markan church occupy an ancillary relationship to the full Gospel of Jesus Christ. Like John (Elijah), they have authority from the Spirit but are not exercising it in accord with the full understanding of Gospel. This parallel or correspondence accounts for the surprisingly lengthy account of John's demise and is consistent with the standard view that the episode is "a prophecy of man's opposition to Jesus and of Jesus' future destiny." Clearly, Mark was doing more than filling in the gap between the sending out of the Twelve (6:7–13) and their return (6:30–34).[119] Mark included the detailed account of John's death primarily to stress the clear separation (not opposition) between John's and Jesus' ministry and Gospel. John's gospel was incomplete; correspondingly the pseudo-prophets' teaching is also inadequate and deficient. But they are not yet cut off from or dead to the truth. Mark does not regard them as irreconcilable schismatics. They require instruction in the meaning of the Gospel, true discipleship and use of spiritual authority.[120] What will be their response? Will unity in the church be restored? The outcome is uncertain and problematic.

Jesus Supports His Disciples

Upon their return the disciples, having been invested with authority from Jesus, are now able to assist in the feeding of the five thousand. As a miracle story, the account seems to demonstrate once more the divine authority of Jesus which is bestowed upon his disciples. Does the story also have Eucharistic overtones, signifying to the reader the abiding spiritual presence of Jesus with the church in the Eucharist? Boobyer thinks not, preferring the view that the feedings "illustrate the fact that the mighty works of God in Moses' day were being repeated in and through Jesus."[121] Best also finds no Eucharistic implications, claiming that Mark "intends us to see the miracle as Jesus feeding the church with his words."[122] However, Quesnell, Bowman, Nineham, and Robbins maintain that to early Christians, the story would be strongly reminiscent of their Eucharistic worship.[123] Quesnell argues that Mark's aim is disclosed in the enigmatic comment in 6:52. Mark intimates to the reader that rightly understood the feedings express "the full meaning of Christianity. It means death and resurrection with Christ. It means the union of all men in one Body. It means his abiding presence."[124] Only the abiding presence of Jesus Christ/Holy Spirit can penetrate and illumine hardened hearts, turning outsiders into insiders. This is the "secret" of the Gospel.

These emphases coincide with Mark's purposes in writing Gospel. The presence and authority of Christ experienced in the Eucharist is vouchsafed in the tradition and is related firmly to his suffering. Immediate revelation and miraculous powers are inadequate for right belief. The full Gospel is required and is contained in germ in the pericope. However, Best is not far wrong in stating that Jesus "feeds the church with his words." He is present through the story as "Gospel" as well as in the Eucharist substantiated by the Gospel. The Gospel links both ways that the church experiences Jesus in the Spirit. The importance of this theme to Mark is demonstrated by the fact that he includes the account of the feeding of the four thousand in 8:1–9 to stress it anew. All ingenious attempts to find deep meaning in the numerology of the feeding accounts have been singularly unpersuasive.[125] The simpler solution is better: Mark utilized two separate traditions to emphasize the relationships between Eucharist, discipleship, and Gospel in a central, common rite of the church. The disciples' lack of understanding (8:14–21) again provides a negative contrast to the positive response Mark expects from the reader. But the point is implicit that by abiding with Jesus they have the opportunity to be illumined, to understand the Gospel, and to exercise the privileges and responsibilities of discipleship. Jesus' presence in the Spirit provides the reader of the Gospel the same opportunity.

The succeeding pericope in 8:11–13 accords well with Mark's general attitude toward miracles: They are valid demonstrations of Jesus' authority and a stimulus for faith and discipleship but are neither ends in themselves nor a substitute for Gospel. Whether the pericope was already joined to the feeding narrative in the pre-Markan tradition[126] or added by the evangelist[127] is uncertain and secondary. Mark uses it to temper excessive enthusiasm over "signs" being performed by charismatic prophets in the church. Mark does not deny the reality of signs, but he minimizes their importance apart from the context of Gospel and the illumination of Jesus/Holy Spirit. Martin notes that the terms (ἀνα) στενάζειν and πνεῦμα are connected in both Mk 8:12 and in Rom 8:23 and suggests hesitantly that Mark is referring to the sighing of the Holy Spirit in Jesus. Hence, Jesus cannot give a sign *from* God (save the cross) as his enemies demand: *he is God* (divine).[128]

We agree that Mark is astute enough to see a reference to the Holy Spirit in the phrase, but think his view of signs is qualified by his "secrecy" concept. Jesus has already performed mighty works which are "signs from heaven" to those who have eyes to see or to whom it is given. Mark makes a distinction between a mighty work (δύναμις) and a sign (σημεῖον). Although the Greek syntax in 8:12 is difficult, the idiom, reflecting the Hebrew manner of making a solemn vow,[129] seems in Mark to mean that no further signs are necessary or would be efficacious. True, Jesus continues to perform mighty works but blind "outsiders" will accept no mighty work as a "sign from heaven." The passage reflects the "secrecy" motif of Mark's Gospel.

Similar to the episode of the Calming of the Storm, the pericope of Jesus' Walking on the Sea (6:45-52) depicts graphically his supernatural authority—a very present help in trouble for the church (cf. 6:50). Indeed, Dodd has pointed out in his form-critical analysis the striking similarity between this pericope and the general type of post-resurrection narrative.[130] This lends credence to the view that the early church understood the passage as an assurance that the Risen Christ was near to protect his church. The eerie form of his manifestation, mistaken for a ghost (φάντασμα) by the disciples, anticipates his appearance in the Spirit (πνεῦμα) to the church. What Jesus has done in the past he can still do in the Spirit in the present. The former lends hope for the future.

The Spirit and the Law

Mark 7:1–23 is a composite, comprised of a collection of sayings or smaller units on the general subject of scribal tradition.[131] The three replies of Jesus (vv. 6–8, 9–13, 14–15) evince only a superficial, forced thematic unity. Dibelius notes that the words of Jesus in vv. 6–14 do not deal with the question posed by the scribes and Pharisees in v. 5.[132] The Markan introductory formula ("and he said to them") in vv. 6 and 9 indicates that Mark has conjoined two independent sayings with the result that vv. 9–13 illustrate the unsupported charge of vv. 6–8.[133]

Mark introduces the crowd in v. 14, which suggests that v. 15 came from another context. Moreover, this saying about true cleanliness relates to eating and not to washing.[134] It is an independent saying inserted by the evangelist to support his own viewpoint. Verses 17–18a show the typical Markan technique of Jesus drawing aside the disciples for private instruction whenever the evangelist wishes to add information or to express interpretation (vv. 18b–19). Verses 21–22 contain a typical Hellenistic catalogue of vices employed here to expound v. 15b.

This analysis indicates that the evangelist has joined disparate materials to construct a polemic against the Jewish Law being binding upon Gentile Christians. The insertion of the quotation from Isa 29:13 as a charge against the vanity of Jewish worship, owing to their substitution of human commands for the divine Law,[135] followed by the tenor of the other sayings, indicates the perspective of Mark. The issue goes beyond the comparatively trifling question of the ritual washing of hands and involves the entire problem of the Christian attitude toward the Jewish Law. Mark's position is unequivocal in the pronouncement in v. 19, "he declared all foods clean." However, Mark's interest goes beyond this issue, which had probably been settled in the church before his time, though the church needed to be reminded of this stance in the polemic with the synagogue. The pericope demonstrates the supreme authority of Jesus in yet another dimension: he sets aside aspects of the Law; hence, he is superior to the Law. On what basis and by what authority? Only the reader knows—by the authority of the Holy Spirit. Yates suggests that Mark contrasts the external means of purification in the Law with the inner purification of the Holy Spirit as the fulfillment of 1:8b.[136] This may be too subtle, but the construction of the entire section and Gospel allows the reader to accept without question Jesus' dictum because of his endowment with the Spirit as the Son of God.

The church still has access to this same authority; however, arbitrary, subjective revelations and dictums delivered by self-proclaimed prophets are unacceptable. The authentic utterance must be substantiated by the tradition contained in the Gospel, which is empowered to provide effective purification and guidance to the church. The appeal to "Spirit and Gospel" as the norm of the church's life and beliefs—this was the overarching purpose of Mark in his treatment of the Jewish Law in his work.

Ministry to the Gentiles

This section of the Gospel (6:6b–8:21) contains two additional healing miracle stories (7:24–30, 31–37) which require little comment. As we have seen, in the first half of his work Mark includes numerous miracle stories to dramatize Jesus' unique authority, attributed ultimately to the Spirit of God, in every realm of the church and world. The striking aspect of these two healing stories is the Gentile territory in which they are performed. No motive is given for the journey, and the route of the return (v. 31) is quite implausible. Hence, in light of Mark's suspect knowledge of geography in Galilee and beyond, vv. 24 and 31 are generally recognized as editorial.[137] Mark has gone to some pains to include direct requests from and responses to Gentiles. Jesus is reluctant to respond to the woman's request, and the deaf-mute is a "Gentile" only by the itinerary (and then marginally!). The first story may reflect the early church's reluctance originally to embark upon a Gentile mission. But these were the best (only?) stories Mark had available to relate Jesus' ministry to Gentiles. Writing to a predominantly Gentile church, Mark considered these accounts especially pertinent in proclaiming the contemporary authority of Jesus/Spirit to his readers via Gospel. Jesus' positive response to Gentiles' needs buttressed the church's condemnation of the Jews' traditions and Jesus' surpassing authority to set aside Jewish Law as illustrated in the preceding pericope (7:1–23).

SECTION FOUR: MARK 8:22–10:45

Markan Structure and Motifs

The section extending from Mk 8:22 or 8:27 through 10:45 is generally recognized by commentators to be the pivotal point in Mark's Gospel. However, the passage is not pivotal in the sense that the disciples or the readers break through to a new, clear comprehension of Jesus and his mission. No, the disciples still fail to understand him (cf. 8:32–33; 9:32; 10:35ff), and the reader has known from the beginning that Jesus is the Spirit-endowed Son (1:1, 9–11). The character development is minimal: "The people and the opponents appear in precisely the same way as before."[138] Yet the evaluation of the passage as pivotal is apropos, due to the evangelist's shift in theological emphasis: From this point he proceeds to heighten the suffering aspect of Jesus' mission and the accompanying concept of a discipleship that involves persecution and "taking up the cross." This motif balances the earlier emphasis on the power of Jesus to effect mighty works and rounds out the full understanding of the Markan Gospel. Although the disciples move only from lack of understanding to misunderstanding (as Tyson and Weeden have shown),[139] Mark expects the reader, aided by a post-resurrection perspective and the Holy Spirit, to grasp the whole Gospel and the full scope and meaning of faithful discipleship.

We view 8:22–26 as a quasi-transitional passage that is loosely joined to and prepares for the transitional passage proper in 8:27–33. Lightfoot[140] and Kuby[141] have drawn attention to 8:22–26 as a transitional pericope in the sense that the way is prepared for the confession of Peter in 8:27–30. Here Peter "sees" something of the identity of Jesus, although it is more accurate to say he sees imperfectly and misunderstands the implications of what he sees. The disciples also need a "second touch," and this will come after the resurrection, promised repeatedly in 8:31, 9:31, and 10:34. For Mark and his readers, the "second touch" is provided by the Spirit of Jesus (Holy Spirit) operating through the Gospel and various means in the church authorized by Gospel.[142]

Tyson is undoubtedly correct in recognizing that Mark has sandwiched this central section on discipleship (8:27–10:45) between two stories that stress the necessity of sight being restored by Jesus if one is to understand Jesus, the Gospel, and discipleship.[143] The reader and candidate for discipleship must understand that the cross is as vital to the Gospel as the miracles. He must realize that only the resurrection of Jesus made possible both good news to hear (content) and the revelation bringing understanding. He must grasp that the Risen Christ/Holy Spirit still gives understanding to the full Gospel as the basis for valid discipleship. The insistence on adherence to these truths implies that some members of the Markan community did not accept this comprehensive view of Gospel. As we have seen, it is likely that they reveled in revelation by the Risen Christ/Holy Spirit but ignored the cross and its ramifications for discipleship. They did not connect Spirit with the Gospel in the manner advocated by Mark. Prophets who hold such views need their eyes opened that they may see (understand) correctly. However, what they see are not new visions from heaven, but the old story of Jesus in a new light of importance, undergirding the church's beliefs and behavior as Christians.

Mark's use of two stories about healing the blind to frame the discipleship section makes it crystal clear that Jesus alone is the giver of sight and insight. As Kee perceives:

> What is most important about these stories is not the substance of the miracles, but the implicit epistemology: for Mark *understanding* of reality is not achieved by availability of evidence, but by revelatory insight. The stories stand, therefore, as illustrations of the dictum set forth in Mark 4:11.[144]

This is the core of the secrecy motif in Mark's Gospel. The secret is not primarily Jesus' messiahship, or the coming of the kingdom or Eschaton, but the revelation by the Risen Christ/Holy Spirit through Gospel that faithful discipleship requires embracing the whole Gospel of Jesus. Mark's Gospel is the textbook; the Holy Spirit is the Teacher. Mark is the author/facilitator who endeavors to aid the readers in making the connection between text and teacher, Gospel and Spirit, that the church may find unity, strength, and protection in "one Lord, one faith, one baptism, one God and Father of us all" (Eph 4:5).

The true transitional passage analogous to 1:14–15, 3:7–12, and 6:6b is 8:27–33, followed by the call to discipleship in a manner parallel to 1:16–20, 3:13–19, and 6:7–13. Although Mark has relied heavily upon traditional material instead of composing a summary passage, the familiar motifs are present—discipleship, revelation and secrecy, conflict with Satan, suffering, gospel—thus preserving the continuity with the first half of the work. As before, Mark interweaves these themes into the fabric of his Gospel in its fullness. But, as intimated in 8:22–26, a shift of emphasis is in the air concerning instruction in discipleship, and consequently, the meaning of Gospel.

Peter's Confession, Passion Predictions, and Gospel

The account of the "confession of Peter at Caesarea Philippi," contains a complicated structure and *Traditionsgeschichte*[145] that requires tracking in order to discern the evangelist's emphasis. Verse 27 contains a double introduction. Verse 27b is closely tied to vv.

28–29; thus, v. 33, which is awkward in its present context, likely formed the conclusion in the pre-Markan tradition.[146] Verse 27a then stood as the introduction to vv. 30–32, which show no close affinities with vv. 27b–29. With his customary formula ("and he began to teach") the evangelist introduces v. 31, an independent Son of Man saying, which contains his interpretation of vv. 27b–29. Hence, Mark has used material from several different sources, supplemented by his own redactional phrases in v. 27 ("on the way"), v. 30, v. 31a, v. 32b, in constructing this passage. A striking result is that Mark has changed the meaning of v. 33 drastically. In its present context Jesus' rebuke of Peter no longer pertains to the confession of Jesus as ὁ χριστός, a title which Mark accepts (1:1), but to Peter's failure to understand and to accept Jesus' suffering as the Son of Man (v. 31). In the traditional account, Peter's confession was likely rejected because to Jesus and the early church the title ὁ χριστός contained strong nationalistic, political connotations. As time passed, the title was reinterpreted and adopted by the church in a non-political sense. The use of the title in this context and throughout the Gospel suggests that it possessed a "positive vagueness" in the time and *Sitz* of the evangelist.[147] Mark believed that Peter confessed Jesus as "the Christ" and from his perspective found the rebuke in v. 33 to be too strong without further clarification. Hence, he inserted v. 31 to justify the rebuke in light of his own theology concerning the meaning of discipleship and Gospel. Verse 31 then emerges as the key verse that expresses the interest of Mark, and the renowned "confession of Peter" actually serves as a framework and foil for conveying the evangelist's own view. In effect, Mark reinterprets ὁ χριστός in terms of the suffering Son of Man[148] (cf. also 13:21–26; 14:61–62).

This leads us back to the question of the evangelist's understanding of the Son of Man as he relates the title to Jesus and the proclamation of Gospel. Since Mark did not create the Son of Man sayings but received them in the tradition,[149] we must rely on our knowledge of background information concerning the Son of Man concept in the early church and insights gleaned from Mark's context for the sayings in determining the evangelist's meaning. One hermeneutical-methodological consideration is essential: The three classes of Son of Man sayings (future, present, suffering) should be kept distinct without assuming that Mark used the title with only one basic meaning.[150] The diverse nature of the three groups of sayings is evidence to the contrary, corresponding to the manifold concepts and connotations of the Son of Man in the OT and intertestamental literature. As we have noted, although Mark had high regard for the Son of Man title, he was not interested in correlating or combining the various traits and roles into a unified, systematic Son of Man Christology. Rather, he employed the sayings, drawn from multiple traditions and origins, according to their present contextual relevance in his larger purpose of proclaiming εὐαγγέλιον without reflection upon their internal consistencies. Failure to recognize this fundamental point accounts for many of the weaknesses in past works on the subject and in commentaries on Mark.[151]

If Mark has no definite Son of Man Christology yet selects suffering Son of Man sayings to insert or to repeat at central points in this section (8:31, 9:31; 10:33; 10:45),[152] then these sayings must constitute a key to the evangelist's purpose. Although the saying in 10:45 is derived from a different tradition than the passion predictions,[153] Mark uses the logion to function as the climax and conclusion to all the Son of Man sayings in this section.[154] In view of its strategic location, it is not surprising that form and redaction critics have centered their analyses primarily upon this saying. Tödt argues that Mk 10:45b was a later addition to the Son of Man saying in 10:45a on the grounds that the theme of Jesus' dying for men's salvation does not appear in the other Son of Man sayings and the concept of serving in 10:45a is complete in itself.[155] Tödt thinks the "ransom" phrase was added in the pre-Markan stage of the tradition, and most commentators concur or attribute it to Jesus himself. In either case, Mark regarded the Son of Man saying and ransom phrase apropos for summing up the message of the preceding thrice-repeated passion predictions. What is the distinctive Markan message conveyed?

The clear, distinctive Markan message in these Son of Man sayings culminating in 10:45 is that Jesus is the authoritative one sent from God whose service and death will "somehow" benefit and save others. Mark was no more interested in explicating a specific doctrine of soteriology than he was in constructing a systematic Christology. Although Mk 10:45 may bring to mind the "suffering servant" of Isaiah 53, it is noteworthy that Mark nowhere calls Jesus the "suffering servant"—a modern phrase which had no clearly defined antecedent in the first century AD.[156] Moreover, Mark does not state that Jesus' death overcomes sin in the manner described in Isaiah 53. If Mark had intended λύτρον to be the exact equivalent of אשם, he would not have left the relationship between the terms so ambiguous. With the exception of Mk 2:1–12, the evangelist does not present the Son of Man as the forgiver of sin, and in this instance, the aspect of suffering is conspicuously absent. And Mark has done little or nothing to merge the concepts and roles into a major motif. As Burkill comments,

> The evangelist does not offer any elucidation of what precisely he understands by the important doctrine of the necessity of the Messiah's sufferings. . . . The evangelist's position, in fact, has all the appearances of being a tentative one. The various parts of his doctrine do not form a harmonious and well-defined system of thought. . . . The writer is really feeling his way after a more adequate and more satisfying statement of the saving truth which the apostolic church discerned in the life and work of its founder.[157]

Perhaps it is more accurate to say simply that Mark's attention was directed elsewhere—toward the theme of suffering itself, not a doctrine of atonement. In the earlier sections, Mark has presented Jesus as the strong Son of God and Son of Man (among other titles)—the victor over sin, nature, demons, and death. Now he portrays Jesus as the suffering Son of Man who must die on behalf of his people. The divine necessity of Jesus' suffering ($\delta\epsilon\tilde{\iota}$, 8:31), seen as an essential ingredient in the redemptive plan of God, was more important to Mark than an explanation of how Jesus' death affects redemption. The efficacy of Jesus' death was already affirmed in the kerygma as a core belief of the church (cf. Acts 2:23ff).

Two related concerns influenced Mark's presentation. One, the sharp shift in thematic emphasis from Jesus' glory to Jesus' suffering in this discipleship section indicates that many of Mark's contemporaries in the church were not prepared to suffer "for my sake and the gospel's" (8:35). Achtemeier argues that the $\ddot{o}\varsigma$ (ϵ)$\ddot{\alpha}\nu$ (whoever) sayings in Mk 8:35–38, when combined with a Markan context, serve as an indication that the sayings were directed by Mark to his community.

> The combination of major intention (the suffering of Jesus and the concomitant suffering of his followers) with generalizing language in the sayings in 8:34–38, therefore, justify us in seeing here another problem Mark is addressing here in his community: some Christians apparently felt compelled by whatever means to avoid suffering which would be incurred because they followed Jesus, and Mark warns that such activity renders any further discipleship invalid.[158]

Each passion prediction is placed in the context of a teaching on discipleship so that "understanding of discipleship and understanding of the death of Jesus go hand in hand."[159] The first teaching defines discipleship as a readiness to take up the cross; the second as a preparedness to be servant of all; and the third presents Jesus as the means and model of a discipleship of servanthood. "This arrangement of the material . . . clearly represents a very strong element of redactional and compositional activity on the part of the evangelist."[160] The probability is high that the misunderstanding of Jesus by Peter was recurring in the Markan church. Excitement over spiritual gifts of prophecy and signs and wonders, coupled with growing anticipation of the parousia and Eschaton, cast into the background the dimension of suffering as a necessary aspect of discipleship. Yet at the same time, the church was threatened with the brutal reality of persecution. Mark saw clearly the artificiality and pretentiousness of the church's response to the situation. He sought to correct the deficiency by depicting clearly that both glorious authority and inevitable suffering are components of discipleship. He does not explain thoroughly how they are related or conjoined but is content to leave the matter as part of the paradox and mystery of God's saving work in Jesus Christ. Discipleship means sharing in both Jesus' glory and Jesus' suffering and in viewing both as expressions of divine necessity and power in God's plan of salvation.

Second, Mark authenticates this understanding of discipleship by appeal to and creation of Gospel. His instruction about the nature of true discipleship is set within the larger context of Gospel. Mark introduces each passion prediction with his favorite redactional phrase, "And he began to teach" (καὶ ἤρξατο διδάσκειν) or an equivalent, saying in effect *nota bene*: Remember! "Teaching" involves both word and act and is based upon tradition from the earthly Jesus that continues to instruct the church.

In 8:35 and 10:29 the evangelist expresses his purpose more explicitly with the insertion of the redactional phrase, "And the gospel's (sake)," (καὶ τοῦ εὐαγγελίου). This phrase, following "for my sake," is too repetitious to have survived in the pre-Markan tradition.[161] Matthew (16:25; 19:29) and Luke (9:24; 18:29) omit it from their Markan source for the same reason. Likewise, in Mk 8:38, which speaks of confessing Jesus and his words, the phrase "and of my words" is redactional, pointing to the post-Easter situation in which Jesus no longer was present in the flesh. Mark contrasts "confessing" with "denying"; only by confessing Jesus and the Gospel (Markan) can the disciple expect to participate in future glory.[162] The evangelist's redactions are consistent with his purpose in composing his work under the rubric of εὐαγγέλιον. By adding the phrase twice (plus "my words"), he brings Jesus and the Gospel into the closest possible relationship without losing the distinction between them. Expressed differently, Mark preserves the continuity between Jesus' past preaching of gospel and his present preaching through the Markan Gospel genre. Marxsen and Weeden recognize correctly that for Mark, Jesus is the content of the Gospel which "qualifies the type of Jesus for whom one dies, loses the world, and risks the disintegrating of his family ties."[163] However, they press the matter too far in claiming that "in Mark's mind, Jesus and the gospel are synonymous....Jesus is the gospel of God."[164] Though we agree with Marxsen (against Weeden) that "the preaching of the gospel produces the reality and presence of its contents (Jesus),"[165] the phrase (καὶ τοῦ εὐαγγελίου) in 8:35 is not epexegetical. Mark knows that in the past preaching of the earthly Jesus, an aspect of Gospel that Marxsen and Weeden virtually ignore, the person of Jesus and the gospel that Jesus preached are not completely identical. Likewise, he knows that his composition of Gospel is based on these traditions from and about Jesus. The new, remarkable feature that Mark incorporated is that the Risen Christ in the Spirit (1:10-11; 3:28-29; 13:10-11) is present in the reading and hearing of the Gospel, functioning as the teacher, revealer, and enabler of true discipleship. It is in the hearing of the Gospel that the miracle of dynamic contact and counsel occurs. Jesus is not encased in the accounts so that the two are identical. The Risen Christ/Holy Spirit gives to disciples (insiders) the understanding of the Word (4:33, 34; 8:38), i.e., the Gospel, that they may experience Jesus spiritually (be given the secret of the kingdom of God, 4:11) through it and comprehend the full meaning of discipleship consistent with the entirety of its content derived from the earthly Jesus. Mark plots his Gospel artistically that the reader may hear the Gospel with the right acoustics to receive the deep vibrations of the living Christ/Holy Spirit.

Weeden contends that Mark makes a clear distinction between the Holy Spirit and Jesus. "Nowhere in Mark is there any suggestion that Jesus and the Holy Spirit are identical."[166] In this statement, Weeden is referring to the relationship between the historical Jesus and the Holy Spirit. In this sense, we agree that the distinction is maintained, though the Spirit resides permanently in Jesus in a way precedented by no prophet. But with respect to the proclamation of Gospel in the post-resurrection era, the relationship between Jesus Christ and the Holy Spirit became blurred and difficult to differentiate. Mark clearly affirms the presence of the Holy Spirit in the church, and to assert that "the reference to the Holy Spirit's intercession in behalf of the Markan faithful (13:11) cannot be construed as an implied reference to the presence of the resurrected Lord"[167] is altogether implausible. Weeden's supposition of a definite separation is supported neither by Mark nor the early church. Mark does not attempt to clarify the relationships among Jesus, the Risen Christ and the Holy Spirit. He is not a speculative theologian. The philosophical issue is not his central interest. Rather, he assumes continuity in establishing the scope and authority of the Gospel as a valid norm for combating and correcting aberrations in the church. Claims to the contrary run counter to the consensus of the NT witness by AD 70.

Transfiguration and Gospel

The somberness of the initial passion prediction and call to a discipleship of suffering is immediately relieved by the reaffirmation of Jesus as the "beloved Son." The phrase is the same as that first declared by the heavenly voice at his baptism by the Holy Spirit. In this way, Mark tells his readers that suffering and glory are compatible aspects of Jesus' mission and destiny; hence, the disciples should anticipate both experiences also. But, as the Holy Spirit empowered Jesus for his ministry, readers-disciples have the assurance of the same divine power present with them for enduring persecution and tribulation, culminating in the glory of the parousia and Eschaton.

The *Traditionsgeschichte* of the Transfiguration pericope is a complex and controversial one.[168] The passage has been viewed as a factual experience (Sweet, Bernardin), a vision (Meyer, Schniewind, Rawlinson), a post-resurrection myth which has been read back into the earthly story of Jesus (Bousset, Bultmann, Lohmeyer). Regardless of the origin of the account, most commentators agree that Mark uses it to anticipate a future event—the parousia (Lohmeyer, Weeden, Kee, Kelber) or an appearance of the Risen Christ (Schniewind, Yates, Lambrecht, Carlston, Petersen). The first interpretation (parousia) is supported by the eschatological references in 8:38–9:1.[169] The second view (post-resurrection) fits better with the statement in 9:9, which presumes that the transfiguration will be understood and proclaimed after the resurrection, that is, in Mark's era. Petersen remarks from a literary perspective that a scene witnessed by only three disciples is hardly as public as the parousia and states in support of an anticipation of a resurrection appearance:

> The narrator provides us with the first hint that the time of the disciples' ignorance will come to an end—after Jesus' resurrection from the dead.... Needless to say, the disciples will have to understand what they saw before they can tell about it. ... Thus, the transfiguration story refers the reader both backward to the literary establishment of Jesus' identity in 1:11 (really 1:1–13), and forward to the disciples' realization of it after his resurrection, a not inappropriate literary function for an incident occurring almost in the midpoint of the narrative.[170]

We agree that the author is thinking first and foremost of resurrection appearances of Jesus, but for Mark the resurrection and the parousia are still connected. In one sense, the resurrection initiates the parousia, and although the final Eschaton has been delayed, it is still expected soon.[171]

C. E. Carlston draws attention to the connection between the transfiguration account and the kerygma. The pericope was told, not to disclose Jesus' miraculous power but rather his divine identity in conjunction with his coming passion and resurrection (8:31). The command, "Listen to him!" is addressed to contemporary hearers also as a call to obedient, perceptive discipleship. This was the core content and function of the kerygma; hence, Mark has used the story "to reflect the conviction that the Christ of the kerygma was not fundamentally different from the historical Jesus."[172] In other words, by skillful editorial ordering of his material, Mark combines the past glory and suffering of Jesus with a present call to discipleship of a similar nature. This call includes the anticipation of the future appearance of Jesus, now already being realized, to aid readers in remaining obedient disciples. We concur with Yates and Lampe, who maintain that the obvious reference to and reminder of the voice and the descent of the Spirit at the baptism (1:10–11) anticipate the time after the resurrection (Mark's era) when the disciples through faith in Christ and the Gospel may share in the glory and power of the Spirit also.[173] Schweizer sums up the matter aptly:

> In short, Mark underlines both sides of the truth: The time after Easter is, even more than the time of the earthly ministry of Jesus, a period in which he and his help are not simply available and visible, but it is a period in which he and his help are to be found in his Word and in his name and in the teaching of the Spirit.[174]

Finally, we note that the title of Teacher (9:38; 10:17; 10:35) and the activity of teaching (8:31; 9:31; 10:1) regularly punctuate the section. Mark 10:1 denotes teaching as the custom of Jesus, though probably no clear distinction is to be made between his preaching (κηρύσσειν) and teaching (διδάσκειν). Mark stresses the title of "teacher" in addition to more exalted ones because he realizes that Jesus' presence as the Teacher instructing the church is the greatest need of his community. Thereby, Mark provides a basis and means whereby the deficient gospel and overzealous activity of pneumatic prophets within the church can be corrected and divine power imparted to cope with persecution from without. To deny the teaching role and function of Jesus in and through the Gospel is to strike at the root of the church; it is to risk blasphemy against the Holy Spirit who endues Jesus with teaching authority for instruction in faithful discipleship (3:29, 35; 4:1ff). The role of Jesus/Holy Spirit as Teacher is essential to Mark's concept of Gospel and to the future survival and triumph of the church. Hence, "Spirit and Gospel" as the basis for perceptive, obedient discipleship is the underlying Markan motif and interest in the pericope and in this central section on discipleship.

SECTION 5: MARK 10:46–52; 11:1–13:37

Bartimaeus and Discipleship

The pericope relating the healing of Blind Bartimaeus (10:46–52) functions as a secondary transitional passage in a manner similar to the pericope describing the healing of the blind man at Bethsaida. Mark received the account from the tradition, and apart from adding the ending phrase "and followed him on the way" (10:52), he employed the account without extensive redaction.[175]

Although the disciples have been given extensive teaching about Jesus, the Gospel, and discipleship, they do not see clearly the full meaning and significance of the teaching. Mark concluded the prior section by contrasting the "seeing" of Bartimaeus with the dimness of the disciples' comprehension. Mark did not intend for Bartimaeus to represent a group or tradition that he considered superior to the disciples.[176] He is not engaging in an anti-apostolic polemic here; rather, Bartimaeus represents the ideal response advocated by the omniscient narrator, and the disciples are like the members of Mark's church: They have their blind spots and often see unclearly what Jesus, the Gospel, and discipleship are all about; yet, they are still disciples, part of the church. Through the Gospel, the Spirit of Christ still teaches, illumines and issues the call to "follow him on the way."

Entry into Jerusalem and the Church

Simultaneously, the transitional passage prepares for the next section relating the entry into and ministry in Jerusalem. Bartimaeus' title, "the Son of David," surprisingly accepted by Jesus, is echoed in the acclaim of the multitude in 11:10 and in the teaching of Jesus in the temple (12:35). The former themes of Jesus' authority amid lowliness and impending death, on the one hand, and spiritual blindness by the Jews and misunderstanding of his mission by the disciples, on the other hand, are continued in the pericopes relating Jesus' ministry in Jerusalem and the attempts of the Jewish authorities to discredit and/or to destroy him. Mark employs the shift in geographical locale—from Galilee to Jerusalem—to mark the initiation of a new section which continues to the Passion Narrative (11:1 – 13:37). Having demonstrated the permeating prominence of the Markan motifs of Spirit and Gospel in the preceding sections, we purport to focus on selected pericopes in this section that show Mark's continuing interest in these themes.

We noted above Jesus' surprising acceptance of Bartimaeus' confession of him as "the Son of David." Surprising, because in the following pericope Mark indicates that the crowd's expectation that Jesus will usher in "the kingdom of our father David" (11:10) is erroneous. The cry, "Blessed be he who comes in the name of the Lord," is a rendering of the Hebrew Ps 118:26 (LXX B A) which was quoted at the regular ritual of the Feasts of Tabernacles and Hanukkah in anticipation of the Davidic Messiah.[177] Also, the shout "Hosanna" appears to have been a part of the Hallel with Psalm 118 as its source. The political-nationalistic expectations of the crowd are intense.

Mark tempers these hopes of a restored Davidic kingdom by inserting vv. 11 – 12, redactional in context and perhaps in content,[178] in which Jesus says and does nothing to acknowledge the acclamation. Instead, he enters Jerusalem alone as the jubilant crowd vanishes. In this adroit way, Mark indicates that they do not really understand Jesus' mission of suffering and are not prepared to enter into his sufferings as faithful disciples. The point is driven home by the change of their shouts soon from "Hosanna" to "crucify him" (15:13 – 14).

The outright political-nationalistic understanding of Jesus as a Davidic Son and Messiah is negated by Mark. But the "Son of David" title itself is not altogether objectionable, as the Bartimaeus account indicates. It is not the case that any man who confesses Jesus as Son of David is summarily rejected. Bartimaeus does not see properly, but he has some insight. The preferred understanding of the episode is that "Son of David" is a title of honor and respect, although it has its limitations and is not the highest title bestowed on Jesus. Within the pericope, Bartimaeus attaches no political connotations to the title. He recognizes in Jesus the power to heal, and it is this divine authority that Mark approves, regardless of the title with which it is associated. As we have seen, Mark is flexible in his use of titles. He accepts in part all honorific designations for Jesus without structuring a definite Christology based on any particular title. Each is valid within limits in the context in which it appears. Mark is careful to make certain that the context discloses the proper meaning and function. In the case of the Entry pericope, he indicates by the abrupt, brusque tenor of the redactional verse (11:11) that the crowd, possibly including the disciples, is wrong in regarding him as the restorer of the kingdom of David, either in a purely temporal, political sense or in an eschatological, messianic sense. Indeed, Mark offers another title, "Lord" (κύριος, v. 3; cf. 1:3), that offsets the erroneous expectations of the crowd. Although κύριος was likely already ingrained in the pericope as a title of simple respect (sir), Mark and his readers undoubtedly invested it with post-resurrection glory.[179] As Mk 11:11 implies, the Lord resides in his church (the Twelve), the new temple not made with hands (14:58), and withdraws from the temple in Jerusalem, which he condemns (vv. 15–19) along with the entire Jewish cultus (cf. vv. 12–14, the unfruitful fig tree). The intercalation of the temple events and the cursing of the fig tree episodes,[180] aided by the addition of temporal and topographical links (vv. 12, 15, 19–20, 27), exhibits a favorite Markan editorial device.[181] Drawing upon the common belief of Hellenistic Christianity (cf. 2 Cor 2:17) and from personal experience, Mark unquestionably knew that the living Christ as Lord speaks through the Holy Spirit. Hence, he uses and redacts the tradition to reject an unworthy Jewish concept of Jesus and to affirm the presence of the living Lord with his church. Or more relevantly, he rejects the synagogue and cultus of Judaism in favor of the disciples and the church as the new realm of the Lord's reign in the Spirit. Hahn contends that the phrase "for all the nations" (πᾶσιν τοῖς ἔθνεσιν, v. 17), omitted in Matthew and Luke, stresses the Markan point in the cleansing of the temple: Judaism is rejected in favor of the Gentiles' acceptance.[182] If Mark was written in Rome, as we advocate, this point would have been especially pertinent to his readers. Mark's unique dual concept of Gospel, authorized by the Spirit past and present, enabled him to accomplish his aim persuasively.[183]

This clarification of Mark's purpose serves as a corrective to the popular interpretation of the Entry pericope in terms of the "messianic secret." Prior studies generally maintain either that the passages give us an accurate insight into the nature of Jesus' messiahship as the unrecognized "Messiah"[184] or that they illustrate the evangelist's "union of the Hellenistic kerygma about Christ... with the tradition of the story of Jesus,"[185] thereby creating the "messianic secret" motif. Our analysis shows that neither of these views about "messiahship" reflects Mark's primary purpose. He is not interested in the title or concept of "secret messiahship" as such, and the "union" of traditions in the pericopes had already occurred before the accounts reached Mark.

This recognition leads to the rejection also of the prevalent position that Mark viewed the Entry in terms of the messianic prophecy of Zec 9:9. Zechariah 9:9 may have constituted the background of the original account, but the Markan version contains no references to Zec 9:9 as does the Matthean account (Mt 21:4, 5, 7).[186] Bauer has established that πῶλον (Mk 11:2ff) used by itself apart from ὄνος (ass, donkey, cf. Mt 21:5) means "horse,"[187] which represents traits of power, authority, triumph. This Markan portrayal of Jesus as the mighty Lord who must suffer is completely contrary to the picture of the humble Messiah-King of Zec 9:9 and Mt 21:5. Mark is interested in depicting the triumphant (though non-nationalistic) authority of Jesus within the context and structure of Gospel, which includes the passion motif, but this interest and concept are not shared by Matthew and Luke in their Entry pericopes. The Markan motif is further supported by the redactional comment in 11:18[188] which contains references to both Jesus' authority and his impending death under the "causal" rubric of "his teaching" (διδαχή), i.e., Gospel for Mark.

The Divine Authority of Jesus

Many commentators consider the pericope concerning the Question of Authority (11:27–33) already to have been joined to the Temple Cleansing passage in the pre-Markan tradition.[189] The account contains little redactional comment from Mark, with the exception of the topographical and character designations in v. 27. The passage came to Mark as one of those rare gems that fitted perfectly into his mounting without extensive cutting and polishing. The question of Jesus' authority is a familiar one; the scribes had answered it earlier: "By Beelzebul . . . the prince of demons, He cast out the demons" (3:22). By so answering, they had sinned against the Holy Spirit (3:28–30), which had resided in Jesus since the baptism by John.[190] The appeal to John's authority (11:29, 30), coupled with the implied reference to Jesus' superior authority, directs the reader's attention back to the baptism event in which the reader is given the answer that the Jewish officials lack: Jesus' paramount authority comes directly from heaven, i.e., from the Holy Spirit.[191] Mark discloses the secret of Jesus' identity and mission to the reader who knows the total Gospel. He is invited and summoned to a responsible discipleship based on the revelation of the Gospel, given to him by the authority of Jesus/Risen Christ/Holy Spirit.

The series of incidents recounted in 11:27–12:40 resembles the complex in 2:1–3:5, wherein Mark makes use of conflict stories to proclaim repeatedly the theme of Jesus' divine authority. As the series in 2:1–3:5 preceded the predictions about Jesus' sufferings, here Mark returns to the theme of Jesus' authority in the *Streitgespräche* before presenting the Passion Narrative. The pattern is repeated to instruct Mark's readers thoroughly in the full content of Gospel.

To the parable (παραβολή) in 12:1–11, Mark attaches the brief introduction (v. 1), similar to 4:2, and provides the conclusion in 12:12. Verses 10-11 indicate that Mark gave or accepted an allegorical interpretation to the "parable" that proclaimed the triumph and glory of the Risen Christ as the cornerstone of the church and the capstone of God's saving plan for the Gentiles ("others," v. 9). Whether the "parable" came originally from Jesus or the early church (based on Isaiah 5),[192] whether Jesus told allegories, whether the evangelist or an earlier redactor added vv. 10–11 in remembrance that Jesus used Ps 118:22 in condemnation of the Jewish hierarchy[193]—these are debatable issues that lie largely outside our scope in interpreting the "parable" in its Markan context. Mark evidently regards it as an allegory derived from Jesus that testifies to his divine authority and power to surmount rejection and death at the hands of the Jewish leaders. From Mark's perspective, of course, the resurrection and triumph of Jesus in the Gentile church is an accomplished reality. The recounting of the "Jesus tradition" serves to substantiate the belief and experience of the church and to convey the lively message of solace and hope to the church faced with rejection and persecution from both the Jewish synagogue and the imperial court.

Mark intends for the reader to identify Jesus as the "beloved Son" (12:6) and to recall that the same title was proclaimed by the heavenly voice at Jesus' baptism (1:11). Again, he provides the reader the clue to the "secret" of the parable, which must be read in light of Mark's view of the nature and purpose of parables in general (4:10–12, 33–34). At his baptism, the beloved Son was given divine authority "to teach" and "to explain everything" by the bestowal of the Holy Spirit. Understanding of the parables that leads to true discipleship comes through revelation by the Holy Spirit, turning "outsiders" into "insiders."[194] Though hearers of the Gospel are held responsible for their blindness and lack of commitment (v. 9), they do not have the innate capacity to perceive and to respond—a paradox that Mark does not resolve. Neither the Jewish officials of Jesus' time or Mark's time have been given the revelation of the Holy Spirit. This is reserved for Jesus' disciples, that is, the church, the heir to Israel's vineyard. Hence, the church should not be surprised at opposition from outside forces, whether synagogue or state. At the same time, the church should not despair; the resurrection and the presence of the Son/Holy Spirit in the church grant assurance that the promise and good news of victory are already in the process of being fulfilled.

The editorial addition in v. 12 may contain an implicit warning to a segment of Mark's church also.[195] In view of our reconstruction of Mark's *Sitz* drawn from multiple references, one can easily envisage pneumatic prophets in the church fastening upon the prophecy of triumph and glory in vv. 10–11 and exulting in the gifts of the Son/Holy Spirit. The era of spiritual power and victory has arrived. Mark does not deny this spiritual experience and truth; but amid such enthusiasm, Mark sounds the note of the Son's suffering and death as the necessary prelude to victory. Attached is an implicit warning to hear the whole Gospel and to respond accordingly in discipleship. Gospel and Spirit are the norm and means for unity and strength in the church against all threats to its welfare and ultimate victory.

The following complex of pericopes (vv. 13–44) reflect minimal Markan redaction, being limited primarily to typical introductory phrases (vv. 13, 18, 28a, 35a, 38a) and concluding comments (vv. 17b, 34b, 37b).[196] Little editorial activity was required, for the content of the stories was already conducive to Mark's purpose of proclaiming Jesus' authority. The concluding comments are instructive in that they indicate the finality of Jesus' teaching. He silences his antagonists and stuns the crowd with a single authoritative word. They are left in amazement, unable to reply.

The lack of editorial conclusions after the statements in 12:27, 12:40, and 12:44 are suggestive. Does Mark signify that the traditions as he received them voice his own interest adequately? The emphasis on "God of the living" in v. 27 and the word of condemnation in v. 40 upon those who accept only a religion of honor and privilege are in complete accord with Mark's own message to his church. Likewise, the woman who put in everything she had, her whole living (ὅλον τὸν βίον, v. 44), constitutes a sterling model for and challenge to true discipleship, exceeded only by the example of Jesus himself.

Son of David and Lord

As we have noted in 10:46–52 and 11:1–11, Mark treats the title "Son of David" with a "positive reserve," clarifying its acceptable and unacceptable meanings. In 12:35–37, Mark states definitely that "Son of David" is at best a secondary, if not inappropriate, title for Jesus. The origin and development of the central saying in vv. 36–37 and the question whether Jesus recognized himself as "the Lord" of the Psalms has been endlessly debated.[197] More germane to our purpose is Mark's understanding and use of the material. The title Messiah (χριστός) was a nebulous term with multiple meanings in Mark's time. Although the church affirmed both "Messiah" and "Son of David," i.e., the Davidic descent, as valid characterizations of Jesus, both titles were subject to misunderstanding in a coarse, nationalistic sense. It is this erroneous view that Mark sought to combat and to replace with a higher view derived from the church's post-resurrection perspective and depiction of Jesus as the Risen Christ. The friction between synagogue and church in Mark's *Sitz* gave impetus to this aim. We need not explicate in detail the rabbinic and Christian presuppositions concerning the inspiration of Scripture (OT) and the messianic nature of Psalm 110.[198] The thrust of the saying is that Jesus (Christ) is much more than the Son of David and the Messiah of Davidic descent. Since Mark has no Davidic genealogy, it is possible that he rejected the claim of Davidic descent altogether. However, since both the early church and the evangelist demonstrate knowledge of a positive aspect of the claim, it is more probable that he simply relegated it a secondary role. Mark knows the positive nonpolitical meaning of "Christ," but the Jewish political connotations attached to "Messiah" plagued the evangelist's and the church's use of the title. Mark overcame this liability by pointing out that David, inspired by the Holy Spirit, calls the Christ (whom the reader knows to be Jesus) "Lord" (κύριος). This is Mark's point and interest in the pericope.[199] He is not concerned solely with showing that "the Messiah" is more than "the Son of David," which may be the point in an earlier stage of the tradition or with Jesus himself. He is doing something much more radical: he is superseding both titles. Mark moves the discussion concerning Jesus' identity beyond the point of defining the relationship between "Messiah" and "Son of David" to the new affirmation that Jesus is "Lord" (without denying the former). In this manner, he divested the church's belief from the limitations and deficiencies of the Jewish concept of the "Davidic Messiah" and introduced a title more meaningful to the Gentile church. By the inspiration of the Holy Spirit, the church now confesses Christ (Jesus) as Lord. The times and theological issues have changed. Mark does not interpret Psalm 110 in terms of the relationship between Yahweh (Lord) and King (Lord) or Messiah (Lord); rather, he identifies Yahweh (Lord) with Christ (Lord) by the inspiration and investiture of the Holy Spirit. Christ (Jesus) is of the same spiritual nature as God.

Mark brings the Risen Christ (Lord) and the Holy Spirit as closely together as his use of tradition allows. He is not interested in explaining further the relationship. The Holy Spirit, the reader now knows, is the source of Jesus' authority and is linked with the confession of his lordship. Without the Spirit's presence and inspiration, right understanding of Jesus and the Gospel remains a "mystery" in parables.

Does Mark go even further and maintain that Gospel is inspired by the Holy Spirit as vitally as the Psalms and the rest of Scripture (OT)? This would appear to be the case, since not only is the inspired quote from Psalm 110 now contained in the Markan Gospel, investing it with the authority of Scripture,[200] but Mark views the Gospel as the medium and content of the Risen Christ's/Holy Spirit's word to the Markan church. The pericope, then, plays a prominent role in the evangelist's theology and purpose in composing the Gospel.

The Markan Apocalypse: Eschatology and Gospel

The problem of identifying the sources that comprise Mark 13 continues to baffle critics, and no clear consensus of opinion has emerged.[201] The Jewish or Jewish-Christian "apocalyptic flysheet" hypothesis has not proved adequate to account for the disparate complexion of the account. There is general agreement that the chapter is composite;[202] it contains older Jewish apocalyptic materials and sayings of Jesus, and both the early church and Mark have altered the contents and structure due to doctrinal interests. We shall attempt to steer a middle course between the extremes of a slavish allegiance to a literary-historical approach that loses sight of the function of the material in its Markan context,[203] on the one hand, and a virtual ignoring of literary and form critical distinctions on the other.[204] With minor differences, the literary and form critics have succeeded in identifying four major types and sources of material in Mark 13:[205] the apocalyptic portions (vv. 7–8, 12, 14–20, 24–27); the verses which in their present form reflect experiences of the early church (vv. 5–6, 9, 11, 13a, 21–23, 30–31); individual sayings from Jesus and the tradition (vv. 2, 3b, 13b, 28–29,

32, 33–37); the Markan redactions (vv. 1, 3a, 4, 10, and the phrase "let the reader understand" in v. 14). Mark is responsible for the finished product, which he places at this juncture for distinct theological purposes.

Keck's question and comments still provide a correct starting point: "Why does Mark suddenly give us an apocalyptic Jesus in contrast with the rest of the gospel? . . . The primary concern of the interpreter is to locate the paraenetic motifs which caused Mark to take up apocalyptic traditions at this point."[206] Mark has shaped vv. 1–5a as an introductory setting for the discourse following. Verse 1 maintains continuity with the preceding section by referring to the temple mentioned previously in 11:11, 15f, 27; 12:10(!), 35; 12:41 (by implication). The eschatological nature of the saying in v. 2, coupled with the reference to the Mount of Olives, a site fraught with eschatological significance in certain Jewish circles, sets the stage for the evangelist's treatment of the topics of eschatology and the parousia. Moreover, this topic is instructive for the meaning of discipleship, for those addressed in the discourse are disciples.

The insertion of the "Christian addition" in vv. 5–6, which bears little relation to the question in v. 4, before the apocalyptic piece in v. 7 (a better response to v. 4), substantiates the instructive, corrective purport of Mark. These observations indicate the following Markan interests in vv. 1–7ff, and prepare the reader for understanding the discourse correctly: (1) The broad topic of concern is eschatology, and more specifically, the delay of the Eschaton. Mark employs apocalyptic material in addressing this issue, since the sources available to him contained both aspects,[207] but his greater concern is with eschatology, i.e., the delay of the Eschaton, or more specifically, the erroneous doctrines it spawned in the church. (2) Mark is not interested in determining the time and manner of appearance of the Eschaton, but in resisting and correcting a growing obsession with these questions among certain enthusiasts in the church, some who looked for an imminent parousia and others who claimed it was already underway.[208]

Against this proclivity, Mark states clearly, "The End is not yet" (v. 7), and follows this with a decisive rejection of all speculation about the time of the End in the dominical saying of v. 32. This firm denial indicates that Mark did not consider the impending destruction of the temple to initiate the Eschaton;[209] on the contrary, he structured the discourse in order to refute this expectation held by these church enthusiasts. The enigmatic phrase in 13:14 ("let the reader understand") may be "Mark's signal to the reader that the following material is not to be taken in its traditional, literal way,"[210] i.e., the profanation of the temple by Antiochus IV (Epiphanes) in 168 BC (Dan 9:27; 11:31; 12:11; 1 Mac 1:54) or the threat to the temple by Caligula in AD 40. Mark collects and presents the apocalyptic material in one central section in order to refute the apocalyptist's extreme claims, though the parable of the fig tree followed by v. 30 may indicate that Mark, too, believed the parousia would occur within "this generation" (ἡ γενεὰ αὕτη).[211] (3) The eschatological problem is related to the motif of the misunderstanding of the discipleship and Gospel, as the statement in vv. 5–6, forcefully intruded into the account, indicates. Heightened expectation of an imminent parousia at the time of the Roman destruction of the temple was creating a deaf ear to the Gospel, which contained a call to a discipleship of suffering and tribulation preceding ultimate victory. In opposition, Mark countered this false teaching that promised immediate glory without suffering by proclaiming a comprehensive Gospel that does not deny the parousia and Eschaton, but states that the traits of suffering and service are part of true discipleship. The disciple must endure in faithfulness before receiving the rewards of the Eschaton. Pesch states that Mark has reworked vv. 5–6, 21–22 and added the references to false christs as a warning against *die Falschpropheten* who pose "als der wiedergekommene Jesus, der Menschensohn (vs. 26), und die somit das Ende der Welt als gegenwärtig behaupten."[212] Keck has explicated this insight in the probable Markan *Sitz*:

> A church facing persecution (13:11ff.) will at the same time face a crisis within (13:5f., 21ff.). How will it know who genuinely represents Christ (ἐπὶ τῷ ονόματι μου λέγοντες ὅτι ἐγώ εἰμι) and who does not?...As a matter of fact, in light of this strong emphasis on the discipleship of the cross, we may ask whether Mark had in mind certain teachers who saw no need of being exposed to death for Christ's sake at all.[213]

Markan Apocalypse: False Prophets and Gospel

Who would proclaim such a perversion of Gospel? In Judea, Zealots of the caliber of Theudas or the grandsons of Judas or John of Gischala (or Josephus?) come to mind,[214] while in Gentile regions, gnostic teachers are a possibility. The available evidence does not sustain the positing of a structured, developed Gnosticism in the church at this early stage.[215] Most likely, pneumatic prophets, exulting in the exercise of present spiritual gifts, tended to focus on motifs that characterized later gnostic teaching without actually holding the cosmology and doctrines of gnostic systems of the second century.

Similarly, Weeden identifies the ψευδόχριστοι and ψευδοπροφῆται of Mk 13:22 as "certain Christian spiritualists," who, based on D. Georgi's study, are akin to the heretics mentioned in 2 Corinthians.[216] Weeden has seen correctly that in Mk 13:6 and 22 the evangelist is issuing an instructive polemic against false prophets within the church who deny the necessity of a suffering discipleship. Verses 8b, 12, and vv. 9, 11, and 13a proclaim the theme of necessary, inevitable suffering involved in preaching the Gospel (v. 10). However, Weeden goes astray in including the disciples within the camp of the heretics who project a *Theios Anēr* Christology. He also overreaches the mark in claiming that the major purpose of the Gospel is to reject this christological heresy. The thesis is not substantiated by persuasive redaction critical analysis. The disciples, for all their failings, remain "on the way" with Jesus and are not rejected, even when they forsake Jesus at his arrest, but are promised a reunion in Galilee. And Mark's purposes extend beyond the combating of a *Theios Anēr* Christology to the presentation of the full Gospel as a norm and means of instruction for faithful discipleship and unity in the church. He does not write an argumentive epistle or apology but confronts the church "with a structured (and selected) version of its own tradition about Jesus."[217] Apparently, he believes that the church will recognize the authority of the Jesus tradition and turn away from excessive charismatic fervor and intense eschatological anticipation and embrace the fullness of the Gospel and its corresponding portrayal of discipleship.

Mark inserts v. 10 into the sayings about the suffering of faithful disciples in order to form the connection between "suffering" and "Gospel," lest "you be led astray." The redactional verse also provides a rationale for the delay of the Eschaton; however, the proclamation of Gospel occupies the limelight. The eschatological problem only forms the backdrop. Mark is not oblivious to the problem of the delay of the Eschaton, but in itself it is a secondary issue. The independent saying from the tradition placed at v. 13b serves as a fitting Markan conclusion to the pericope. The emphasis is not upon the Eschaton, but upon *enduring* to the End (ὁ δὲ ὑπομείνας εἰς τέλος) for salvation. To endure as a faithful disciple requires two gifts: the Holy Spirit and the Gospel.

If the false claimants to superior prophetic powers can appeal to the Spirit for authority, so can Mark.[218] Indeed, Swete states:

> It (13:11) guarantees to Christian confessors, in the moment of need, the presence of an Advocate within who will speak by their mouth as truly as he spoke by the mouth of David or Isaiah. We have here the germ of the doctrine of the "other Paraclete" or Advocate which is developed in the fourth Gospel.[219]

Mark makes three distinctive departures from the false prophets' appeal to the Holy Spirit in proclaiming their message and performing "signs and wonders" (13:21, 22). First, he places the saying (13:11) within the context of discipleship and Gospel firmly established by the redactional statement in v. 10. The implication is that the Holy Spirit is not necessarily given to everyone on trial, but to disciples, that is, to those who stand before governors and kings *for my sake* (v. 9) and *preach the Gospel* (v. 10), intentional Markan phrases almost tautological. To preach the Gospel as a disciple presupposes understanding the Gospel, and understanding the Gospel presupposes the mystery being given to you (4:11). In 13:11, Mark states that for the reader in the post-resurrection *Sitz,* the Holy Spirit provides the revelation, that is, gives the understanding and power of utterance. What are the means and content of the Spirit's utterance? It can be none other than the Gospel itself. The Gospel contains the fullness of the truth about the Spirit's work in Jesus and the nature of discipleship. The testimony disciples will bear, the Gospel they will preach, and the inspired speech given by the Holy Spirit are all the same "word" or at least representative of the same "word" which Mark designates Gospel (1:1, 14–15, 8:35; 10:29; 13:10). For Mark, there is no higher revelation, no other truth, no other Gospel. If the truth were something different, then Mark's Gospel would have a different form and content. "Whatever is given to you" to speak must be consistent with the concept and content of Gospel advocated by Mark. To preach or to accept anything less is to be beguiled by "false prophets," "to be led astray" (13:22), to be in opposition to the Holy Spirit and in danger of committing the eternal sin (3:29).[220]

Second, Mark structures the Gospel which the Holy Spirit will give (i.e., reveal) out of traditions which he and the church respected as authentic teachings from reports about the earthly Jesus. This is a Markan apologetic tactic derived from his theological convictions. It expresses his fundamental belief that for a teaching to be a part of Gospel and to be regarded as true, it must have its origin in or be consistent with the gospel proclaimed by the earthly Jesus. This appeal to Jesus and the tradition placed a stringent check upon the authority and validity of the teachings of the pneumatic prophets, who tended to ignore both the earthly Jesus and the tradition. Mark makes it clear that this kind of theological teaching and activity is inadequate and injurious. Adroitly, he does not enter into a personality contest or a polemic over leadership ability or the comparative authority of various church offices or spiritual gifts—matters of contention in congregations from the time of the early church (e.g.,

Corinth) to the present. No, he centers the debate or discussion on the topics "Spirit and Gospel" and defines the role and meaning of each in interrelationship. The Gospel of Jesus Christ (past and present), inspired by the Holy Spirit, is the divine norm of true discipleship, of the church's belief and activity, of its very life. Mark's unique view of Gospel was a first step toward the canonization of the Gospels as Holy Scripture equal in authority, if not superior, to the OT writings.

Third, Mark indicates as clearly as his use of tradition and concept of Gospel allow that Jesus/Risen Christ and the Holy Spirit are inseparable if not identical.[221] The Holy Spirit empowered Jesus at the baptism for the proclamation of Gospel. The same Holy Spirit now empowers disciples for the proclamation of Gospel, which has Jesus' teaching (word and act) or gospel as its essential content. In light of the Gospel's proclamation of the resurrection of Jesus and the general belief of the church in the indissolvable association of the Risen Christ and the Holy Spirit, the reader knows with certainty that the Holy Spirit continues the presence of Jesus Christ with the church.[222] The parallel verse to Mk 13:11 in Luke (21:15; cf. 12:12) speaks of the exalted Jesus instead of the Spirit. This clarification by Luke shows that the church was sure "that no one other than Jesus Christ himself addressed it in the Holy Spirit."[223] For Mark, this was already obvious and mandated by his concept of Gospel, but Luke, operating with a different view of Gospel as something more akin to "faith-history,"[224] considered clarification necessary.

From a literary critical perspective, i.e., narrative criticism, Petersen maintains that the references to the Holy Spirit speaking through the disciples are "the story-time fulfillment of the Baptist's prediction that Jesus would baptize with the Holy Spirit (1:8) . . . and, also, the commencement of the mission to the nations."[225] Since Jesus possesses the Spirit and promises—virtually bestows—the Spirit upon the disciples in the tradition and story-world, the reader associates the two (Jesus and the Spirit) as one divine reality and power. The reader regards this passage (13:11) as the "moment" which authenticates and gives insight into what the present experience of the Holy Spirit means and entails: obedience to Jesus Christ, who is still associated with the Holy Spirit and somehow present in the experiencing of the Spirit. The Gospel content and quality of narrative-time, which are constructed by combining tradition with a post-resurrection perspective, make it clear that a mission to the nations (Gentiles) is the prime responsibility of obedient disciples. The Markan church, by its very existence and experience, knows that it is charged with this command from Jesus for the future (in the continuing story-time). Thus, the Gospel addresses Mark's church directly as "the elect" (13:22, 27), the favored ones who have the power and benefits of Jesus/Holy Spirit to endure tribulation and persecution. Yet, the conditions of the continuing privilege of the Spirit's aid are clear: embracing the complete Gospel as a guard against false claimants to Christ's authority or prophetic powers (13:5ff), intense imminent apocalyptic-eschatological predictions (13:7, 32ff), division within households (13:12), and the temptation of succumbing to worldly cares and riches (4:19). When the community realizes that the Gospel contains the message of the Son who must die and understands the implications of that message for discipleship, then the church is prepared to continue the mission to the nations and is empowered by the Holy Spirit to overcome all adversaries. In support of this insight, R. Schnackenburg points out that εὐαγγέλιον appears in the context of mission in 13:10 and 14:9 and in the context of suffering discipleship in 8:35 and 10:29. He states further that εὐαγγέλιον in Mark should be understood as the "later preaching of the message of Jesus, but with special emphasis on the way of the cross, which Jesus had to undergo and to which he now calls all his followers."[226]

Mark understood, perhaps as no other, the gravity of the offense of stressing the ecstasy of spiritual experience and powers without an accompanying commitment to mission and service, even suffering service. The result is the inevitable quenching of the Spirit, even blasphemy and the demise of the church. However, he approached this theological and practical problem in his church, not in a vindictive or harshly polemical manner, but pastorally. He corrected, instructed, and taught the fullness of Gospel through the traditions and mouth of the supreme Teacher: Jesus Christ, who still reigns in the Spirit as the Lord of the church.

The conclusion to the apocalyptic discourse, strategically placed by Mark, states his own conclusion concerning the issues associated with false apocalyptic-eschatological views in his church: Watch! Only the disciple who is watchful and receptive to the coming of the Master, i.e., Christ/Holy Spirit, is privy to the "secret of the kingdom of God" (4:10–11; 13:11), i.e., the meaning of Gospel and discipleship, and eligible for the final gathering of the elect (13:27), i.e., the glories of heaven.[227] The alternative to watchfulness is spiritual blindness leading to false pretentious claims, resulting in idolatry, blasphemy, and death.

Best suggests appropriately that Mk 13:37 in its present position is not only a fitting conclusion to the apocalypse but to all the teaching of Jesus addressed to both the historical disciples and the

members of Mark's own community.[228] Mark has carefully guided
the reader into an understanding of the Gospel and the Spirit and the
meaning of discipleship. But Mark's skill as an author and redactor
in molding a "Gospel" as an oral or literary creation had its limits.
The Gospel as a new genre does not command, capture, or encap-
sulate the Christ/Holy Spirit. The Master/Spirit comes and speaks
with power through those readers or hearers who watch expectantly
with awareness of all that Mark has disclosed. To these, the Spirit
gives something beyond human understanding and capacity—a
divine persuasion and assurance accompanied by commitment.[229]
This factor Mark could not manufacture; he could only provide the
opportunity for reception of this gift by summoning his community
to enter seriously into the pilgrimage which continues until the
unknown time of the Eschaton: "What I say to you, I say to all:
Watch!" (13:37).

Markan Apocalypse: The Presence of Jesus in the Spirit

Our view of Mark's purposes in the Little Apocalypse runs counter
to the interpretation offered by W. Kelber on two central points: One,
Kelber claims that Mark in chapter 13 seeks "to protect the present
from a prematurely contrived presence of Jesus. There is a deep
sense in which the resurrected Jesus must not make an appearance in the gospel."[230] Kelber thinks Mark structured the apocalypse around this aim: In the first part (vv. 5b–23), he rejects
the false prophet's concept of realized eschatology (parousia); in the
second part (vv. 24–27), he announces the presence of Jesus as a
future event; in the third part (vv. 28–37), "he protects the reconstructed future against prophetic errors by assuming the unpredict-
ability of future fulfillment."[231]

Kelber has misconstrued Mark's disavowal of radical imminent
eschatological hopes to mean that Jesus is totally absent from the
present community. But he is able to achieve this result only by
totally ignoring 13:11 (no index references), and by interpreting
13:33–36 as commands to vigilance, which are ineffectual since
the disciples disobey. Kelber does not reckon with Mark's concept
of the Spirit as the guarantor of the presence of Jesus, and he
does not entertain the view that although the historical disciples
disobeyed, the Markan community has an open-ended opportunity
to obey, fortified by Spirit and Gospel.

Second, Kelber holds "that by reproducing the Jesus tradition in
written form, Mark has sought to bring to an end the free-wheeling
transmission of the Jesus tradition by wandering prophets who

place their claims on at least as lofty a level as that of Jesus."[232] Kelber proposes that by committing the tradition to *writing*, Mark robs the prophets of the authority and immediacy of the oral proclamation and also relegates Jesus to the past while pointing to the future as the time of fulfillment. To the contrary, as we have shown, Mark by no means relegates Jesus to the past and future, but proclaims his presence in the Spirit in the church, mediated through Gospel, which reveals his identity and mission and calls for the desired, appropriate response. Moreover, the mode of conveying Gospel, written or oral, was not a matter of major importance to Mark. He likely used both forms, and the majority of the members of his church would be *hearers*, not readers, of the Gospel. The crucial matters were the content and authority of the Jesus traditions and the wholistic theology and continuing power of the new genre of Gospel, due to the mediation of the Holy Spirit. By virtue of Mark's skillful molding of the traditions into a complete, unified Gospel and theology quickened by the presence of the Holy Spirit, the Markan genre of Gospel was more than the sum of its parts. It was an utterly unique creation. The genre and content of Gospel itself mitigated and controlled the excessive claims of the overzealous pneumatic prophets.

ENDNOTES

CHAPTER 3: THE BODY OF THE GOSPEL (MARK 1:16–13:37)

1. N. R. Petersen, "Point of View in Mark's Narrative," *Semeia* 12 (1978): 118, attempts to distinguish between redaction criticism and narrative criticism. However, since Mark is the designer of the narrative, it seems better to regard narrative criticism as an aspect of redaction criticism.

2. Taylor, *The Gospel According to St. Mark*, p. 164, though in Isa 40:25, 57:15 God is "the Holy One," and ἅγιος is applied to Christ in Acts 3:14, 4:27, 30, 1 Jn 2:20, Rev 3:7.

3. J. Dewey, *Marcan Public Debate* (SBLDS 48, Chico: Scholar's Press, 1980), argues for a pattern of concentric parallelism in the section and identifies Mark as the unifying hand. Best, *Mark: The Gospel as Story*, pp. 104–106, doubts that Mark was aware of any pattern.

4. Kee, *Community of the New Age*, p. 56 (with the exception of 3:6).

5. Yates, *The Spirit and the Kingdom*, pp. 50–51.

6. Bultmann, *History of the Synoptic Tradition*, pp. 209, 339–341.

7. R. H. Stein, "A Marcan Seam in Mc 1:21f.," *ZNW* 61–62 (1970–71): 90–91; H. D. Knigge, "The Meaning of Mark," *Int* 22 (1968): 55; Hahn, *Christologische Hoheitstitel*, p. 296.

8. The literature is extensive. For examples: Trocmé, "Is There a Marcan

Christology?" p. 8; R. P. Meye, "Messianic Secret and Messianic Didache in Mark's Gospel," *Oikonomia,* ed. Felix Christ (Hamburg: Herbert Reich, 1967), p. 61, sees a connection between "teaching" in this pericope and "disciples" in 1:16–20; R. T. France, "Mark and the Teaching of Jesus," *Gospel Perspectives I,* eds. R. T. France and D. Wenham (Sheffield: JSOT Press, 1980), 1:128–129; Robbins, *Jesus the Teacher,* pp. 197-213.

9. Achtemeier, "He Taught Them Many Things," p. 475.

10. Hengel, *The Charismatic Leader,* p. 45.

11. Dunn, *Jesus and the Spirit,* pp. 187, 237.

12. G. F. Hawthorne, "Christian Prophets and the Sayings of Jesus: Evidence of and Criteria for," *SBL Seminar Papers,* Vol. 2 (Missoula: Scholar's Press, 1975), pp. 105–129, sets forth eleven considerations which he regards as cummulative evidence for the creative role of Christian prophets.

13. Boring, *Sayings of the Risen Jesus,* pp. 233–234.

14. Ibid., p. 233-234. Earlier W. D. Davies, *Paul and Rabbinic Judaism* (London: S.P.C.K., 1958), p. 142, argued that Mark was written in reaction to the overemphasis in "Q" upon the teachings of Jesus.

15. D. Hill, *New Testament Prophecy* (London: Marshall, Morgan, and Scott, 1979), pp. 179-180. Boring has responded to the demand for "absolute certainty" in classifying prophetic sayings as unrealistic in "Christian-Prophecy and the Sayings of Jesus: The State of the Question," *NTS* 29 (1983): 104–112.

16. R. Kysar, *John, the Maverick Gospel* (Atlanta: John Knox Press, 1976), Ch. 1; J. L. Martyn, *History and Theology in the Fourth Gospel* (New York: Harper & Row, 1968), pp. xix-xx.

17. Cf. Dunn, *Jesus and the Spirit,* p. 284.

18. E. E. Ellis, *Prophecy and Hermeneutic in Early Christianity* (Tübingen: J. C. B. Mohr, 1978), pp. 34–35.

19. Scott, *The Spirit in the New Testament,* p. 169.

20. Barrett, *The Holy Spirit and the Gospel Tradition,* pp. 71–79; Burkill, *Mysterious Revelation,* p. 35.

21. Taylor, *The Gospel According to St. Mark,* p. 174.

22. Suggested in part by W. Manson, *Jesus and the Christian* (London: James Clarke & Co., 1967), pp. 42–43, though Manson attributes Messianic significance to the title and the term "authority."

23. Hooker, *The Message of Mark,* p. 35.

24. L. Williamson, Jr., *Interpretation: Mark* (Atlanta: John Knox Press, 1983), p. 51.

25. N. Perrin, "The Creative Use of the Son of Man Traditions by Mark," *A Modern Pilgrimage in New Testament Christology* (Philadelphia: Fortress Press, 1974), p. 88; earlier in *Union Seminary Quarterly Review* 23 (1968): 353, who states further that 2:10 and 2:28 are constructions by Mark designed "to stress the authority of Jesus and to claim that he exercised that authority as Son of Man."

26. N. Perrin, "The Christology of Mark," *JR* 51 (1971): 478–79, 484–85.

27. G. Lindeskog, "Das Rätsel des Menschensohnes," *Studia Theologica* 22 (1968): 149–175; G. Vermes, *Jesus and the World of Judaism* (London: SCM Press, 1983), p. 96; R. Leivestad, "Exit the Apocalyptic Son of Man," *NTS* 18 (1972): 243–267; J. Bowker, "The Son of Man," *JTS* 28 (1977): 26.

28. Vermes, *Jesus and the World of Judaism*, p. 96.

29. Bowker, "The Son of Man," p. 26.

30. A. J. B. Higgins, *The Son of Man in the Teaching of Jesus* (Cambridge: University Press, 1980), p. 132, n. 107, who quotes Paul Winter's remark in *Deutsche Literaturzeitung* 89 (1968), col. 784, "If Perrin's interpretation of the Son of Man sayings in the Synoptic Gospels is correct ... then the place of origin of the [Son of Man] myth is not to be sought in Iran, or in Judea, or even in Ugarit, but in the German universities."

31. Manson, *Jesus the Messiah*, pp. 164–65; Taylor, *The Gospel According to St. Mark*, pp. 199–200; Cullmann, *The Christology of the New Testament*, p. 161.

32. Bultmann, *Theology of the New Testament*, 1:26ff; Dibelius, *From Tradition to Gospel*, p. 226.

33. Higgins, *The Son of Man in the Teaching of Jesus*, p. 126, and earlier, "Son of Man—*Forschung* since 'The teaching of Jesus,'" *New Testament Essays*, ed. A. J. B. Higgins (Manchester: University Press, 1959), pp. 123–124; H. E. Tödt, *The Son of Man in the Synoptic Tradition* (Philadelphia: Westminster Press, 1965), p. 218; M. D. Hooker, *The Son of Man in Mark* (Montreal: McGill University Press, 1967), pp. 190-194.

34. Higgins, *The Son of Man in the Teaching of Jesus*, p. 126.

35. Martin, *Mark: Evangelist and Theologian*, p. 191; italics original.

36. Best, *The Temptation and the Passion*, pp. 35–36.

37. R. T. Mead, "The Healing of the Paralytic—A Unit?" *JBL* 80 (1961): 353.

38. Dunn, *Jesus and the Spirit*, p. 89.

39. See the treatment in Weeden, *Mark—Traditions in Conflict*, pp. 150–151, who advocates the torturous thesis that ὁ λόγος was Mark's opponents' term for "gospel," which he appropriated, altered, and employed against them. The word occurs 15 times in the singular, and 8 of these occurrences are in 4:14–20.

40. Kee, *Community of the New Age*, p. 164.

41. Bultmann, *History of the Synoptic Tradition*, pp. 14–15, ascribes the activity to the early church, and Dibelius, *From Tradition to Gospel*, p. 66, terms vv. 6–10 "a fictitious conversation introduced by the narrator."

42. Hooker, *The Son of Man in Mark*, p. 90.

43. D. Juel, *Messiah and Temple: The Trial of Jesus in the Gospel of Mark* (SBLDS 31, Missoula: Scholar's Press, 1977), p. 102.

44. Bowman, *The Gospel of Mark*, p. 113, who notes that the objections are not voiced. Yates, *The Spirit and the Kingdom*, p. 114, views πνεῦμα in 8:12, 14:38 functioning in the way described here in 2:8.

45. Hooker, *The Son of Man in Mark*, p. 102.

46. In agreement with Taylor, *The Gospel According to St. Mark*, p. 182, and Schweizer, *The Good News According to Mark*, p. 56.

47. Keck, "Mark 3:7–12 and Mark's Christology," pp. 342–344.

48. T. A. Burkill, "Mark 3.7–12 and the Alleged Dualism in the Evangelist's Miracle Material," *JBL* 87 (1968): 409–417, convincingly counters Keck's arguments for 3:7–12 as a concluding summary but does not consider a later article by Keck, "The Introduction to Mark's Gospel," *NTS* 12 (1966): 358–362, in which contrary to Burkill's implication, Keck rejects any notion of Mark presenting Jesus simply as a *Theois Anēr*.

49. Bultmann, *History of the Synoptic Tradition*, p. 29. Hengel, *The*

Charismatic Leader, p. 65, is attracted to the view that the verse shows Jesus to have been an "ecstatic."

50. Bultmann, *History of the Synoptic Tradition*, p. 13; Dibelius, *From Tradition to Gospel*, p. 220, Hahn, *Christologische Hoheitstitel*, p. 298.

51. R. Holst, "Reexamining Mk. 3.28f. and Its Parallels," *ZNW* 63–64 (1972–73): 122–124.

52. Anderson, *The Gospel of Mark*, p. 124.

53. There is no consensus of opinion among scholars on this controversial issue. Boring, *Sayings of the Risen Jesus*, p. 284, n. 39, provides a convenient summary of positions of scholars on both sides of the issue. The Steeter "Four Source Documentary Hypothesis" assumes that Mark did not know Q, and this is still the majority view in spite of Boring's case to the contrary.

54. Higgins, *The Son of Man in the Teaching of Jesus*, p. 116, who thinks both developed from "one Aramaic logion." J. G. Williams, "A note on the 'Unforgivable Sin' Logion," *NTS* 12 (1965): 75–77, argues that it is basically an authentic saying of Jesus.

55. Schweizer, *The Good News According to Mark*, p. 84.

56. J. D. Crossan, "Mark and the Relatives of Jesus," *NovT* 15 (1973): 81–113 (esp. 93f).

57. Ibid., pp. 92–95.

58. Bultmann, *History of the Synoptic Tradition*, p. 14; Taylor, *The Gospel According to St. Mark*, p. 244.

59. J. Lambrecht, "The Relatives of Jesus in Mark," *NovT* 16 (1974): 255f.

60. Crossan, "Mark and the Relatives of Jesus," p. 111. Cf. Kelber, *The Kingdom in Mark*, pp. 22, 25–27, 53–54.

61. É. Trocmé, *The Formation of the Gospel According to Mark* (Philadelphia: Westminster Press, 1963), p. 136.

62. Lambrecht, "The Relatives of Jesus in Mark," p. 258. Cf. also Best, *Mark: The Gospel as Story*, pp. 52, 56, 84.

63. F. C. Burkitt, *The Earliest Sources for the Life of Jesus* (Boston: Houghton Mifflin Co., 1910), pp. 50–57. Cf. also Keck, "Mark 3:7–12 and Mark's Christology," pp. 356–358, who thinks Mark wanted "to check and counterbalance this way of understanding Jesus' life and work."

64. Schweizer, "πνεῦμα," *TDNT*, 6:397–398; Aune, *Prophecy in Early Christianity*, pp. 241–242.

65. Scott, *The Spirit in the New Testament*, p. 76.

66. Dunn, *Jesus and the Spirit*, p. 53.

67. Boring, *Sayings of the Risen Jesus*, p. 160.

68. J. W. Drane, "Why Did Paul Write Romans?" (essay supplied privately by the author, Stirling University, 1984), p. 217.

69. Kee, *Community of the New Age*, p. 139.

70. Cf. Taylor, *The Gospel According to St. Mark*, p. 236, for fuller discussion.

71. Theissen, *The First Followers of Jesus*, p. 28.

72. Barrett, *The Holy Spirit and the Gospel Tradition*, p. 107.

73. Ibid., p. 105.

74. Boring, *Sayings of the Risen Jesus*, pp. 161–162.

75. Ibid., p. 162.

76. Hill, *New Testament Prophecy*, pp. 182–183.

77. Ibid., p. 183, note 11.
78. Aune, *Prophecy in Early Christianity,* pp. 241–242.
79. Ibid., p. 242.
80. Against E. Schweizer, *The Holy Spirit* (Philadelphia: Fortress Press, 1980), p. 51, who goes too far in stating that the "dire threat of judgment is therefore aimed at figures who like the Antichrist want to put themselves in the place of God."
81. P. J. Achtemeier, "Mark as Interpreter of the Jesus Traditions," *Int* 32 (1978): 343–344.
82. Schweizer, *The Good News According to Mark,* p. 92.
83. Ibid., pp. 92, 97. Cf. Dibelius, *From Tradition to Gospel,* p. 228, and Bultmann, *History of the Synoptic Tradition,* who terms vv. 10–12 "quite secondary." Taylor, *The Gospel According to St. Mark,* pp. 254–255, thinks vv. 10–12 are based on tradition but have been joined and placed here by Mark, a view with which we concur.
84. C. A. Evans, "The Function of Isaiah 6:9–10 in Mark and John," *NovT* 24 (1982): 132.
85. Schweizer, *The Good News According to Mark,* p. 97.
86. E. Linnemann, *Gleichnisse Jesu: Einführung und Auslegung* (Göttingen: Vandenhoeck & Ruprecht, 1966), p. 125.
87. Martin, *Mark, Evangelist and Theologian,* p. 176. Against Betz, "The So-Called 'Divine Man' in Mark's Christology," p. 235, who claims unpersuasively that Mark intends a parallel with the miraculous "going-across" of Israel at the Red Sea (Exodus 14).
88. K. M. Fisher and U. C. von Wahlde, "The Miracles of Mark 4:35–5:43: Their Meaning and Function in the Gospel Framework," *Biblical Theology Bulletin* 11 (1981): 15.
89. B. M. F. van Iersel and A. J. M. Linmans, "The Storm on the Lake, Mk. 4:35–41 and Mt. 8:18–27 in the Light of Form-Criticism, 'Redaktionsgeschichte' and Structural Analysis," *Miscellanea Neotestamentica,* eds. T. Baarda, A. F. J. Klijn, and W. C. van Unnik (Leiden: E. J. Brill, 1978), p. 23. Cf. also Best, *Mark: The Gospel as Story,* p. 53, who thinks 6:45–52 functioned in the same way.
90. Robinson, *The Problem of History in Mark,* p. 40; T. A. Burkill, "The Notion of Miracle with Special Reference to St. Mark's Gospel," *ZNW* 50 (1959): 42.
91. Best, *Mark: The Gospel as Story,* pp. 93, 95.
92. Weeden, *Mark–Traditions in Conflict,* pp. 144, 148.
93. Best, *Mark: The Gospel as Story,* p. 48.
94. R. C. Tannehill, "The Disciples in Mark: The Function of a Narrative Role," *JR* 57 (1977): 386–405. However, in a more recent publication, "The Gospel of Mark as Narrative Christology," *Semeia* 16 (1979): 82, Tannehill focuses more on Jesus as the central character.
95. Cf. Dibelius, *From Tradition to Gospel,* p. 15. Bultmann, *History of the Synoptic Tradition,* pp. 368–371.
96. Quoted by Kelber, *The Oral and the Written Gospel,* p. 184.
97. Kelber, *The Oral and the Written Gospel,* p. 99.
98. Ibid., p. 209.
99. W. H. Kelber, "Mark and Oral Tradition," *Semeia* 16 (1979): 42.
100. Ibid., p. 45.
101. Kelber, *The Oral and the Written Gospel,* p. 210.

102. Best, *Mark: The Gospel as Story*, pp. 19–20.

103. Kelber, ed., *The Passion in Mark*, in which Donahue, Robbins, Perrin, Dewey, Weeden, and Cross contribute articles in which they subscribe to the same position.

104. Taylor, *The Gospel According to St. Mark*, p. 255; Schweizer, *The Good News According to Mark*, p. 93.

105. Dibelius, *From Tradition to Gospel*, p. 230.

106. Bultmann, *History of the Synoptic Tradition*, p. 346, holds the second view and "Wrede thought the same"; against Burkill, *Mysterious Revelation*, p. 321.

107. D. E. Aune, "The Problem of the Messianic Secret," *NovT* 11 (1969): 25.

108. Bultmann, *History of the Synoptic Tradition*, p. 210; Taylor, *The Gospel According to St. Mark*, p. 272.

109. P. J. Achtemeier, "Toward the Isolation of Pre-Marcan Miracle Catenae," *JBL* 89 (1970): 265–91, and reaffirmed in "He Taught Them Many Things," p. 476.

110. Achtemeier, "He Taught Them Many Things," p. 477.

111. Best, *The Temptation and the Passion*, p. 106. See the analysis by Hahn, *Christologische Hoheitstitel*, pp. 282, 301.

112. Bultmann, *History of the Synoptic Tradition*, p. 419, who cites Dibelius in agreement.

113. E. Grässer, "Jesus in Nazareth (Mark vi 1–6a)," *NTS* 16 (1969): 1–23. Cf. also F. W. Beare, *The Earliest Records of Jesus* (Nashville: Abingdon Press, 1962), p. 124, who differs in viewing v. 6a as the conclusion to the original account.

114. Ellis, *Prophecy and Hermeneutic*, pp. 65–66.

115. Contrary to Grässer, "Jesus in Nazareth (Mark vi 1–6a)," p. 15, who sees in vv. 2–3 the paradox of the messianic secret, i.e., that the man of God in v. 2 is at the same time the carpenter of v. 3, a correction of a *Theios Anēr* Christology.

116. Keck, "The Introduction to Mark's Gospel," p. 355, echoing an objection also raised by E. Schweizer, "Mark's Contribution to the Quest for the Historical Jesus," *NTS* 10 (1964): 426, who, nevertheless, does regard 6:6b as the introduction to the succeeding section.

117. Cf. Bultmann, *History of the Synoptic Tradition*, p. 332. Taylor, *The Gospel According to St. Mark*, p. 306, provides the linguistic evidence.

118. Anderson, *The Gospel of Mark*, p. 165, against Lightfoot, *History and Interpretation in the Gospels*, p. 106, n. 2, and Nineham, *Saint Mark*, pp. 170–171, who recognize only a message of repentance, similar to John the Baptist's, until after the resurrection.

119. Schweizer, *The Good News According to Mark*, p. 132. Contrary to Taylor, *The Gospel According to St. Mark*, p. 307, and Nineham, *Saint Mark*, p. 172.

120. If Mark knew the tradition in Acts 19:1–7 referring to disciples of John who had never heard of the Holy Spirit, his treatment might be taken as a sharp rebuke of the activities of the pneumatic prophets, implying that they did not have the Spirit. But we cannot assume uncritically that he knew the story.

121. G. H. Boobyer, "The Eucharistic Interpretation of the Miracle of The Loaves in St. Mark's Gospel," *JBL* 3 (1952): 167.

122. Best, *Mark: The Gospel as Story*," p. 63.

123. Q. Quesnell, *The Mind of Mark*, p. 276f., quoted in H. C. Kee, "Mark's Gospel in Recent Research," *Int* 32 (1978): 356; Bowman, *The Gospel of Mark*, p. 100; Nineham, *Saint Mark*, p. 179; V. K. Robbins, "Last ·Meal: Preparation, Betrayal, and Absence," *The Passion in Mark*, pp. 21–22.

124. Quesnell, *The Mind of Mark*, p. 276f.

125. For example, A. Farrar, *A Study in St. Mark* (Philadelphia: Westminster Press, 1951), and his subsequent work, *St. Matthew and St. Mark*, 1954.

126. Anderson, *The Gospel of Mark*, p. 197, who notes that a partial parallel is found in Jn 6:5–14, 22–30.

127. Taylor, *The Gospel According to St. Mark*, p. 361.

128. Martin, *Mark, Evangelist and Theologian*, pp. 169, 174.

129. Anderson, *The Gospel of Mark*, p. 198.

130. C. H. Dodd, "The Appearances of the Risen Christ: An Essay in Form-Criticism of the Gospels," *Studies in the Gospels* (Oxford: Basil Blackwell, 1955), pp. 23–24.

131. See the analysis in Grant, *The Gospel According to Mark*, p. 747.

132. Dibelius, *From Tradition to Gospel*, p. 221.

133. C. G. Montefiore, *The Synoptic Gospels* (London: Macmillan, 1927), pp. 162–163.

134. Beare, *The Earliest Records of Jesus*, p. 130.

135. The quote is from the LXX, which alone clearly renders the desired meaning of substitution. The Hebrew text charges the people with fearing God only in obedience to a human commandment. Cf. E. P. Gould, *A Critical and Exegetical Commentary on the Gospel According to St. Mark* (ICC, New York: Scribner's, 1905), p. 128.

136. Yates, *The Spirit and the Kingdom*, pp. 61–62.

137. Beare, *The Earliest Records of Jesus*, p. 133; Schweizer, *The Good News According to Mark*, p. 154. Some MSS omit "and Sidon," but its inclusion in ℵ A B and other MSS merit acceptance.

138. Bultmann, *History of the Synoptic Tradition*, p. 350.

139. J. B. Tyson, "The Blindness of the Disciples in Mark," *JBL* 80 (1961): 261–68; T. J. Weeden, "The Heresy that Necessitated Mark's Gospel," *ZNW* 59 (1968): 146–150.

140. Lightfoot, *History and Interpretation in the Gospels*, pp. 90f.

141. A. Kuby, "Zur Konzeption des Markus-Evangeliums," *ZNW* 49 (1958): 54, 58.

142. E. S. Johnson, "Mark viii. 22–26: The Blind Man from Bethesda," *NTS* 25 (1978–79): 380–383, although he does not see the connection between the Spirit and the Gospel.

143. Tyson, "The Blindness of the Disciples in Mark," pp. 261–68.

144. Kee, *Community of the New Age*, p. 58.

145. The following analysis follows largely Hahn, *Christologische Hoheitstitel*, pp. 174, 226–230, with whose position we basically concur.

146. Also affirmed by E. Dinkler, "Petrusbekenntnis und Satanswort —Das Problem der Messianität Jesu," *Signum Crucis* (Tübingen: J. C. B. Mohr, 1967), pp. 289–330.

147. U. B. Müller, "Die christologische Absicht des Markusevangelium und die Verklarungsgeschichte," *ZNW* 64 (1973): 159–193, goes too far in

claiming that Mark regards Peter's Christology to be false and issues a corrective by Jesus' word at the transfiguration, "Hear Him."

148. In agreement with F. C. Grant, *The Gospels: Their Origin and Their Growth*, pp. 96–97, and Best, *The Temptation and the Passion*, pp. 79–80.

149. P. Vielhauer, "Jesus und der Menschensohn," *Aufsatze zum Neuen Testament*, ed. E. Dinkler (Münschen: Chr. Kaiser Verlag, 1965) pp. 92–93, who offers a summary and critique of the positions of Bultmann, Cullmann, Jeremias, and Tödt in support. Against Perrin, "The Creative Use of the Son of Man traditions by Mark," p. 357–365, whose contention that the Son of Man sayings in Mk. 2:10–10:45 are creations of the evangelist lacks firm evidence.

150. Against Higgins, *Jesus and the Son of Man*, p. 26.

151. For examples: (1) Hooker, *The Son of Man in Mark*, pp. 108–109, 163, who attempts to explicate the Markan Son of Man sayings in light of Daniel 7. She encounters difficulty in demonstrating a parallel because of the absence of suffering as a trait of the Son of Man in Daniel 7 (and in Enoch). (2) Higgins, "Son of Man—*Forschung* since 'The Teaching of Jesus'" pp. 125–129, names Mowinckel, Bowman, N. Johansson, C. C. McCown, E. Stauffer as scholars who interpret the Son of Man too narrowly on the basis of eschatological, apocalyptic sources only. (3) Schweizer, *The Good News According to Mark*, pp. 168–170, identifies Ezekiel as the primary source for the title, while C. K. Barrett, "The Background of Mark 10:45," *New Testament Essays*, ed. A. J. B. Higgins (Manchester: University Press, 1959) pp. 12–13 refers to passages in 2 and 4 Maccabees and in selected rabbinic writings as decisive. (4) J. Jeremias, *Servant of God* (Naperville: Alec R. Allenson, 1957), p. 60, holds that the Gospel's concept is based on the glorious Son of Man of the apocalyptic sources invested with traits of the Suffering Servant of Isaiah 53. But we have no firm evidence that such a synthesis occurred in the pre-Christian era or that Mark received such a portrayal of the Son of Man from the tradition.

152. Possibly Mark knew only one passion prediction which he repeated at appropriate points; however, F. H. Borsch, *The Son of Man in Myth and History* (Philadelphia: Westminster Press, 1967), pp. 348–349, upholds "the probability that the sayings came to him from separate sources in his own traditions," though Borsch thinks Mark was more concerned with Jesus as the Christ than as the Son of Man.

153. Tödt, *The Son of Man in the Synoptic Tradition*, p. 211, believes the name Son of Man was added by the early Palestinian community to a saying from Jesus.

154. Perrin, "The Creative Use of the Son of Man Traditions by Mark," p. 364.

155. Tödt, *The Son of Man in the Synoptic Tradition*, pp. 206ff; cf. W. J. Moulder, "The O.T. Background and the Interpretation of Mark x. 45," *NTS* 24 (1977): 120–127, who argues that the ransom saying originated with Jesus.

156. Scholars often fail to notice that the "servant" of Isaiah is not a uniform concept; in fact, the "servant" of Isaiah 42 does not suffer at all.

157. Burkill, *Mysterious Revelation*, pp. 175–176.

158. Achtemeier, "He Taught Them Many Things," p. 470.

159. Best, *Mark: The Gospel as Story*, p. 84.

160. Perrin, "The Creative Use of the Son of Man Traditions by Mark," p. 363.

161. Evidently some later copyists had the same opinion, since several MSS omit ἐμοῦ καί, notably p^{45} D 28 it sy^s, though the majority of MSS include the phrase.

162. Tödt, *The Son of Man in the Synoptic Tradition*, p. 45. Again Mark blends a Son of Man saying into a portrayal of the Risen Christ/Holy Spirit already present in the community through the Gospel. The apocalyptic aspect is softened, and the aspect of sovereignty is heightened.

163. Weeden, *Mark–Traditions in Conflict*, p. 84.

164. Ibid., p. 82. Since he views Jesus as absent from the church, Weeden attempts to make a distinction between Jesus and Gospel by stating obscurely that "the term 'gospel' is an equivalent for Jesus himself *theologically*" (underlining added).

165. Marxsen, *Mark the Evangelist*, p. 126ff.

166. Weeden, *Mark–Traditions in Conflict*, p. 85.

167. Ibid., p. 87.

168. Cf. Taylor, *The Gospel According to St. Mark*, pp. 386–388, who summarizes the following positions.

169. E. Käsemann, *Essays on New Testament Themes* (London: SCM Press, 1964), p. 36, thinks that Mark 8:34 "reflects the language of Palestinian Christian prophets uttering maxims of holy law for the guidance of the community and laying down the future consequences of obedience or disobedience here and now." Taylor, *The Gospel According to St. Mark*, p. 383, favors an original saying from Jesus overlaid with apocalyptic expectation. In any event, Mark considers the saying to be from Jesus and, therefore, does not use it to describe the teaching of false prophets, for Jesus does not speak falsely.

170. Petersen, *Literary Criticism for New Testament Critics*, pp. 64–65.

171. H. Anderson, "The Easter Witness of the Evangelists," *The New Testament in Historical and Contemporary Perspective*, eds. H. Anderson and W. Barclay (Oxford: Basil Blackwell, 1965), pp. 43–44.

172. C. E. Carlston, "Transfiguration and Resurrection," *JBL* 80 (1961): 240.

173. Yates, *The Spirit and the Kingdom*, p. 129; G. W. H. Lampe, "The Holy Spirit in the Writings of St. Luke," *Studies in the Gospels* (Oxford: Basil Blackwell, 1955), p. 168.

174. E. Schweizer, "The Portrayal of the Life of Faith in the Gospel of Mark," *Int* 32 (1978): 398–399.

175. Dibelius, *From Tradition to Gospel*, pp. 52–53, holds that the name "Bartimaeus" was a secondary addition, and Bultmann, *History of the Synoptic Tradition*, p. 213, suspects the title "Son of David" was a later insertion; but if so, both were added in the pre-Markan tradition.

176. Meye, *Jesus and the Twelve*, pp. 164–166, emphasizes the favored status of the Twelve, but his concern with the historical situation prevents him from seeing the theological significance of the passage for Mark.

177. Hahn, *Christologische Hoheitstitel*, p. 265.

178. Ibid., p. 171.

179. Ibid., pp. 87–90. Mark does not use the title extensively because it was not originally a divine name for Jesus and did not appear often in

the tradition.

180. R. H. Hiers, "Not the Season for Figs," *JBL* 87 (1968): 394–400, thinks the title-phrase means that Jesus expected the messianic age to begin; for in the messianic age, figs would always be in season. Even if this speculation were true, this would not necessarily be Mark's meaning. Best, *Mark: The Gospel as Story,* p. 70, suggests that the phrase indicates that Mark was aware that he was using the phrase in an unusual manner. Perhaps; or perhaps he was not bothered by the phrase at all.

181. Best, *The Temptation and the Passion,* p. 83.

182. F. Hahn, *Mission in the New Testament* (Naperville: Alec R. Allenson Inc., 1965), p. 115, who states further that the Parable of the Vineyard makes the same point. Cf. also Burkill, *Mysterious Revelation,* pp. 12–22.

183. Against H. Conzelmann, "Gegenwart und Zukunft in der synoptischen Tradition," *ZTK* 54 (1957): 295, who states, "Die Geheimnistheorie ist die hermeneutische Voraussetzung der Gattung 'Evangelium'."

184. E.g., Lohmeyer, Schniewind, T. W. Manson, Taylor.

185. Bultmann, *History of the Synoptic Tradition,* p. 347.

186. G. Bornkamm, G. Barth, and H. J. Held, *Tradition and Interpretation in Matthew* (Philadelphia: Westminster Press, 1963), pp. 37, 106, who hold that Matthew wished to affirm the humbleness of the Messiah-King who is correctly understood by the disciples.

187. W. Bauer, "The 'Colt' of Palm Sunday," *JBL* 72 (1953): 229.

188. Bultmann, *History of the Synoptic Tradition,* p. 63; Burkill, *Mysterious Revelation,* p. 200. Neither scholar assesses the theological significance of the verse.

189. Bultmann, *History of the Synoptic Tradition,* p. 20. Schweizer, *The Good News According to Mark,* pp. 236–237, thinks that in the tradition 11:15–17 formed the antecedent to ταῦτα ποιεῖς in v. 28.

190. Cf. Bowman, *The Gospel of Mark,* p. 222.

191. Yates, *The Spirit and the Kingdom,* pp. 34–35. Cf. Hill, *New Testament Prophecy,* p. 49.

192. See the treatment by C. A. Evans, "On the Vineyard Parables (Jes. 5; Mk. 12)," *Biblische Zeitschrift* 28 (1984): 86.

193. Taylor, *The Gospel According to St. Mark,* pp. 476–477, gives a full discussion. Schweizer, *The Good News According to Mark,* pp. 239–240, points out that vv. 10f are quoted word for word from the LXX and were frequently cited in the church to portray Jesus and the church as the fulfillment of OT prophecy.

194. Recognized in part by Kazmierski, *Jesus the Son of God,* p. 136.

195. Seen also by Schweizer, *The Good News According to Mark,* p. 242.

196. Cf. Nineham, *Saint Mark,* p. 314ff, who sees a similar ordering of materials.

197. E.g., Taylor, *The Gospel According to St. Mark,* p. 493, holds that Jesus is the author, while Bultmann, *Theology of the New Testament,* 1:121f, 145f, attributes the saying to the early church.

198. See Nineham, *Saint Mark,* pp. 329–332.

199. Recognized in part by Schweizer, *The Good News According to Mark,* pp. 254–258.

200. This insight was stimulated by Barrett, *The Holy Spirit and the*

Gospel Tradition, p. 108, who remarks that belief in David's inspiration "arises from the fact that the Psalm was contained in a book the whole of which was believed to be inspired."

201. See the reviews and critiques in G. R. Beasley-Murray, *Jesus and the Future* (London: Macmillan, 1954), Ch. 1, and *Commentary on Mark 13* (London: Macmillan, 1957) p. 18. In a later article, "Second Thoughts on the Composition of Mark 13," *NTS* 29 (1983): 414–420, the author alters his position and affirms the composite nature of Mark 13.

202. W. G. Kümmel, *Promise and Fulfillment* (Naperville: Alec R. Allenson, Inc., 1957) p. 98. Against J. Lambrecht, *Die Redaktion der Markus-Apokalypse* (Rome: Päpstliches Bibelinstitut, 1967), pp. 299–300, who adheres to the unity of Mark 13 as Jesus' teaching.

203. Exemplified by L. Hartmann, *Prophecy Interpreted* (Lund: CWK Gleerup, 1966), pp. 145–147.

204. Exemplified by F. Busch, *Zum Verständnis der synoptischen Eschatologie Markus 13 neu untersucht*, p. 8, quoted by Marxsen, *Mark the Evangelist*, p. 153.

205. Cf. Bultmann, *History of the Synoptic Tradition*, p. 122; E. Grässer, *Das Problem der Parusieverzögerung in den synoptischen Evangelien und in der Apostelgeschichte*, Beihefte zur *ZNW* 22 (Berlin: Alfred Töpelmann, 1960), p. 159; R. Pesch, *Naherwartungen: Tradition und Redaktion in Mk 13*, KBANT.(Düsseldorf: Patmos Verlag, 1968), pp. 117–118, 242–243.

206. Keck, "The Introduction to Mark's Gospel," p. 365.

207. Theissen, *The First Followers of Jesus*, pp. 8, 18, 25, 76, who holds that "homeless, wandering charismatics" handed on much of the apocalyptic-eschatological material in Ch. 13 and elsewhere which was later "to take independent form as Christianity." Boring, *Sayings of the Risen Jesus*, pp. 189, 193, also attributes the bulk of Mk 13:5b–31 to Christian prophets. This is too sweeping a generalization.

208. R. Scroggs, "The Exaltation of the Spirit by Some Early Christians," *JBL* 84 (1965): 363, 373, suggests that overenthusiastic prophetic elements accepted the belief that the beginning of the End was already underway and would soon culminate in the Lord coming from heaven to rule over his kingdom—beliefs also held in the churches at Corinth and Thessalonica.

209. Against Marxsen, *Mark the Evangelist*, pp. 182–184, who views the temple destruction as the signal to flee to the mountains (v. 14), that is, to Galilee to await the parousia.

210. Keck, "The Introduction to Mark's Gospel," p. 366.

211. A. L. Moore, *The Parousia in the New Testament* (Leiden: E. J. Brill, 1966), pp. 132–133, argues that "all these things" (ταῦτα πάντα) in v. 30 refers to ταῦτα in v. 29 and means the entire complex of signs and events experienced by but not exhausted by this generation. This may be too subtle.

212. Pesch, *Naherwartungen*, pp. 117–118.

213. Keck, "The Introduction to Mark's Gospel," pp. 365–366.

214. W. L. Knox, *Some Hellenistic Elements in Primitive Christianity*, (London: H. Milford, 1944), p. 26. The uprising of Theudas occurred in AD 44, and Josephus (*Ant.* 20.97, 102) describes an uprising by the grandsons of Judas soon afterward.

215. R. McL. Wilson, *Gnosis and the New Testament* (Philadelphia: For-

tress Press, 1968), pp. 52–59, contrary to Reitzenstein, Bousset, Bultmann, Betz, Georgi, and Schmithals who argue for a developed Gnosticism in the early church.
216. Weeden, "The Heresy That Necessitated Mark's Gospel," pp. 145–158. Weeden also cites the Lucan combination of "signs and wonders" (cf. Mk 13:22) with the activity of the Theios Anēr in Acts 2:19, 7:36. As indicated, Georgi, Die Gegner des Paulus im 2. Korintherbreif, has influenced Weeden's perspective.
217. Keck, "The Introduction to Mark's Gospel," p. 366.
218. Boring, Sayings of the Risen Jesus, p. 189, speculates that Mark is acquainted with the revelatory formulae ἐγώ εἰμι and ἐπὶ τῷ ὀνοματί μου used by Christian prophets but does not use them because they have been appropriated by his opponents
219. H. B. Swete, The Holy Spirit in the New Testament (London: Macmillan, 1909), p. 122.
220. Cf. Gal 1:6–9, in which interestingly the same motifs appear.
221. Marxsen, Mark the Evangelist, p. 175; against Winstanley, The Spirit in the New Testament, pp. 18–19, who claims that the Spirit is a Jewish hypostatization distinct from Jesus and the Father.
222. Against Boring, Sayings of the Risen Jesus, p. 190, who thinks the saying implies only the occasional gift of the Spirit to particular persons in times of crisis.
223. Schweizer, The Good News According to Mark, p. 271.
224. I. H. Marshall, Luke: Historian and Theologian (Grand Rapids: Zondervan, 1971), p. 52.
225. Petersen, Literary Criticism for New Testament Critics, pp. 70–71.
226. R. Schnackenburg, "Das Evangelium," p. 318, quoted by Kazmierski, Jesus, The Son of God, p. 18, n. 59. Cf. also Hooker, The Son of Man in Mark, pp. 156–157, who asserts that Mark 13 is an explication of Mk 8:34.
227. Kee, Community of the New Age, p. 161, recognizes the relationship between watchfulness and revelation but does not perceive the role of the Spirit. He alludes to prayer (cf. 14:34–38) as the link.
228. Best, Following Jesus, p. 246.
229. Seen in part by Tannehill, "The Gospel of Mark as Narrative Christology," pp. 83–84, although he does not stress the connection between Jesus and the Spirit.
230. W. H. Kelber, "Mark and Oral Tradition," Semeia 16 (1979): 42.
231. Kelber, The Oral and the Written Gospel, pp. 99–100.
232. H. C. Kee, "Mark's Gospel in Recent Research," Int 32 (1978): 365, makes this observation about Kelber's position.

—4—

THE PASSION AND RESURRECTION
NARRATIVES (MARK 14:1–16:8)

Introduction

Past scholarship generally advocated the view that the Passion Narrative was the earliest unit in Mark's Gospel and had attained a definite form as an independent composition before the evangelist incorporated it into his Gospel.[1] Kähler's provocative statement that the Gospels are "passion narratives with an extended introduction" became a commonplace.[2] However, the rise of redaction criticism challenged the fixity of the pre-Markan Passion Narrative. Recent redaction studies have established that the hand of Mark is clearly observable in the Passion and Resurrection Narratives as in the earlier sections, although critics differ in their estimation of the extent of redaction discernible.[3] Amid the swirl of opinions and positions, we maintain that Mark received a connected Passion Narrative, but has reworked it and inserted additional logia in order to preserve continuity with prior themes and interests within a wholistic concept of Gospel. Our analysis substantiates this position.[4] However, since the major motifs and purposes of Mark have already been delineated in the preceding sections, it is not necessary for us to exegete the entire Passion-Resurrection Narrative. We purport to focus on selected pericopes and complexes which reflect Mark's interest in the related themes of "Spirit and Gospel."

The Anointing: Gospel in Miniature

Mark 14:3–9 (the Anointing) has been intercalated by the evangelist between the introduction in vv. 1–2 and the natural continuation in v. 10.[5] The reference to "Gospel" in the redactional verse that concludes the pericope (v. 9) discloses the evangelist's understanding of the passage: First, he contrasts those at table (perhaps including the disciples), who misunderstand Jesus and the act of anointing, with the woman who in humble obedience anoints Jesus as the authoritative Son who must suffer and die. Second, Mark proclaims that the telling (and hearing) of this act (for those who have ears to hear) is to preach the fullness of "Gospel" (εὐαγγέλιον). Not only is the episode a part of Jesus' past gospel and Mark's book; it is the whole Gospel in miniature in the present in that it proclaims Jesus' divine authority and death and the call to perceptive, persistent discipleship consistent with Jesus' nature and mission.

The claim of V. K. Robbins and company that Mk 14:7, 9 assure the absence of Jesus from the community until the parousia[6] exhibits a remarkable tour de force in bringing the text into conformity with a preconceived position. It is evident that 14:7 alludes to the earthly Jesus and his impending death, not to his resurrected form and state. The Greek term for "remembrance" (μνημόσυνον) is an especially vivid word, and contrary to Robbins, denotes not a mere memory, and hence real absence of Jesus, but his actual presence in the telling of the Gospel. Interestingly, Robbins explains the lack of the Pauline phrase, "Do this in remembrance of me" (1 Cor 11:23–26) in the Markan Last Supper pericope as evidence that Mark stresses the absence of Jesus.[7] Apart from the strained exegesis that interprets both the inclusion and the exclusion of the term to mean Jesus' absence, Robbins does not seem to realize that Mark is utilizing another strand in the tradition in recounting the Last Supper and is not drawing directly from Paul. In the Markan context, the absence of Jesus was not the problem, but the misunderstanding of his presence experienced in the Holy Spirit.

The Last Supper: Basis for Discipleship

The core tradition of the Last Supper (vv. 22–25) has been bracketed by two related but originally independent units[8] that establish a context of discipleship modeling in which negative examples are used for positive instruction by the evangelist. The original *Sitz im Leben*, form, and meaning of the Last Supper pericope (vv. 22–25) is an extremely controversial issue that is not immediately germane to our purpose. Taylor, Behm, and Best interpret the pericope in light of sacrificial concepts found in Ex 24:1–11;[9] Manson and Cullmann view the "'ebed Yahweh" of Deutero-Isaiah as the key to the meaning.[10] Lightfoot thinks the point for Mark is the "pledge of a future great deliverance."[11] Danker argues for Psalm 40 as the basis for the narration of Mk 14:1–25,[12] and Bowman maintains that the Passover Haggadah provided the pattern for this pericope and the entire Gospel.[13] All these suggestions run aground on one methodological shoal: Mark has done nothing to indicate that he saw these posited parallels and patterns as determinative for his own viewpoint. The fact that Mark included the account of a Last Supper in a Passover setting indicates that he believed Jesus' death had atoning, reconciling efficacy and was to be followed by a future triumph in glory. But Burkill is correct:

> The evangelist does not offer any elucidation of what precisely he understands by the important doctrine of the necessity of the Messiah's sufferings, and he makes no attempt to explain the nature of the connection between the passion and the parousia, on the one hand, and between the resurrection and the parousia, on the other.[14]

The evangelist's attention is directed elsewhere—toward the proclaiming of the Gospel and the elucidation of discipleship. Jesus must die, but he will emerge victorious in the coming kingdom of God. His death will establish a (new)[15] covenant with a new community (the church). It is perhaps a moot point whether Mark is adopting a prophecy and fulfillment pattern based on the OT, as Rohde maintains, or is merely using OT phrases in his description determined foremost by the Easter faith, as Suhl claims.[16] In either case, the evangelist retains basically the language of the tradition to express the dual-pronged thrust of Gospel that informs the Christian community about the nature of true discipleship. Whereas the Twelve were unable to fathom the meaning of the Last Supper, the Markan readers have the advantages of a post-resurrection perspective and the presence of the Lord in the Spirit in the celebration of the Lord's Supper to understand Jesus, the Gospel, and the requirements of discipleship. Though suffering is inevitable, the persevering disciple will ultimately attain the victory and the reward of the eternal kingdom. The promise of 14:25 is reaffirmed in the Markan saying in v. 28 which assures a reunion in "Galilee." (We shall defer treatment of this passage and consider it in conjunction with 16:7.)

Gethsemane: Sonship and Suffering

Views concerning the origin and construction of the Gethsemane pericope range widely. Taylor approvingly quotes Klausner: "The whole story bears the hallmark of human truth. . . . It must have been transmitted to the Evangelist (or their sources) direct from Peter, James, or John. . . ."[17] Kelber comes to the opposite conclusion: "With the possible exception of a Gethsemane lament and prayer tradition, the pericope is fully explicable in terms of Markan linguistic and syntactical features, literary devices, as well as religious motifs."[18] We accept the majority view that the account rests upon a historical nucleus but has undergone accretion in the tradition and by Mark's redactions, e.g., the threefold prayers (cf. 2 Cor 12:8; Dan 6:10, 13), possibly corresponding to Peter's threefold denial, and the closing verses (vv. 41–42), which heighten the Markan paradox between the suffering Son of Man and the victorious Son who boldly advances to meet his adversaries.[19] The statement in v. 42 is especially suggestive. The verse points ahead to 16:6b–7 in which Mark uses two verbs, ἐγείρω and (προ)άγω, derived from the same roots (stems) found in 14:42. Mark intimates to the reader that Jesus, who is risen, bids the disciples to arise and to resume their mission of going with Jesus after his death and resurrection. The reunion in "Galilee" is already anticipated and pronounced. In the same account, Mark reminds his readers who this Jesus is. On the one hand, he is the one who says, "Abba, Father" (v. 36); that is, he is the unique Son. Moreover, he is the Son who submits to the divine necessity (v. 41) because he has the very Spirit of God (v. 38). As Schweizer states:

> Once it is seen that the expression "willing Spirit" comes from the Hebrew of Ps. 51:12, that it is identical there with God's holy spirit, and that it is here used in a prayer for endurance in temptation, it is plain that what is present is the Spirit of God which is given to man and which strives against human weakness.[20]

Kelber notes, too, that in the apocalyptic discourse, "the hour" of the "delivering up" of Christians (παραδίδωμι, 13:11; 14:41) coincides with the intercession of the Holy Spirit.[21]

In the Gethsemane pericope, Mark brings together several major motifs. He connects the reference to Jesus and the Spirit in Gethsemane with the post-resurrection promise of the Holy Spirit in 13:11 and refers to the baptism of the Son with the Holy Spirit in 1:9–11, who equipped Jesus for the proclamation of Gospel. Jesus, by virtue of the Spirit, is the authoritative Son and the authentic basis of Gospel. Yet, Mark presents him also as the Son of Man who has been betrayed and must suffer and die (v. 41). These are the two poles of the Markan Christology in paradox. As Boring has perceptively insisted, Mark is not interested in resolving the paradox, but in affirming both aspects as true and valid from his particular perspective and logic.[22] However, Christology per se is not Mark's overarching concern, but is integral to the very nature of Gospel itself and its instructive role about the meaning of discipleship. Boring's identification of Christology as Mark's major concern leads him to misconstrue Mark's use of the secrecy motif as a literary device to conjoin and to hold in tension two opposing Christologies. This is the penultimate function of the secrecy motif. The ultimate purpose is to disclose the Risen Christ's/Holy Spirit's revelation of the concept of Gospel, which includes Mark's Christology as one among several important motifs.

Mark stresses the Gospel's twin motifs of divine authority and human suffering as dual components of discipleship, but he is not content simply to preserve venerable statements from a past, dead Jesus. No, he intimates in the story-line, confirmed by his actual experience in the church, that the disciples will rise from their stupor through encounter with the Risen Jesus (ἐγείρεσθε), who will lead (ἄγωμεν) his disciples in triumph over all foes. This was a needed message of hope to a dispirited church facing persecution. But the reader and church must accept the prerequisite: mature discipleship, possible only through understanding the Gospel, which requires the aid of the Risen Christ/Holy Spirit. Thereby the heavily laden eyes of the disciples can be fully opened (v. 40). C. H. Bird contends that the function of the Markan γάρ clauses here and elsewhere is to allude to a concept or purpose already familiar to the reader.[23] This insight may point to Mark's purpose and point in the conclusion to the Gethsemane pericope (14:43–50).

The original disciples failed Jesus: "They all forsook him and fled" (14:50). Tannehill is right:

> A clear choice is placed before the readers, represented by Jesus, on the one hand, and the faithless disciples on the other. . . . Choosing to stand with Jesus means accepting Jesus' words in 8:31–10:45, and living them out as Jesus does in the passion story.[24]

However, he falls short of comprehending the Markan conclusion in stating that "the disciples' story-line stops at this point of failure." Instead, Mark points toward a promised reunion and restoration of the disciples with Jesus in Galilee—depicted as a future event but still within the story-line of the Gospel, which regards Jesus' promises as certain of fulfillment. Also, Mark is not writing in isolation from the everyday world of his community. He and his readers know that the promise of restoration of the disciples has indeed occurred, and the church and Gospel are among the firstfruits.

Arrest, Trial, Crucifixion: The Paradox of Gospel

In relating the arrest and trial of Jesus, Mark has interpolated the account of Jesus before the Council (14:55–65) into the story of Peter's denial by rewriting the introduction in vv. 53–54 to apply to both accounts and by composing vv. 66–67a as a fresh introduction.[25] The result of this familiar literary technique is that the Markan Jesus discloses his identity and mission within a framework of (failing) discipleship. Peter follows "at a distance," far behind in theological strides also, but he does still follow. He is still related to Jesus, and hence, all hope is not lost. This is Mark's message to his readers as well.

D. Juel has argued strongly in *Messiah and Temple*[26] that the royal Messiah motif is central in the trial narrative. All other titles are secondary, serving to supplement the content of the confession that Jesus is the Messiah-King. The title is tied to the Temple theme to provide further testimony to Jesus as the Messiah and to proclaim that the Christian community is the new temple of God.[27]

There are a number of objections to this thesis. First, as we have shown above, there is no evidence that Mark presents Jesus exclusively or primarily as the Messiah-King. Mark is not adverse to the Messiah title, but he is wary of it. Writing to a predominantly Gentile church, he used the title sparingly and supplemented it with other designations. The title "Son of the Blessed" in v. 61 is unique in the NT and in Jewish sources. Juel's explanation that it is a "pseudo-Jewish expression created by the author" to buttress the Messiah title[28] is altogether unconvincing. It is more likely that the phrase means "Son of God" (cf. 1:1). Juel recognizes this possibility and makes a futile effort, on the basis of the use of the title in the midrash on 2 Samuel 7 in 4Q Florilegium, to establish that the title was used "in pre-Christian Jewish circles as a designation for the Royal Messiah."[29] The obscure posited parallel is unconvincing. Nor does Juel take account of Mark's *Sitz* and prior use of titles. Mark juxtaposes at this climatic place in the Gospel (14:61–62) three key titles: Christ, Son of the Blessed, Son of Man[30] (possibly also "I am," ἐγώ εἰμι). Here Mark uses the same technique he employed in the Prologue, namely, piling up titles from the tradition, not to structure a systematic Christology, but to demonstrate the divine sovereignty of Jesus as the "Son" who must die but who will ultimately triumph.[31] The evangelist was not able to be more specific and remain true to his commitment to Gospel. This is the message his supporters and antagonists in the church needed to hear in order to practice discipleship with unity and hope in the face of misunderstanding and oppression.

Juel's contention that the Markan Jesus is the Messiah who will build the eschatological temple "not made with hands"[32] (14:58) is equally suspect. It is likely that Mark was aware of the temple prophecy in 2 Sam 7:13–16 and assimilated this tradition into his depiction of Jesus' mission in so far as it was applicable. However, he has done nothing to place special emphasis on the connection between Messiah and temple. It should be noticed that the OT also speaks of God as the builder of the temple at the end of days (Ex 15:17; Ezk 37:26ff) This parallel is in closer accord with Mark's eschatology and Christology. Jesus, by the endowment of the Spirit of God and by his resurrection, is "the Son of the Blessed," i.e., the divine Son, inseparably related to God himself. As in 12:36, though he may legitimately be called Messiah, he is more than Messiah: He is the Lord, the Son of God who replaces the temple and its mediating, reconciling function.

The charge of blasphemy against Jesus by the high priest (14:63–64) and the passers-by at the cross (15:29), both related to the temple charge, support our denial of the "Messiah" category as central for Mark. Juel recognizes rightly that Mark intends the reference about the building of a "temple not made with hands" to refer to the church.[33] However, Mark's emphasis is not confined to the future eschatological dimension. It also includes a reference to the resurrection as the basis for the new "body of Christ," the new "temple of the Spirit,"[34] concepts with which Mark indicates familiarity, although he has no tradition using the phrases. The mention of "three days" is an obvious reference to the resurrection for the benefit of the reader and is linked with the Passion sayings (8:31; 9:31; 10:33ff). Through his resurrection, Jesus will build a new community, and he will be with it.[35] To fail to see this effect of Jesus' death and resurrection as the divine Son is to be irreparably blind and lost. Contrary to surface appearances, it is the chief priest and passers-by who are guilty of blasphemy. And Mark has already made it clear that blasphemy against Jesus is an eternal sin against the Holy Spirit (3:28–29). Interestingly, Mark uses the same term (βλασφήμειν) in 3:29 and 15:29 instead of the word (ἐκμυκτηρίζειν) from the LXX to describe the mockery.[36] Jesus and the Spirit are inseparably related. Persons past and present who fail to confess that the Holy Spirit experienced in the church embodies the crucified and Risen Jesus, the cornerstone of the church (12:10), are guilty of blasphemy against the Holy Spirit. This warning constituted an urgent appeal to pneumatic prophets, devoid of a Passion

Narrative in their gospel, to view the Spirit and Gospel through new eyes opened by the same Holy Spirit. Mark may have inserted the rare term $(\alpha)\chi\epsilon\iota\rho\sigma\pi\sigma\acute{\iota}\eta\tau\sigma\varsigma^{37}$ (14:58) into the tradition of the temple saying or deliberately retained it, instead of using the more familiar word $\pi\nu\epsilon\upsilon\mu\alpha\tau\iota\varkappa\acute{\sigma}\varsigma$ (spiritual), because the latter smacked too strongly of the false orientation of the pneumatic prophets. They would understand it as a reference to "a private spiritual experience" or a prediction of the spiritual church at the Eschaton, not the mundane, visible church that is, contrary to appearances, "not made with hands."[38]

The sequel to the temple charge and Jesus' reply is found in the *velum scissum* (15:38), followed by the centurion's confession (15:39). These two verses afford insight into Mark's understanding of the cries and death of Jesus on the cross (15:34–37). The pericope probably came to Mark intact in the tradition, except for the concluding confession which contains the distinct Markan title, "Son of God." Various interpretations have been given to the cry in 15:34, whether attributed to Jesus or to the early church[39]: A cry of desolation, as Jesus became the Suffering Servant[40] and/or the substitute for sinners; a final utterance of faith in the light of Psalm 22; a cry of triumph in expelling a demon which had possessed Jesus;[41] a cry of triumphal obedience; a shout of victory over demonic powers by the exalted *Theios Anēr*.[42] Though all these interpretations can be defended by reference to the OT background or the context of Hellenistic Christianity, Mark's redactional activity does not favor any particular interpretation. The lack of editorializing at this high point in the narrative is instructive. Apparently, Mark was not interested in expressing either a specific soteriology or systematic Christology. Either he assumed that everyone knew the "right explanation" or he assumed that, though differences and ambiguities existed, the efficacy of the cross was a widely accepted article of faith. It was sufficient for his purposes to proclaim the more general good news that Jesus' death removed the veil or barrier, however interpreted, between humanity and God, making reconciliation and restoration possible.[43] The confession of the centurion, a Gentile, signifies that the temple cult has been superseded and the way opened for the Gentile church to experience direct communion with God—a pertinent theme of assurance to the predominantly Gentile community of Mark. Lightfoot remarks, "It is not likely to be accidental that the Greek word for 'to rend' ($\sigma\chi\acute{\iota}\zeta\epsilon\iota\nu$) occurs in Mark only in two places (1:10, 15:38).... As the earlier verse described the incarnation ... so this verse ... describes the at-one-ment between God and man (*sic*).... "[44] Again, Mark connects the christological nature and soteriological mission of Jesus with his baptism by the Holy Spirit and the pronouncement by the heavenly voice that he is the beloved Son. From the beginning of Jesus' ministry to his final cry, Mark explicitly and implicitly emphasizes the presence of the Spirit within Jesus as the empowering divine force giving efficacy to his words, deeds, and death. Mark is limited by the paucity of Holy Spirit sayings at his disposal. The fact that he inserts or redacts terms and phrases in the tradition in order to refer specifically to the Holy Spirit in a post-resurrection sense four times at opportunely spaced places in the Gospel (1:8; 3:29; 12:36; 13:11) demonstrates his strong interest in this motif. At the conclusion to the Passion Narrative, Mark's use of the title "Son of God" reminds the reader that Jesus' death is efficacious because he dies as the Spirit-endowed Son. The past tense of the confession (ἦν) indicates that this is a retrospective statement. It declares that Jesus has fulfilled the mission for which he was equipped at his baptism.[45] The adverb "truly" is the evangelist's confirmation of the verity of the earlier traditions about the Son which formed the basis of Gospel. From Mark's and the reader's perspective, the confession discloses that "this man" who died in weakness was also the Son of God who, having been baptized in the Spirit and proclaimed divine,[46] has been raised and is alive. However paradoxical and contrary to appearances it may seem to "outsiders," the reader (insider) knows that Jesus died as the Son of God because the Holy Spirit resided in him. How can the centurion possibly have known this, based upon a fleeting acquaintance with Jesus? Mark dramatizes the human impossibility of the confession by placing it upon his lips while the disciples scatter. The shocking contrast accents Mark's answer: The centurion knew Jesus' identity because it had been given to him to see by the presence of the Risen Christ/Holy Spirit who still resides within the church to grant perception and protection. Indeed, the reader who knows the secret of the fullness of Gospel identifies with the centurion and finds his confession natural and plausible. Mark has now explicated the full content of the Gospel that the reader and church are to accept by the revelation of the Spirit. The Spirit can only teach what Jesus has taught, for they are for all practical purposes one and the same. The challenge to the church is boldly clear: Hear and see the revealed meaning of the Gospel of Jesus (objective and subjective genitive) and follow in perceptive, obedient discipleship.

Rhoads and Michie draw attention to the consummate narrative skill of Mark, although they do not grasp clearly the role of Spirit and Gospel.

Throughout the story, there is a transition from the ancestral community of Jesus to the new grouping comprised of those who do the will of God by following Jesus, and those who have the mystery of the rule of God are distinguished from those on the outside. Jesus sees his death as the crucial turning point for this transition.... Only when Jesus has "died like this" does the narrator allow a human character in the story to acknowledge Jesus as Son of God, for it is by dying for the good news that Jesus fulfills his role as Son of God.[47]

The Resurrection: Spirit and Gospel

As the reader already knows, the mission of Jesus did not end with the cross and burial. But Mark considered it important to announce the resurrection and the promise of a reunion in Galilee as a vital part of the story, i.e., Gospel. It was not necessary for him to describe the resurrection appearance and reunion in detail, for the promise sufficed to bring the Gospel up-to-date, that is, to the current experience of the Risen Christ/Holy Spirit by the church. The past gospel of Jesus and the present proclamation of Jesus coalesces in Mark's Gospel when it is heard correctly.

The earlier view that a redactor, possibly Mark, connected an independent resurrection account to the Passion Narrative,[48] has recently been challenged by redaction and narrative critics who claim that Mark created the entire narrative as a parousia story. Crossan's expression of this hypothesis is summarized approvingly by Kelber:

Crossan argues the thoroughgoing redactional nature of the Empty Tomb narrative (16:1–8) both on the basis of the history of tradition and in view of a thematic coherence with the minutiae and fundamentals of Markan theology. As for the details, for example, Jesus' journey to Galilee defined by the term *proagei* (16:7) is in continuation of his earlier journey to Jerusalem (10:32, *proagōn autous ho Iēsous*) while the women's reaction to the Galilean invitation (16:8, *ephobounto gar*) equals the follower's previous response to Jesus' leadership role (10:32, *kai hoi akolouthountes ephobounto*).... As for the fundamentals of Mkan theology, 16:1–8 enunciates the Mkan motifs of Jesus' absence from the community (4:13–20, 26–29; 13:1–23; 14:7, 25), the Galilean reorientation (1:14–15; 14:28), and discipleship failure (1:35–38; 4:40–41; 6:52; 8:14–21; 8:32–33; 9:5–6, 32; 10:35–37).[49]

A close examination of the hypothesis shows that it is based on two major principles: the redactional character of 16:7, 8 (the abrupt ending), and an interpretation of 16:1–8 which emphasizes Markan creative conformity to prime theological themes running throughout the Gospel. The latter principle is countered by recognizing Mark's skill in using and adapting older *tradition* to fit his purposes, and by offering alternative interpretations concerning Mark's meaning, e.g., 16:7 and 14:28 (see below). Concerning 16:7, most commentators agree that Mark's hand is evident in the reference to "Galilee,"[50] though his intent and meaning are strongly debated. The crucial matter then is the theological interpretation given to the Empty Tomb pericope, especially 16:7–8, in relationship to the rest of the Gospel. The claim that Mark composed the entire narrative reflects unwarranted skepticism toward the pre-Markan origin and historical nucleus of the tradition.

Lohmeyer was the first to interpret Mk 14:28 and 16:7 as referring to the parousia, but Marxsen, Weeden, Perrin, and Kelber have popularized the motif as a major Markan theological motif. Marxsen stressed the symbolic use of "Galilee" to stand for "Jesus' home in a far deeper sense than the historical. It is the place where He worked, where—hidden in the proclamation—he is now working, and will work at his Parousia."[51] Marxsen is inconsistent in asserting that Galilee means both the parousia and the "place in the proclamation" where Jesus is now working. Marxsen haltingly attempts to resolve the conflict by maintaining that the proclamation "represents the Exalted Lord whose Parousia is at the door."[52] The matter remains ambiguous. Does Mark view Jesus as already present or anticipated in the near future or both? Weeden and Kelber cut the Gordian knot by insisting that Mark proclaimed the absence of Jesus until the parousia. Kelber contends that Mark forced the church to come to grips with the reality of the times (Roman persecution culminating in the destruction of Jerusalem) and not to expect Jesus to return in apparitions to rescue his followers. Rather, the Markan church in Galilee was summoned to faithfulness in suffering, service, and mission to the world in preparation for his return.[53] Kelber also claims that Mark was disowning the disciples and dislodging their authority in Jerusalem as "guarantors of the tradition" in favor of the Galilean church. Weeden thinks Mark was discrediting the *Theios Anēr* Christology of false prophets by undermining the source of their authority: union with the exalted Lord in their own experience.[54]

Although Marxsen, Weeden, and Kelber are partially correct in their assessments of Mark's intents—to present Jesus as present in the proclamation, to summon the church to obedience in service, and to resist false prophets—they misconstrue his basic approach and theology. Their fundamental mistake is the failure to recognize that Mark is referring to a resurrection appearance and reunion in 14:28, 16:7, not the parousia. This understanding is supported by the fact that the passion predictions associate the resurrection with Jesus' sufferings, and no mention is made of the parousia.[55] Moreover, as Knigge points out, it is not at all certain on linguistic grounds that the verb "see" (ὄψεσθε) in 16:7 can be related to the parousia.[56] It is used more often in the NT with respect to appearances of the Risen Christ (Lk 24:34; Jn 20:18; Acts 9:17; 13:31; 26:16; 1 Cor 9:1; 15:5–8; 1 Tim 3:16). In support, Kee notes that the visions of the exalted Jesus, the cosmic woes of the end time, and the final triumph of the Son of Man are all offered as public events.

> But the resurrection is a private event: ἐκεῖ αὐτόν ὄψεσθε. By implication, you alone, as his once faithful, recently scattered flock, will see him risen from the dead. That is implicit in 14.28 . . . : the flock will be reconstituted by the once smitten shepherd. They *have* seen him risen from the dead, Mark is telling his reader.[57]

Mark's interest in the teaching ministry of Jesus and his parabolic "secrecy" motif inveigh against the imminent parousia as his principal concern. Mark envisions an extended time of teaching in the church during which the Risen Christ, present in the Spirit, will reveal the secret of the kingdom through the Gospel. The parables of growth (e.g., 4:3–32) and the eschatological discourse (13:7, 10) give impetus to the extended time needed and anticipated for the task.[58] This mission required announcement of a resurrection reunion in which Jesus validates the teaching that continues in the church and authorizes Mark's own mission through the proclamation of Gospel.

In order to perceive fully Mark's purpose, the commentator must employ two approaches to Mark's work: the literary-narrative approach that assesses the narrative-world and the story-line of the Gospel, and the literary-historical approach that assesses the role of the Gospel in the Markan community. Since the story of Jesus' resurrection and appearances was well established in the kerygma and church by the time of Mark, it would be unnatural and incredible for Mark's readers not to understand the angel's declaration (16:7), following the announcement that "He is risen," as the promise of a resurrection appearance. If Mark had intended the promise to pertain to the parousia, he would have realized the necessity of being much more explicit. Further redaction would have been required to negate the more obvious reference to the resurrection reunion. The statement that the women did not tell the disciples cannot be interpreted as a permanent situation. Obviously, if they had never told, we would not have the story![59] There are no sound grounds for assuming that the Markan community was so removed from the mainstream of the church and kerygma that they did not know about the resurrection and resurrection appearances.

The absence of an account relating the appearance in Galilee does not prove that Mark did not have the resurrection in mind. There are other instances where Mark does not relate the sequel to events: The fulfillment of the promise that Jesus will baptize with the Holy Spirit is never described explicitly, but Mark is aware of the presence of the Holy Spirit in the church (e.g., 1:8; 3:29; 12:36; 13:11). Indeed, the reunion in Galilee in all likelihood comprised the initial appearance of Jesus in the Spirit and the bestowal of the Holy Spirit upon the disciples. That Jesus overcame Satan in the testing or in the cross-resurrection is not narrated, but it is apparent from the tenor and context of the Gospel. Mark was not writing to readers totally ignorant of the basic tenets of Christianity. He could assume that his readers had some general, common knowledge of central events and beliefs, as every author does.

Stein states that "the strongest argument in favour of the traditional view, however, is the reference to Peter in Mark xvi.7."[60] Peter was already dead when Mark wrote; knowing this, Mark's readers would not have understood a reference to Peter's meeting with Jesus in Galilee to be the parousia. The argument that we must understand Peter and Galilee as primarily symbolic terms[61] in Mark is much too abstract. Though the names may have symbolic meanings, Mark and his readers know that they also pertained to a historical person and a geographical place. Indeed, if Peter came to Rome and Mark wrote in Rome (alias Galilee), it is probable that Peter himself told of a resurrection appearance. The traditional association of Peter and the Gospel with Rome better accounts for the reference to Peter in 16:7 than the claim of Trocmé and Kelber that Mark is opposing "Cephasites." If the latter position is asserted,

> one wants to see some corroboration for these historical implicates, some explanation of why an allegedly anti-Petrine/anti-Jerusalem Gospel became the core of the pro-Petrine Matthew, and why any Galilean would have polemicized against Peter in Jerusalem when, by Mark's time, it was James who had been in charge there. In other words, the historical reconstruction . . . seems to hang in mid-air.[62]

Following a literary-narrative critical approach, Kingsbury observes that the prophecies of Jesus (8:31; 9:31; 10:33–34), of John the Baptist (1:7–8), and of Scripture (1:2–3; 9:12–13; 14:49) are trustworthy and come to fulfillment. The reader is assured that the prediction of the projected meeting in Galilee will come to pass also when "the disciples at last 'see' what previously they had been unable to 'see.'"[63]

Petersen[64] has addressed most directly from a literary approach the issue of the women's silence and the lack of a resurrection appearance story in Mark. He replies: In the plotting of the narrative, Jesus' words come to pass despite the statements and misunderstandings of the disciples (cf. 14:27–30).

> Indeed, since all but Jesus, the narrator, and the reader stand under a cloud of ignorance until Galilee, the fearful flight of the women is no more determinative of what Jesus will make happen than Judas' betrayal, the flight of the ten, and Peter's default on his promise. The flight of the women belongs to the scattering of the sheep...the silence of the women is broken by Jesus' words, which "will not pass away" (13:31).[65]

Petersen maintains that the development of events in "plotted time" anticipates fulfillments in "story-time." The meeting in Galilee is the first and is prerequisite for others: for the overcoming of the disciples' ignorance; for the baptism of the disciples with the Holy Spirit—presumably empowerment for the mission of preaching the Gospel to all nations;[66] for the seating of the Son of Man at the right hand of Power. "Thus, the meeting in Galilee cannot be the parousia of the Son of man."[67]

If Mk 14:28, 16:7 promise a resurrection reunion in Galilee, as we have argued, why doesn't the evangelist include an appearance pericope? Why this strange abrupt ending? These questions still deserve treatment. We maintain that the answer emerges from the awareness of his purpose in writing Gospel in his particular *Sitz*. Mark faced a dilemma in ending his work. On the one hand, a resurrection appearance was needed to resolve the pending fulfillment of promises and plot in the Gospel. Also, to omit a report of this central event in the kerygma would be an intolerable offense to the reader. Mark's Gospel would not be "good news" at all. On the other hand, to describe a resurrection appearance would play into the hands of the pneumatic prophets who appealed to immediate revelation and ecstatic experiences in the Spirit for their prestigious role and inspired teachings in the Christian community. Mark had to guard against this misuse of the Gospel by antagonists "picking this plum" for exploitation. To give undue emphasis to resurrection appearance would detract from Mark's entire understanding of Gospel. It would minimize the importance of the past Jesus traditions as a check upon subjective expressions of truth. It would jeopardize his own genre of Gospel as the content and medium of the Risen Christ's/Holy Spirit's disclosure of the "mystery of the kingdom of God" (4:11), i.e., the secret that "the community is already living in a proleptic way the life of the kingdom of God."[68] It would blunt the sharp insistence upon suffering and service as necessary correlatives of discipleship. Finally, it would "wrap up the story" as a completed unit in the past and destroy the effect Mark has carefully constructed that the story continues into the present time of the reader. Mark desired theological concord and committed disciple-ship within the church as the proper response to the hearing of Gospel. This response would guarantee the continuing presence of the Holy Spirit and the future of the church against all adversaries. But the story and outcome remain open and undetermined.[69] Will the readers and community realize the presence of Jesus in the world through the Spirit and Gospel as he was once present in human form? The outcome is not stated, and the women's failure, at least initially, to heed the proclamation has its parallel among members of Mark's own community. There can be no absolute assurances in such matters; there is, however, a cautious optimism afforded by the angelic announcements that the resurrection has occurred and that Jesus will meet and lead his disciples in Galilee. This was as far as Mark could go in recounting tradition without defeating his purpose, as the relating of an appearance story would have done. Mark's readers regard themselves as part of the continu-ing ranks of disciples of Jesus. Their awareness that the original disciples have met the Risen Christ gives them confidence that they, too, have the opportunity of encountering the same Jesus,[70] though they are astute enough to realize that he now comes in the form of the Holy Spirit. Mark has confidence in the Spirit and Gospel to instruct the reader-disciple correctly. But he is aware of the require-ment of discipleship and the necessity of revelation to the elect—a paradox he does not attempt to resolve. Thus, the story and out-come remain open-ended, but hopeful. Mark has engaged the depth of his resources as an author and a Christian teacher to cre-ate "a spiritual Gospel" capable of serving as a theological norm for the beliefs and practices of the Christian community.

The Longer Ending: Sequel to the Drama

Today, it is generally accepted among scholars on both textual and theological grounds that Mark ended his Gospel at 16:8. Excep-tions to this position are W. R. Farmer, who holds that vv. 9–20 "likely belonged to the autograph and was excised by Alexandrian scribes,"[71] and E. Schweizer, who thinks the original ending was lost.[72] Farmer's thesis runs counter to the textual evidence, which is solidly against the authenticity of vv. 9–20. Schweizer's contention that Mark continued beyond 16:8, on the grounds that the prophecies and the story of Peter's denial demand fulfillment, is effectively turned aside by the recognition of Mark's purpose and method in composing Gospel in his *Sitz*. Indeed, the understanding of Mark's purpose and concept of Gospel makes intelligible the inevitable addition of the "longer ending." We suggest two possible scenarios. (1) The pneumatic prophets were not persuaded by Mark's "Gospel." They considered it an attack upon their positions of authority and their teaching of Christian tenets focusing on direct experiences of the Spirit. Accordingly, perceiving correctly the intent of Mark's abrupt, abortive ending, they negated his thrust by simply appending an account of resurrection appearances accompanied by pneumatic gifts and signs. Again, the traditions from the historical Jesus calling for a suffering discipleship were relegated to the past—once required but quite irrelevant in the present context. Rather, of first importance is seeing him "after he had risen" (v. 14) and performing "signs" as evidence "accompanying those who believe" (v. 16). In the last analysis, Mark's Gospel failed to achieve the author's purpose. (2) Mark's Gospel found acceptance in the church, at least to the extent that it was considered worthy of preservation. In time, the challenge and threat posed by the false prophets were overcome. "Orthodoxy" triumphed in the (Roman) church, and the exercise of spiritual gifts in a functional, charismatic style of church leadership no longer constituted a danger to the hearing of Gospel. At this point, the "omission" of appearance stories in Mark's work, the only complete Gospel known to the community, became a noticeable defect. The church knew reports of resurrection appearances and desired to incorporate them into the church's Gospel. Accordingly, they composed the "longer ending" which contained themes consistent with the body of the Gospel—preaching the Gospel; mission to the world; belief and baptism; unbelief and condemnation—coupled with unique pneumatic, charismatic motifs (vv. 17b–20). Thereby, the Gospel story was filled out and finished as the basis for the church's beliefs.

Since we do not know exactly when and where the longer ending was appended,[73] we cannot determine definitely which scenario more nearly approximates the actual situation. We favor the latter since the external evidence supports a second-century date for the addition of vv. 9–20. In either instance, however, the ending is best explained as an appendix to a Gospel composed as a "pastoral teaching" to correct the unbalanced, erroneous proclamations of false pneumatic prophets in the Markan community.

ENDNOTES

*CHAPTER 4: THE PASSION AND RESURRECTION NARRATIVES
(MARK 14:1–16:8)*

1. See Dibelius, *From Tradition to Gospel*, p. 180, and Taylor, *The Gospel According to St. Mark*, pp. 524–526, who refers to the analyses of Schmidt and Bultmann in support.
2. M. Kähler, *The So-Called Historical Jesus and the Historic, Biblical Christ* (Philadelphia: Fortress Press, 1964), p. 80, n. 11.
3. E.g., Beare, *The Earliest Records of Jesus*, pp. 219–220, and J. Jeremias, *The Eucharistic Words of Jesus*, rev. ed. (Oxford: Basil Blackwell, 1966), pp. 89–96, argue for a pre-Markan account which became fixed relatively early; to the contrary, E. Linnemann, *Studien zur Passionsgeschichte* (Göttingen: Vandenhoeck & Ruprecht, 1970) pp. 41–45, and L. Schenke, *Der gekreuzigte Christus*, Stuttgarter Bibelstudien 69 (Stuttgart: Katholisches Bibelwerk, 1974) pp. 15–23, ascribe extensive creativity to Mark in the Passion Narrative. Kelber, *The Passion in Mark*, pp. 8–20, gives a helpful survey of diverse positions. Recently the discussion has moved to consideration of the role of the Passion-Resurrection narrative within the narrative drama of Mark—cf. Rhoads and Michie, *Mark As Story*, pp. 86–89.
4. F. Nierynck, *Duality in Mark: Contributions to the Study of the Marcan Redaction* (Leuven: University Press, 1972), passim, shows that the narrative reflects Mark's wording and style.
5. Lohmeyer, *Das Evangelium des Markus*, p. 289; Burkill, *Mysterious Revelation*, p. 228. The story appears in variant forms and contexts in Lk 7:36–50 and Jn 12:1–8.
6. V. K. Robbins, "Last Meal," *The Passion in Mark*, p. 36.
7. Ibid., p. 36.
8. Anderson, *The Gospel of Mark*, pp. 308, 310, 315, and Schweizer, *The Good News According to Mark*, pp. 294, 298, 306, although they confess uncertainty as to whether Mk 14:12–16, 17–21 were joined by Mark or in the earlier tradition.
9. V. Taylor, *Jesus and His Sacrifice* (London: Macmillan & Co., 1951), pp. 137–138, 261–262; J. Behm, "διαθήκη," *TDNT* (1964), 2:133–134; Best, *The Temptation and the Passion*, pp. 146–148.
10. Manson, *Jesus the Messiah*, p. 201; Cullmann, *Christology of the New Testament*, pp. 63–65.
11. Lightfoot, *History and Interpretation in the Gospels*, pp. 140–141.
12. F. W. Danker, "The Literary Unity of Mark 14:1–25," *JBL* 85 (1966): 468–472.
13. Bowman, *The Gospel of Mark*, p. 165.
14. Burkill, *Mysterious Revelation*, pp. 176–177.
15. The textual evidence does not warrant the acceptance of the term (καινῆς), but the context indicates that this is the intended meaning, as scribes soon saw.
16. Rohde, *Rediscovering the Teaching of the Evangelists*, p. 141.
17. Taylor, *Jesus and His Sacrifice*, p. 148.

18. W. H. Kelber, "Mark 14:32 – 42: Gethsemane," *ZNW* 63 – 64 (1972 – 73): 176.

19. See Beare, *The Earliest Records of Jesus*, pp. 229 – 230; Anderson, *The Gospel of Mark*, pp. 317 – 321.

20. Schweizer, "πνεῦμα," *TDNT*, 6:397.

21. W. H. Kelber, "The Hour of the Son of Man and the Temptation of the Disciples," *The Passion in Mark*, p. 44, although Kelber disassociates the Spirit and Jesus.

22. M. E. Boring, *"Truly Human/Truly Divine: Christological Language and the Gospel Form* (St. Louis: CBP Press, 1984), pp. 79ff.

23. C. H. Bird, "Some γάρ Clauses in St. Mark's Gospel," *JTS* 4 (1953): 173.

24. Tannehill, "The Gospel of Mark as Narrative Christology," p. 82.

25. Schweizer, *The Good News According to Mark*, pp. 321; Anderson, *The Gospel of Mark*, pp. 324 – 325.

26. Juel, *Messiah and Temple*, passim; cf. also Donahue, "Temple, Trial, and Royal Christology," *The Passion in Mark*, p. 78.

27. Juel, *Messiah and Temple*, pp. 57 – 58, 93.

28. Ibid., pp. 78 – 79.

29. Ibid., p. 80.

30. Against N. Perrin, "The High Priest's Question and Jesus' Answer," *The Passion in Mark*, p. 92, who confines Mark's interest to the Son of Man sayings as an anticipation of the parousia.

31. Tödt, *The Son of Man in the Synoptic Tradition*, pp. 39 – 40. Tödt points out that the allusions to Ps 110:1 and Dan 7 are consistent with the emphasis on "sovereignty," if indeed, they do form the background for 14.62. N. Perrin, "Mark XIV.62: The End Product of a Christian Pesher Tradition?" *NTS* 12 (1966): 155, also argues this uncertain position.

32. Juel, *Messiah and Temple*, pp. 57 – 58.

33. Ibid., pp. 154 – 157.

34. Yates, *The Spirit and the Kingdom*, p. 143, declares with respect to 1:10, "that some relation was intended to 'the temple not made with hands' (Mark 14.58) is obvious."

35. Best, *Mark: The Gospel as Story*, p. 75.

36. Juel, *Messiah and Temple*, p. 103.

37. The term does not occur in the LXX and only in Col 2:11, Eph 2:11, Heb 9:11, 24 in the NT.

38. Against Juel, *Messiah and Temple*, p. 157, who thinks ἀχειροποί-ητος contains the stronger supernatural connotations.

39. See Taylor, *Jesus and His Sacrifice*, pp. 161 – 162, who summarizes the views of Bacon, Loisy, Bultmann, and Lightfoot.

40. C. Maurer, "Knecht Gottes und Sohn Gottes im Passionsbericht des Markusevangeliums," *ZTK* 50 (1953): 35.

41. F. W. Danker, "The Demonic Secret in Mark 15:34," *ZNW* 61 – 62 (1970 – 71): 67.

42. J. Schreiber, "Die Christologie des Markusevangeliums," *ZTK* 58 (1961): 158 – 159; rebutted by Best, *The Temptation and the Passion*, pp. 100 – 101.

43. G. Lindeskog, "The Veil of the Temple," *Coniectanea Neotestamentica 11* (1947): 132 – 137, presses (too hard) a parallel between the pattern of Mk 15:38 and Heb 10:19f.

44. Lightfoot, *The Gospel Message of Mark*, p. 56.
45. Tannehill, "The Gospel of Mark as Narrative Christology," p. 88.
46. Boring, *Truly Human/Truly Divine*, pp. 78–79, who overestimates the role of the christological paradox in Mark's Gospel.
47. Rhoads and Michie, *Mark as Story*, pp. 114–115.
48. Dibelius, *From Tradition to Gospel*, p. 190.
49. Kelber, "Conclusion: From Passion Narrative to Gospel," *The Passion in Mark*, p. 156. Cf. also N. Q. Hamilton, "Resurrection Tradition and the Composition of Mark," *JBL* 84 (1965): 417, who states speculatively, "The final statement that the women did not tell anyone shows that Mark is apologizing for a story which no one knew until he created and published it to the church."
50. Lohmeyer, *Das Evangelium des Markus*, p. 356; Lightfoot, *Locality and Doctrine in the Gospels*, pp. 63ff, 73ff; Marxsen, *Mark the Evangelist*, pp. 75ff; Best, *Mark: The Gospel as Story*, p. 44.
51. Marxsen, *Mark the Evangelist*, p. 94.
52. Ibid., p. 94.
53. Kelber, *The Kingdom in Mark*, pp. 11–12, 23.
54. Weeden, *Mark–Traditions in Conflict*, esp. Ch. 6.
55. R. H. Stein, "A Short Note on Mark XIV. 28 and XVI. 7," *NTS* 20 (1973–74): 448.
56. H. D. Knigge, "The Meaning of Mark," *Int* 22 (1968): 65–66, against Lohmeyer and Marxsen who allege that "ὄψεσθε" refers to the parousia and "ὤφθη" to the resurrection.
57. Kee, *Community of the New Age*, pp. 174–175.
58. Best, *Mark: The Gospel as Story*, p. 42.
59. Ibid., p. 72.
60. Stein, "A Short Note on Mark XIV. 28 and XVI. 7," p. 450; cf. also Bilezikian, *The Liberated Gospel*, p. 97, n. 16.
61. Tyson, "The Blindness of the Disciples in Mark," pp. 261–268; cf. Trocmé, *The Formation of the Gospel According to Mark*, pp. 125–137.
62. L. E. Keck, "Major Book Reviews: *Mark and the Passion*," p. 434, whose objections also apply to J. Schreiber, "Die Christologie des Markusevangeliums," *ZTK* 58 (1961): 176f, who sees Mk 14:28 and 16:7 as a polemical message of the Markan Exalted Jesus to Jewish Christians in Jerusalem who rejected the kerygma of the Hellenistic church.
63. Kingsbury, *Jesus Christ in Matthew, Mark, and Luke*, p. 38.
64. Petersen, *Literary Criticism for New Testament Critics*, pp. 76–78, is the basis for the following discussion.
65. Ibid., p. 78; cf. also Hooker, *The Message of Mark*, pp. 120–121.
66. C. F. Evans, "I Will Go Before You Into Galilee," *JTS* 5 (1954): 4–5 argues on the basis of a linguistic analysis of πρόαξω that the Gentile mission is the point of Mk 16:7, not the resurrection or the parousia. But for Mark the mission presupposes the resurrection!
67. Petersen, *Literary Criticism for New Testament Critics*, p. 77.
68. Kee, *Community of the New Age*, pp. 174–175.
69. Rhodes and Michie, *Mark as Story*, pp. 96–100, who view the imminent parousia and final rule of God as the end of the story.
70. See also Best, *Mark: The Gospel as Story*, p. 30.
71. J. N. Birdsall, "Critique of W. R. Farmer, *The Last Twelve Verses of Mark*," *JTS* 26 (1975): 151–160.

72. Schweizer, *The Good News According to Mark*, p. 366.

73. F. W. Beare, "Sayings of the Risen Jesus in the Synoptic Tradition," *Christian History and Interpretation: Studies Presented to John Knox*, eds. W. R. Farmer, C. F. D. Moule, and R. R. Niebuhr, (Cambridge: University Press, 1967), p. 162, states: The longer ending of Mark (16:9–20) without the Freer interpolation "appears in nearly all Old Latin manuscripts, is mentioned by Irenaeus, and is included in the Arabic Diatessaron; it must therefore have been framed and attached to some copies of Mark by the middle of the second century." Schweizer, *The Good News According to Mark*, p. 374, refers to a tradition which attributes the conclusion to the Presbyter Austion around AD 100. An earlier date is equally possible. Cf. T. E. Boomershine, "Mark 16:8 and the Apostolic Commission," *JBL* 100 (1981): 225, for a brief history of interpretations of Mark's ending with a list of major publications.

—5—

ROME—A BRIDGE BETWEEN
PAUL AND MARK

Introduction: Mark, Paul, and Rome

Our analysis and exegesis of Mark's Gospel has disclosed the prominent role of the dual theme of "Spirit and Gospel" in the evangelist's presentation. We have contended that a purely literary (e.g., rhetorical and reader-response) approach to Mark is inadequate to plumb fully the author's meaning and purpose. The Gospel was not written in a vacuum, but addressed conflicts that the church faced in the "real" world. Hence, we maintain that a reassessment of the evidence concerning the general provenance and specific situation of Mark's Gospel and community will substantiate further the results gleaned from our analysis of the form and content of the Gospel. We purport to demonstrate that the description of Mark's *Sitz im Leben* serves to explain and to confirm the permeating role accorded the motif of "Spirit and Gospel" in the evangelist's work.

We shall pursue two tracks of inquiry, both of which run through Rome, leading to the following conclusions: (1) Mark's Gospel was written in Rome in the late 60s, shortly before the destruction of Jerusalem by Titus in AD 70. The Gospel is best understood against the backdrop of events that impacted a mixed Jewish-Gentile church in Rome during this turbulent period; in particular, the threat of renewed persecution from both the Roman state and the Jewish synagogue. Mark's related motifs of "Spirit and Gospel" afforded the community the assurance of ultimate victory beyond the temporary suffering to be borne in obedient discipleship. (2) Mark's Gospel reflects a number of striking affinities with Paul's Letter to the Romans. We maintain that Rome was the bridge that linked common concerns and motifs found in both Mark's Gospel and in Paul's Letter to the Romans. Indirectly, Romans reflects light upon Mark's *Sitz* and theology by the letter's references to and intimations of similar problems encountered by the church at Rome over a decade earlier, specifically the misunderstanding of Gospel by ecstatics and false prophets. Though the intervening years had altered the situation somewhat, the Markan church still faced essentially the same challenges—internal dissension and external oppression. Mark's Gospel addressed both these challenges by proclaiming a "Good News" stemming from the historical Jesus and quickened anew by the Holy Spirit. The provenance of Rome accords best with the totality of external and internal evidence pertaining to the origin of the Gospel. The ancient maxim applies appropriately to Mark: "All roads lead to Rome."

The Roman Provenance of Mark's Gospel: Early Traditions

We do not purport to present an exhaustive evaluation of all the early sources, but to treat the central traditions and issues. The crux of the matter lies in the validity of and interpretation given to Papias' statement that Mark was the interpreter ($\dot{\epsilon}\rho\mu\eta\nu\epsilon\upsilon\tau\dot{\eta}\varsigma$) of Peter.[1] Papias composed this note about AD 120–130 and reportedly received his information from the presbyter John, who exercised his ministry well before AD 100. Papias' testimony is credible and is reiterated and confirmed by references in the Anti-Marcionite Prologue,[2] Justin,[3] Irenaeus,[4] Clement of Alexandria,[5] Origen,[6] and the *Chronicon Hieronymi*[7]—works which state specifically that Mark was associated with Peter in Rome. Are these witnesses based on independent traditions from Papias, or have they only amplified Papias' terse statements? B. W. Bacon held the latter view while M. Hengel in a recent reassessment maintains that the testimonies are based on several independent traditions.[8]

The results of these conflicting conclusions are self-evident. If Bacon is correct that we have "an unbroken line backward from the later writers to Clement, from Clement to Papias, and from Papias to the 'Elder,'" then there is only one general tradition in support of the association of Mark with Peter. Indeed, "in reality there is nothing back of Papias save $\dot{\epsilon}\nu$ $\beta\alpha\beta\upsilon\lambda\tilde{\omega}\nu\iota$ in I Peter 5.13 to suggest that Peter ever set foot in Rome."[9] Accordingly, scholars such as Marxsen and Kelber, Kee and Kingsbury, and S. Schulze, who contend respectively that the Gospel was composed in the regions of Galilee, Syria or the Decapolis,[10] unhesitatingly dismiss the early tradition as erroneous or inconclusive.[11] However, Hengel rightly insists that the Papias note "must be taken very seriously" and not rejected without firm evidence simply because it does not fit with one's theological and "ahistorical" convictions about Mark's origin derived from form-critical considerations.[12] Hengel states strongly,

> The claim that Papias invented the link between Mark the evangelist and Peter on the basis of his reading of I Peter 5.13, which has proved particularly popular, is nonsense.... Both traditions are independent and provide reciprocal confirmation.[13]

The essential issue is whether the Elder's oral tradition that was passed on to Papias was reliable and reliably reported by Papias. In the absence of compelling evidence to the contrary, we maintain with Hengel that it was.[14] It is generally recognized that "Babylon" was often used as a cryptogram for Rome and that Papias referred to 1 Pet 5:13[15] in understanding the Elder's assertion concerning the association between Mark and Peter.[16] In all probability Papias would not have passed on the tradition if he had not believed on other grounds that the Gospel of Mark was derived from the association of Mark with Peter in Rome. Moreover, it appears unlikely that this view could have been maintained virtually unopposed if some definite knowledge of the facts had not lain behind the tradition and position. Though the Papias passage and subsequent testimonies do not definitely prove the Roman provenance of Mark's Gospel, the evidence favors this point of origin and should not be lightly set aside.

Furthermore, it is easier to explain the early dissemination and inclusion in the NT canon of a non-apostolic Gospel—soon superseded by others in the church—if one assumes a special connection with a prominent disciple of Jesus and a center of authority such as Rome. The tradition is virtually unassailable that Peter met his death in Rome. Since originally the work was known simply as τὸ εὐαγγέλιον (and only later entitled Κατὰ Μάρκον to distinguish it from other rival Gospels), it evidently was for a time the only Gospel acknowledged in a particular area. The church in Rome gained prominence early, and no other gospel was strongly associated with this leading Christian center; hence, it is likely that Mark, linked with the name and authority of Peter, was the original εὐαγγέλιον in that area.[17]

Whether the author of the Second Gospel was identical with the Mark mentioned in 1 Pet 5:13, Phm 24, Col 4:10, 2 Tim 4:11 and with John Mark (Acts 12:12; 25; 15:37, 39) is uncertain. As mentioned above, scholars who reject the validity of the traditions preserved in the early church sources generally deny that the author of the Gospel was John Mark. The reputed deficient knowledge of the author about the geography of Palestine, especially Galilee, is advanced as further evidence against that claim.[18] However, Mark's geographical deficiencies may be explained in part by the awareness that he was from Jerusalem, not Galilee, and had been away from Palestine a lengthy period before he wrote the Gospel. Finally, Hengel offers the rejoinder that "the second Gospel was not written anonymously by just anyone, but by a theological teacher with authority, behind whom there was an even greater authority."[19] There are no other known contenders by the name of Mark mentioned in the existent literature. John Mark remains the most plausible candidate, though for our purposes the name of the author is not as important as determining the locale in which the Gospel was written.

The date of the composition of the Gospel cannot be determined precisely by the external evidence. Hengel surveys anew the relevant sources and calculates on the basis of chronological information given in Lk 3:1 (Tiberius, 28/29) and the *Chronicon Hieronymi* that Mark wrote his Gospel about AD 69. The calculation proceeds as follows:[20] Luke 3:1 dates the emergence of John the Baptist in the fifteenth year of Tiberius (AD 28/29). The *Chronicon Hieronymi* places the passion of Jesus in the eighteenth year of the emperor (AD 32/33) and relates that Peter came to Rome in the second year of Claudius (AD 42/43) and was bishop there for twenty-five years (AD 67/68). A year later the apostle's companion Mark is said to have proclaimed in Egypt this Gospel based on Peter's words (confirmed by Eusebius, *H. E.* 2.16.1; 2.17.1) Hence, the most likely date for the composition of the Gospel is AD 68–69, a time of turbulence and threatened persecution of the church in Rome. This date accords with internal evidence in the Gospel implying these conditions and concerns. Irenaeus states that Mark wrote after the deaths of Peter and Paul (*Adv. Haer.* 3.1.1), which, coupled with references in 1 Clem 5:1–6:2 and in Tertullian (*Adv. Marcionem* 4.5.3), imply that Peter was put to death during the Neronian persecution. Even if this disputed tradition is correct, a date around AD 68–69 is still plausible for the composition of the Gospel.

Though other traditions and sources suggest earlier and later dates for the origin of the Gospel,[21] the weight of the external evidence favors the years AD 68–69, shortly before the fall of Jerusalem, as the probable period for the writing of the Second Gospel.

The Roman Provenance of Mark's Gospel: Internal Evidence

The internal evidence in the Gospel for a Roman provenance may be categorized under the following major headings: Latinisms and explanations of Jewish terms, the prominence of Peter, the persecution motif, the Apocalyptic Discourse, and Markan theological themes. We shall focus succinctly on the pivotal points.

(1) *Latinisms.* The presence of a number of Latinisms in Mark which do not appear in the parallel passages in Matthew and Luke suggest that the Gospel was written in a Latin speaking region; for examples: κεντυρίων, 15:39, 44, 45; σπεκουλάτωρ, 6:27; ξεστή, 7:4. However, these expressions may have been assimilated into the current speech of Hellenistic Judaism throughout the empire by the Christian era. Hence, their occurrence in Mark falls short of proof that the terms were supplied by Mark in a Latin-speaking region, though this remains highly probable. Rohde's point is persuasive:

> Above all, we consider Marxsen's objection that the Latinisms in Mark's Gospel belong to the tradition, not to the redaction (*Evangelist Markus*, p. 41, note 1) ill founded: in that case, we would ask why the redaction did not eliminate them. We consider them on the contrary to be editorial additions in order to make the gospel more intelligible to readers in Rome, whom we have assumed to be Gentile Christians.[22]

In two instances, Zahn terms it "decisive" that Mark explains Greek by Latin: αὐλὴ by πραιτώριον, 15:16; λεπτώ δύο by κοδράντης, 12:42.[23] Hengel contends that in Mk 7:26 the two descriptions of the women in Tyre, Ἑλληνίς, Συροφοινίκισσα τῷ γένει, would be "geographically vague (and) would seem nonsensical" if the Gospel came from Syria. Ἑλληνίς to designate the language and the ethnic φοινί(κι)σσα would have been sufficient. This was not the case in Rome, where "it was possible to make a clear distinction between the much more familiar Carthaginians ... and the Phoenicians, who belonged to the province of Syria."[24]

A related linguistic aspect is the evangelist's explanation of Jewish customs and practices for non-Palestinian readers, e.g., ἀββα (ὁ πατήρ, 14:36), ταλιθα κουμ (τὸ κοράσιον ... ἔγειρε, 5:41), ἐφφαθα (διανοίχθητι, 7:34). These interpretive glosses would have been unnecessary in a Palestinian environment but were needed in a distant locale such as Rome.

The occurrence of multiple Latinisms and explanations of Jewish terms deserves more consideration in identifying the provenance of Mark than has been given in contemporary scholarship. More recent commentators have concentrated almost exclusively on the theological and sociological features of the Gospel and have virtually ignored the linguistic evidence.

(2) *The Prominence of Peter.* The witness of the church fathers attests strongly to the association of Mark and Peter in Rome. Consistent with this tradition, the Gospel itself projects Peter as the most prominent disciple among the Twelve.[25] He is mentioned twenty-five times, proportionally more often than in the other longer Synoptic Gospels. In Markan parallel passages, Matthew has omitted the name Simon Peter nine times and Luke fifteen times. Simon Peter is the first disciple to be named in Mark's Gospel (1:16), and he stands at the head of the lists of the Twelve (3:16ff), the Three (5:37, 9:2), and the Four (13:3). Peter is the spokesman who confesses Jesus' "messiahship" and is sharply rebuked by Jesus (8:29, 32f). His failure is singled out at Gethsemane (14:37), and he is the only one to follow Jesus after his arrest (14:54, 66–72). Finally, the angel commands the women to announce the resurrection "to his disciples and to Peter" (16:7).

The preeminence of Peter in Mark's Gospel is obvious. Most likely the "Petrine stories" stemmed from the disciple himself, for the church would hardly have portrayed his failings so graphically. Indeed, it is noteworthy that Mark does not whitewash Peter and present him as a model disciple. Instead he lets Peter remain as one who, like Mark's readers, has his shortcomings and must be instructed by Jesus/Holy Spirit in the truth of the Gospel and the meaning of discipleship. For the reader, he is a type of the flawed but teachable follower who has the potential to become a faithful stalwart of the faith and the church. The prominence of Peter in Rome and the character portrayal of the disciple in Mark's Gospel coincide and mutually support the tradition that the Second Gospel was composed in Rome.

(3) *The Persecution Motif.* The motif of persecution of Jesus and the disciples (the Markan church) is clearly expressed in the Gospel in striking sayings, e.g., 8:31, 8:34ff; 8:38; 9:31; 10:30; 33; 10:45; 13:8, 10. The inevitability of Jesus' death is stated as early as 3:6, and from the time of Peter's confession (8:27–30) the related themes of suffering and discipleship permeate the narrative, leading to the climactic account of Jesus' death on the cross. Though persecution of the church occurred sporadically in diverse parts of the empire, it was most intense in Rome during the reign of Nero (d. AD 68). The Markan Gospel presupposes persecution or the threat of persecution as a reality and offers encouragement to the church to persevere in faithful discipleship in anticipation of eventual triumph.

Martin argues that Mark's characterization of John the Baptist constitutes a vivid message to a church facing martyrdom. John is depicted as the martyred prophet whose fate prefigures the death of Jesus. As John was handed over to a cruel, undeserved death, in parallelism Jesus must suffer a similar treatment at the hands of harsh, ungodly men. Martin concludes, "The inference is that followers of Jesus in the church in Rome can expect no less."[26] Though we cannot be as certain as Martin that the persecution motif points specifically to Rome, the church's plight in the imperial city in the late 60s stands as the most likely occasion and site for the heightened emphasis upon this theme in the Gospel.

(4) *The Apocalyptic Discourse—Correcting False Prophets.* The Apocalyptic Discourse (Mark 13) has become a hotbed of controversy for determining the date and provenance of the Gospel. We have argued above that Mark constructed the discourse as a polemic against and corrective of the extremist views of false prophets who, misinterpreting the authority of their "signs and wonders," proclaimed that the Eschaton was imminent. Can we go further and establish the identity of these "false prophets?" Are there any available sources and clues?

Kee claims that the rural references and apocalyptic thrusts of the Gospel are similar to the traits which would characterize an itinerant charismatic community; namely,

> a community which is influenced both by the Jewish-Hasidic-Essence-apocalyptic tradition . . . and the Cynic-Stoic style of gaining adherents by itinerant preaching, healing, and exorcisms from village to village.[27]

Kee thinks the context that best accords with this sociological-theological description is southern Syria and locates the Gospel's origin there. Kee's sociological reconstruction of the context of the Markan community from references in the Gospel is imaginative but contains two assumptions that render his conclusion suspect: (1) The description of the Markan community is fashioned from tradition and redaction alike without any attempt to distinguish between or to evaluate separately the two types of material. (2) The identification of Syria as the probable locale is arbitrary. Even if Kee's sociological analysis should be accepted, there is no compelling reason why Rome would not qualify equally well as the setting for the community and Gospel. The influence of Jewish apocalyptic concepts, the appearance of charismatic prophets, the admission of Gentiles, and the manifestation of esoteric behavior (compare the mystery religions) fit a Roman context as acceptably as a Syrian one. Nor do the "rural" features constitute an exception. The whole social and economic structure of the empire was primarily agricultural in nature. (Even today urban preachers commonly employ rural images to illustrate their sermonic points.) Kee's sociological analysis is inconclusive in determining the definite provenance of Mark.

The same result ensues when Galilee is identified as the place of composition as Marxsen and Kelber advocate on different grounds. The theological approach takes precedence in their reconstructions of the locale. Marxsen holds that Mark's Gospel was written to encourage the church in Jerusalem to flee to Pella (Galilee) following the outbreak of the Jewish War in AD 66.[28] Mark composed chapter 13 to subdue intense eschatological expectations while assuring the church that the Risen Lord will appear in this generation at the parousia (16:7) and reward his faithful.

Marxsen's case rests primarily upon the theological importance that he accords the references to "Galilee" in 14:28, 16:7. But it is difficult to find in the verses any indication of a flight to Pella, which was located in the Transjordan, not Galilee proper.[29] Nor are the verbs ὁρᾶν, ὀφθῆναι used exclusively with reference to the parousia in the Gospels (cf. Mt 28:7, 10; Jn 20:18, 20).[30] Indeed, the symbolical significance that Marxsen attaches to "Galilee" supports the view that the evangelist was referring to the Gentile mission and church as the people of the promise. This understanding would fit the context of the church in Rome more plausibly than a hypothetical community in Galilee about which the external sources are silent.

Kelber's case is fashioned almost totally from his theological exegesis of Mk 14:28, 16:7, with only passing mention of external sources and evidence. The witness of the church fathers in support of Rome is summarily dismissed as inconsistent with the internal evidence of the Gospel.[31] Latin loan-words are accounted for by the sweeping generalization that they are exclusively military and economic terms. "This reflects the situation not of Rome, but of an occupied country, because it is there that the imperial power imposes its military might and economic structure most tangibly upon the people."[32] However, to banish this category of terms from Rome so brusquely requires a stronger edict. These terms probably pervaded the empire.

Only Josephus is cited by Kelber as a credible witness. His description of false prophets displaying signs and wonders and preaching a miraculous deliverance from apparent disaster in the "apocalyptically aroused milieu of the beseiged Jerusalem" echoes strains heard in the Markan apocalypse.[33] However, Josephus' comments constitute meager support for Kelber's claim that the entire Gospel was written after the fall of Jerusalem (and the failure of Jerusalem Christianity) "to urge Christians to go back to the origin, the Galilean starting point" to await the kingdom at the parousia.[34] Though Kelber describes perceptively the tension between Mark and false prophets, his case for the date, provenance and tenor of the Gospel remains unsubstantiated. Hengel's terse critique of Kelber's position is apropos: "Unbridled redaction criticism makes everything possible in this way."[35]

Hengel's analysis of Mark 13 (especially 13:23, 37; cf. 14:38) "shows that in the time of the evangelist the saying of Jesus . . . has become a saying for a persecuted and threatened church which is eagerly awaiting the parousia of the Son of Man."[36] He concludes that the Gospel was written in Rome in ca. AD 69,

> for the destruction of the temple is not yet presupposed: rather the author expects the appearance of Antichrist (as Nero *redivivus*) in the sanctuary and the dawn of the last, severest stage of the messianic woes before the parousia.[37]

By his own admission Hengel's position remains "hypothetical,"[38] and the Nero *redivivus* motif, while imaginative, is problematic. Nevertheless, he does attempt to relate the text to a definite historical situation that seems more plausible than any alternative in accounting for the Markan apocalyptic discourse.

Paul and Mark: Spirit and Gospel

Our cursory investigation of the external and internal evidence for the provenance of Mark indicates that all roads lead toward Rome. Though a conclusive case cannot be established, Rome satisfies the relevant historical, sociological, and theological criteria. Can anything more be said to make the identification more positive? In light of the consensus of opinion among recent Markan scholars (e.g., Marxsen, Weeden, Kelber, Boring, and this author) that the apocalyptic discourse reflects the evangelist's endeavor to temper intense eschatological expectations of false prophets, the question resurfaces, Can we learn anything further about the teachings of these false prophets? What sources provide insight into the Markan community and the "gospel" of these ecstatics? We maintain that Paul's Letter to the Romans bears striking theological resemblances to Mark's Gospel and provides indirect attestation to our contention that Mark was countering the teaching of false prophets in Rome in his presentation of the wholistic Gospel. We hold that unfortuitous lines of correspondence exist between Paul and Mark in their understandings of "Spirit and Gospel."

The point merits reiteration that one cannot assume that Mark was influenced directly by Paul or the Pauline corpus. The possibility that the author of the Gospel was John Mark, the erstwhile traveling companion of Paul (Acts 12:12, 25), makes this view appealing. However, the continuing impact of M. Werner's influential study[39] disclaiming any direct influence necessitates a cautious approach to the topic. As in most instances, we establish degrees of probability, not absolute proof.

"Gospel" in Paul and Mark

The origin and use of the substantive εὐαγγέλιον in the church before the time of Paul is cloaked in controversy. Mark is responsible for the seven appearances of the term (excluding 16:15) in the Second Gospel, and Matthew parallels Mark in his four retentions of the word. Luke does not use the noun at all in his Gospel, though he employs the verb and inserts two references to εὐαγγέλιον in Acts (15:7, 20:24). Paul emerges as the earliest NT writer to use the noun (56 instances, excluding the Pastoral Epistles).[40] However, it is improbable that Paul introduced the term into the church. He nowhere attempts to define τὸ εὐαγγέλιον but assumes that his readers already know its meaning. A perusal of the Pauline passages discloses that for the apostle it meant both the preaching and content of the Good News of Jesus' suffering, death, and resurrection (cf. Rom 1:1, 3–4; 16:25ff; 1 Cor 9:14, 18; 15:1ff). Evidently in the church at Rome, as in other churches visited by Paul, τὸ εὐαγγέλιον was commonly understood to designate the proclamation of the kerygma of Jesus Christ (objective and subjective genitive). Both Jewish and Gentile sources likely contributed to the church's and Paul's understanding of the term. The Septuagint employs only the verbal forms of εὐαγγελίζεσθαι, and the contexts in which they appear contribute little to our understanding of the NT concept of εὐαγγέλιον. Friedrich concludes, "The NT use of εὐαγγέλιον does not derive from the LXX. . . ."[41]

Rabbinic Judaism used the verb בשׂר ("to proclaim good news") and taught that the proclamation of the message brought about a new event.[42] This usage forms a likely background for the early Palestinian church's employment of the Greek verb εὐαγγελίζεσθαι and the development of the substantive εὐαγγέλιον for both the act and content of the Christian proclamation.[43] From this point the term spread with the missionary expansion of the church and described the kerygma of passion and resurrection which Paul received as paradosis.

Simultaneously, in classical Greek literature εὐαγγέλιον was a technical term for "good news of victory," and the message was considered to be instrumental in effecting "good fortune." In the imperial cult the divine emperor proclaimed good news, and the proclamation effected the stated action.[44] The similarity to the church's understanding of εὐαγγέλιον is apparent, though in the NT Christ constitutes the center and content of the message.

This brief linguistic analysis shows the widespread preparation in rabbinic Judaism and in Greek culture for the early Christian and Pauline concept of τὸ εὐαγγέλιον. The specific references by Paul in Romans (e.g., 1:1, 3–4; 16:25ff) without further clarification indicate that εὐαγγέλιον was a familiar term and concept in the Roman church a decade before Mark composed his Gospel. Mark followed the basic outline and content of the kerygma, expanding and illustrating central tenets with traditions from Jesus' ministry.[45] Indeed, the basic difference between Paul's and Mark's expressions of τὸ εὐαγγέλιον was that Mark committed himself to the use of prior Jesus traditions, including accounts of Jesus' early ministry, to proclaim the kerygma, whereas Paul composed freely his understanding of central tenets of the kerygma, focusing primarily on the cross-resurrection event and motif.[46]

Mark, like Paul, also appropriated the earlier conviction that the Gospel transcends conceptual content. It contains divine power to effect change, action, and aid within the community. Mark also sharpened the locus of authority of the kerygma-Gospel, locating its power in the Holy Spirit who empowered Jesus' preaching (word and deed) and who continued to address the reader and church through the Markan Gospel.

Mark's Gospel was unique in form and specific content, but it was in continuity with the accepted basic concept of Gospel in his Roman provenance and church. With respect to the meaning of τὸ εὐαγγέλιον, the lines of correspondence between Paul and Mark converge. Marxsen correctly states the relationship in affirming that "Paul's understanding is the presupposition for Mark's, though we need not assume direct dependence."[47] Koester[48] and Fitzmyer concur, the latter contending that "Paul's use of εὐαγγέλιον . . . may have been the presupposition of the Marcan introduction of the term into his account of what Jesus did and said."[49]

A related parallel is found in Paul's and Mark's use of λόγος to designate the Gospel. The term ὁ λόγος is equivalent to τὸ εὐαγγέλιον in 1 Cor 14:36; 2 Cor 2:17, 4:2; 1 Thes 1:6, 8, 2:13;

Gal 6:6. In Romans, Paul prefers τὸ ῥῆμα (10:8) instead of ὁ λόγος to refer to the Gospel, but there is no significant difference between the two terms in this context.[50] In Mark the word λόγος occurs 15 times in the singular as a designation for the Gospel. Eight references appear in 4:13–20. As Kee observes, "It is obvious that by the time Mark writes his Gospel, the term λόγος includes the fuller Christian message of both kingdom and passion."[51]

The parallels between Paul and Mark in their uses of εὐαγγέλιον and λόγος are striking. They were the first Christian writers to our knowledge to use εὐαγγέλιον in the absolute, and they did so in a manner that assumed general understanding by their readers. The church at Rome emerges as the likely bridge that conveyed this common understanding of εὐαγγέλιον to Mark for his unique form of proclamation.

"Spirit" in Paul and Mark

Another line of correspondence between Paul and Mark via the bridge of Rome may be seen in their similar views concerning the nature and work of the Holy Spirit in relationship to Gospel. In the preserved authentic tradition, Jesus himself did not speak extensively of the nature and work of the Holy Spirit, though it is clear that he launched his ministry with the conviction that he was endowed with the power of the Spirit of God. His authority in teaching and in performing mighty works, his exorcisms and his proclamation of the advent of the kingdom—all testify to his awareness of the Spirit empowering him for ministry. Indeed, Windisch may be correct in postulating that our present Synoptic tradition has suppressed the pneumatic element to some extent.[52] Indeed, Mark likely contributed to the suppression in order that the Gospel would not be misunderstood improperly in his community as an account of pneumatic signs and wonders. However, in the period before Mark, proceeding from the time when the church came to view itself as the eschatological, Spirit-filled community (cf. Acts 2) in fulfillment of OT prophecy, theological reflection upon the work of the Holy Spirit became greatly intensified. Beasley-Murray comments pertinently:

> The appreciation of the relation of Jesus to the Spirit affords a bridge between Jesus and the post-resurrection community of his followers. Whatever our views about the narrative of the Pentecostal effusion of Acts 2, it is indisputable that the earliest communities of the risen Lord were charismatic groups... assured that they possessed the Spirit of the new age, and in due time they called that Spirit not only the Spirit of God, but the Spirit of Christ, and even the Spirit of Jesus (Acts 16, 7).[53]

By the era of Paul and Mark the nature and role of the Spirit had been extensively developed and appropriated by the church at large. Indeed, Scott affirms, "It was cardinal to the life and thought of the church everywhere, and no Christian, however ignorant or conservative, can have left it wholly out of account."[54] Of especial interest for our topic is the correspondence between Paul's view of the Spirit in Romans and Mark's portrayal.

Paul explicitly reflects the view that to experience the Spirit is to experience Jesus himself. Jesus Christ is present in the church's life in the form of the Holy Spirit. Moule and Ellis are probably correct in holding that in 1 Cor 3:16f the Spirit refers to God and that in 2 Cor 3:17f the Lord (κύριος) refers to Yahweh, though christological connotations are close at hand.[55] However, in Rom 8:9–11 (cf. 1 Cor 15:45) the apostle clearly identifies the Risen Christ with the divine life-giving Spirit. Indeed, θέος, κύριος, and πνεῦμα appear together as virtually interchangeable titles. Dunn may well be right in stressing that Paul is speaking in terms of his experience, not in ontological terms. "But so far as the religious experience of Christians is concerned Jesus and the Spirit are no different. The risen Jesus may not be experienced independently of the Spirit."[56] Even if a metaphysical identity is not asserted, for all practical purposes the Risen Jesus/Christ is linked with the presence and power of the Holy Spirit. This indissoluble relationship proclaimed by Paul typified the view held by the Roman church in the period preceding Mark's composition. Although Mark did not contribute significantly to that theological issue and clarification, he reflects familiarity with the (Pauline) concept of functional identity between Jesus and the Spirit. He assumes that his readers also hold this view. But his interest is directed elsewhere, towards instruction of members of his community who were not aware of the full scope and authority of the Gospel as the medium of the Spirit for the empowerment of the church.

"Spirit and Gospel" in Paul and Mark

Paul's conflict with ecstatic pneumatics in Corinth over abuse of spiritual gifts affords insight into the manner in which he linked Spirit and Gospel as a corrective to a serious theological aberration. D. Georgi has argued persuasively that the pneumatic "false prophets" whom Paul opposed in Corinth were "Christian missionaries who had adopted the patterns of Hellenized Jewish propaganda; . . . in powerful miracles and spiritual performances they demonstrated that the *christus praesens* transcended the limitations of human life."[57] Less convincing is Georgi's contention that Paul's opponents in 2 Corinthians regarded themselves as "divine men" who proclaimed a "divine man" Christology.[58] As we have seen, the concept of a "divine man" was extremely vague and tenuous in the first century. It is not necessary for our purposes to resolve the thorny problem of the origin and source(s) of their Christology and theology. It is clear that Paul denounced these arrogant "false prophets" because, in addition to challenging Paul's apostleship and favoring libertine practices, they were perverting the gifts of the Spirit under the guise of proclaiming another Jesus, another Spirit, another gospel (2 Cor 11:4). How did Paul seek to counteract the influence of these heretical ecstatics? He pulled all the rank he could muster and appealed to the following authorities as the basis of his own authority and the validity of his Gospel:[59] (1) apostolic authority due founders of the church (1 Cor 9:1–6; 12:28); (2) apostolic authority due to personal commissioning by the Risen Christ (1 Cor 15:8ff); (3) the authority inherent within the kerygma of Gospel itself (cf. 1 Cor 9:12, 14, 16, 23; 15:1f). What constitutes the continuing authority of the Gospel? The Risen Christ who manifests and makes himself known through the Gospel (1 Cor 4:1, 2 Cor 2:14; 4:4ff) in the unity of the Spirit (1 Cor 12:4–6; 15:45). Indeed, Ellis points out that it was the proclamation of a fleshly wisdom, a wisdom of this age (1 Cor 1:20; 3:18f; cf. 2 Cor 1:12) by false prophets that "caused Paul to underscore the unity of the Spirit with the exalted Christ specifically with reference to the prophetic gift of inspired speech and discernment."[60] The true prophet speaks under the inspiration of Christ/Holy Spirit, and his speech will conform to the tenets of the kerygma.[61]

This inspired, authoritative Gospel in accord with kerygmatic tradition provided a norm for the testing of charismatic interpretations and proclamations. Because the preaching of the "false prophets" deviated from the kerygma with its stress on the cross and resurrection of Christ, it was by definition rendered invalid: indeed, so far removed from the kerygma was this "gospel" that Paul declared that their preaching pertained to another Jesus, another Spirit, another gospel—in fact, constituted no gospel at all (cf. Gal 1:7).

This same understanding of the unity of Christ/Spirit/Gospel was also expressed by Paul in Romans, evidently with the assumption that his concept of "Spirit and Gospel" would be intelligible and acceptable to his Roman readers. Before proceeding with this line of investigation, we note first G. Klein's observation that there are two major contemporary interpretations of Paul's orientation in Romans, "those which argue that Paul is primarily occupied with his own concerns and those which argue that Paul is primarily occupied with the concerns of the Roman church."[62] In agreement with the multimethodological approach and conclusion of K. Donfried, we maintain that Romans is best understood from the latter perspective.[63] Moreover, we concur with Donfried that Romans 16 is an integral part of the original letter. Though the textual evidence is inconclusive, the editorial committee of the United Bible Societies' *Greek New Testament* retained the traditional location of chapter 16 at the end of chapter 15 "on the basis of good and diversified evidence" supporting the sequence of 1:1–16:23 and the doxology.[64] "The burden of proof rests with those who would wish to argue the contrary."[65]

Perhaps the strongest objection against the integrity of Romans 16 is the claim that Paul would not have known some 26 persons by name (non-Jewish primarily) in Rome in a church that he had never visited. However, if Paul were addressing specific problems in Rome, such as a crisis occasioned in the Gentile church by the return in AD 54 of Jews and Jewish Christians after the relaxation of Claudius' edict issued in AD 49,[66] one would expect the apostle to marshal all the support available in Rome by listing persons he had met throughout the course of his lengthy ministry.[67] In response to the supposed difficulty arising from the non-Jewish names, H. Leon established in his study the high probability that the names in Romans 16 belonged to Roman Jews since the Jews often acquired Greek, Latin, and Egyptian appellations.[68]

This approach to Romans is consistent with the analyses by Dunn, Bruce, and Drane concerning the situation of the Roman church. Bruce and Drane find evidence of several house-churches addressed in chapter 16.[69] According to Drane's analysis[70] of the synagogue-church relationships in Rome, these house-churches faced internal and external problems which are reflected in the body of the letter. Romans 16:17–19 discloses that the church contended with dissension created by deceitful persons who opposed the Pauline teaching (διδαχή). They are described in terms similar to those used in 2 Corinthians 11. Ellis suggests that they may have been pneumatics who promoted a wrong kind of "wisdom" and boasted of visions and revelations.[71] Such references are not confined to Romans 16. Throughout the letter Paul implicitly and explicitly cautions the church to beware of a contentious faction that exhibited attitudes and values similar to those held by the Corinthian pneumatic ecstatics (cf. Rom 6:1 and 1 Cor 5:6; Rom 13:13 and 1 Cor 11:17–22; Rom 14:1–15:6 and 1 Cor 8, 10:23–33; Rom 16:17f; and 1 Cor 1–4).[72] Though the abuse of spiritual gifts and emphasis on immediate revelation do not seem to have been as pronounced in Rome as in Corinth, in germ the same unbalanced teaching appears to have been present. Dunn notes in particular Rom 6:4f, "where Paul deliberately refrains from stating that believers already participate in the resurrection of Christ."[73] Instead, he regards this participation as a future event. This stance was likely "occasioned by the danger, real or suspected, of a gnostic or enthusiastic view of the resurrection such as we find in I Cor. 15.12."[74] While the meager evidence in Romans does not allow a positive identification of the disruptive element, the tenor of Paul's counsel points toward the presence of a faction that emphasized inspiration and *charismata* in ways detrimental to the church's unity.

Paul, aware of a potentially schismatic ecstaticism in Rome, asserted his apostolic authority and addressed the issue by expressing his own understanding of central tenets of the Gospel. On the other hand, Mark, facing a similar challenge at a later date, was obligated to take a different literary tack and form: he simply omitted descriptions of resurrection appearances and delivered only the momentous announcement that the reapproachment with the Risen Christ was assured. For disciples who identified with both Jesus' crucifixion and his resurrection, that is, hearers and readers who responded to the true Gospel, the presence of the Risen Christ was a continuing reality. Both Paul and Mark appealed to the Spirit as the authenticator and quickener of the Gospel (cf. Rom 1:16–17; 16:25f).

ENDNOTES

CHAPTER 5: ROME—A BRIDGE BETWEEN PAUL AND MARK

1. Eusebius, *H.E.* 3.39.15.
2. See the discussion in Taylor, *The Gospel According to St. Mark*, pp. 3–4.
3. Justin, *Dial.* 106, 3.
4. Irenaeus, *Adv. Haer.* 3.1.1.
5. Clement, *Hypotyposeis* 6, in Eusebius, *H.E.* 2.1.3f.
6. Eusebius, *H.E.* 6.25.5.
7. Cf. Eusebius, *Werke* vii, GCS 47, upon which the work is dependent.
8. M. Hengel, *Studies in the Gospel of Mark* (Philadelphia: Fortress Press, 1985), pp. 2–6, 47–53. Cf. Bacon, *Is Mark A Roman Gospel?*, pp. 20–21.
9. Bacon, *Is Mark A Roman Gospel?*, pp. 20–21.
10. Kingsbury, *Jesus Christ in Matthew, Mark, and Luke*, p. 56.
11. Earlier, J. Wellhausen, *Einleitung in die drei ersten Evangelien*

(Berlin: Georg Reimer, 1911), pp. 41, 78, suggested Jerusalem as the place of an original Aramaic composition, and J. V. Bartlet, *St. Mark* (New York: H. Frowde, Oxford Univ. Press, 1922), pp. 36–37, supported Antioch as the provenance. W. C. Allen, *The Gospel According to St. Mark* (New York: Macmillan Co., 1915), claimed that the Gospel was originally written in Aramaic in Jerusalem and later translated into Greek at Antioch. These theories have been discredited by later scholarship.

12. Hengel, *Studies in the Gospel of Mark*, p. 47.
13. Ibid., p. 150, n. 56.
14. So also W. Bauer, *Orthodoxy and Heresy in Earliest Christianity* (Philadelphia: Fortress Press, 1971), p. 107. The debate over the meaning of ἑρμηνευτής is not as important in exploring the provenance as assessing the extent and validity of the Papias tradition.
15. In Eusebius, *H.E.* 3.39.17.
16. Argued by Zahn, *Einleitung in das Neue Testament*, pp. 19f, 214f, and more recently by W. R. Farmer, *Jesus and the Gospel* (Philadelphia: Fortress Press, 1982), p. 160, though he raises the possibility that a tradition existed that "the Gospel of Mark was written by an associate of Peter." Best, *Mark: The Gospel as Story*, p. 25, is skeptical of the connection in Rome in the Papias tradition, but grants that "there is probably some relation between Peter and the Gospel."
17. See the insight and discussion by Hengel, *Studies in the Gospel of Mark*, pp. 81–84.
18. Best, *Mark: The Gospel as Story*, p. 26.
19. Hengel, *Studies in the Gospel of Mark*, p. 155, n. 71.
20. Ibid., pp. 5–6.
21. Ibid., pp. 6, 117–118 (n.9).
22. Rohde, *Rediscovering the Teaching of the Evangelists*, p. 138, n. 50.
23. Cited in Bacon, *Is Mark a Roman Gospel?* pp. 53–54.
24. Hengel, *Studies in the Gospel of Mark*, p. 29.
25. Ibid., pp. 50–53, 59–63, notes the following statistical points.
26. Martin, *Mark: Evangelist and Theologian*, p. 69.
27. Kee, *Community of the New Age*, p. 105. See Ch. 4 for a full description of the social and cultural traits to which Kee finds allusions in the Gospel.
28. Marxsen, *Mark the Evangelist*, p. 107, who cites the reference to the flight in Eusebius, *H.E.* 3.5.3.
29. Cf. F. Neirynck, *Evangelica*, BETL 60 (1982), pp. 566ff, 597, for a discussion of the location of Pella and the historical accuracy of the note in Eusebius, *H.E.* 3.5.3.
30. Martin, *Mark: Evangelist and Theologian*, p. 72.
31. Kelber, *The Kingdom in Mark*, p. 129.
32. Ibid.
33. Ibid., p. 133.
34. Ibid., pp. 132–147.
35. Hengel, *Studies in the Gospel of Mark*, pp. 156–157, n. 76.
36. Ibid., p. 41.
37. Ibid., p. 28.
38. Ibid., p. 25.
39. Werner, *Der Einfluss paulinischer Theologie im Markusevangelium*,

passim.
    40. G. Friedrich, "εὐαγγέλιον," TDNT (1964), 2:727, supplies these statistics.
    41. Ibid., p. 725.
    42. Ibid., p. 726.
    43. Cf. Schulz, Die Stunde der Botschaft, p. 34. who argues that "lange bevor Paulus Christ wurde, ist im frühen Christentum Syriens 'Evangelium' der Inbegriff für die christliche Botschaft überhaupt geworden."
    44. Friedrich, "εὐαγγέλιον," p. 724. Schweizer, The Good News According to Mark, p. 30 also views this concept impacting the church's understanding of gospel.
    45. Cf. Lightfoot, The Gospel Message of St. Mark, p. 20. See the discussion above in Ch. I.
    46. Reploh, Markus-Lehrer der Gemeinde, p. 19, correctly stresses Mark's expansion of kerygmatic material beyond the cross and resurrection: "Auch das Leben Jesu gehört zum εὐαγγέλιον, zur Botschaft vom Heil."
    47. Marxsen, Mark the Evangelist, p. 147.
    48. H. Koester, "One Jesus and Four Primitive Gospels," Trajectories Through Early Christianity, eds. J. Robinson and H. Koester (Philadelphia: Fortress Press, 1971), p. 161, states, "Mark's basic concept of the Gospel is Pauline...."
    49. J. A. Fitzmyer, To Advance the Gospel: New Testament Studies (New York: Crossroad, 1981), p. 159. Kelber, The Oral and the Written Gospel, pp. 213–214, as we noted above, stresses the lack of continuity between the oral Pauline Gospel and the written Markan Gospel, but he overlooks the fact that Paul also wrote and the probability that Mark's Gospel was heard.
    50. Cf. W. Bauer, A Greek-English Lexicon of the New Testament and Other Early Christian Literature, ed. and transl. by W. F. Arndt, F. W. Gingrich, and F. Danker (Chicago: Univ. of Chicago Press, 1979, 2nd rev. ed.), pp. 479, 735.
    51. Kee, Community of the New Age, p. 164. Weeden, Mark—Traditions in Conflict, pp. 150–151, cites J. Schreiber and T. A. Burkill as advocates of this position, though Weeden's opinion is that ὁ λόγος is Mark's opponents' term for their secret gospel.
    52. H. Windisch, "Jesus und der Geist nach synoptischer Überlieferung," Studies in Early Christianity, p. 231f; cited in Dunn, Jesus and the Spirit, p. 88.
    53. Beasley-Murray, Jesus and the Future, p. 478.
    54. Scott, The Spirit in the New Testament, p. 151.
    55. E. E. Ellis, "Christ and Spirit in I Corinthians," Christ and the Spirit in the New Testament, eds. B. Lindars and S. Smalley (Cambridge: University Press, 1973), p. 273, citing C. F. D. Moule, "2 Cor. 3:18b," Neues Testament und Geschichte (Tübingen, 1972), pp. 235f; against Dunn, Jesus and the Spirit, pp. 320–21, who only states that "the experienced Spirit is seen in terms of Jesus."
    56. Dunn, Jesus and the Spirit, p. 323.
    57. Cited in H. Koester, "One Jesus and Four Primitive Gospels," HTR 61 (1968): 233–34.
    58. Georgi, Die Gegner des Paulus im 2. Korintherbrief, pp. 210, 213–216.
    59. Cf. Dunn, Jesus and the Spirit, pp. 271–80.

60. Ellis, "Christ and Spirit in I Corinthians," p. 275.

61. Kelber, *The Oral and the Written Gospel*, pp. 144–45, 157–58, correctly perceives that Paul reconnected "the Spirit of the Living God/Christ with Word" (2 Cor 3:1–6; cf. 1 Cor 2:4, 13; 1 Thes 1:5), but his acute distinction between the written word (*gramma*) and the oral word (*pneuma*) is unconvincing.

62. K. P. Donfried, ed., *The Romans Debate* (Minneapolis: Augsburg Publishing House, 1977), p. xiii.

63. Donfried, "False Presuppositions in the Study of Romans," *The Romans Debate*, pp. 120–122, who draws upon P. Minear, W. Marxsen, and W. Wiefel for support in opposition to T. W. Manson, G. Bornkamm, and R. J. Karris, who represent the "non-historical" view.

64. Ibid., p. 122.

65. B. M. Metzger, *A Textual Commentary on the Greek New Testament* (New York: United Bible Societies, 1971), p. 536.

66. W. Marxsen, *Introduction to the New Testament* (Philadelphia, Fortress Press, 1970), pp. 99–104.

67. Donfried, "A Short Note on Romans 16," *The Romans Debate*, p. 58.

68. Ibid., pp. 55–56.

69. F. F. Bruce, *Paul: Apostle of the Heart Set Free* (Grand Rapids: Eerdmans, 1977), pp. 384–385. Drane, "Why Did Paul Write Romans," p. 217; cf. ch. 3 above.

70. Ibid.

71. Ellis, *Prophecy and Hermeneutic*, p. 109.

72. Cf. Dunn, *Jesus and the Spirit*, p. 268.

73. Ibid., p. 261.

74. Ibid.

—SUMMARY—

"SPIRIT AND GOSPEL" IN MARK

Our investigation and exegesis has established that the dual theological motif of "Spirit and Gospel" occupies a prominent role in Mark's unique presentation. The internal evidence indicates that Mark composed a new genre called "Gospel" that was based on traditions derived from Jesus' preaching of the gospel of the kingdom. The evangelist redacted and re-presented this material as the medium through which the Risen Christ in the form of the Spirit continued to address and to aid the Markan community. Mark had neither the material nor the inclination to clarify the precise relationship between the Risen Christ and the Holy Spirit. He did not contemplate or speculate about the ontological relationship that later occupied the church's attention. Rather, he assumed a functional unity on the basis of the church's experience and theological consensus. Mark's concern was more practical than theoretical. He was disturbed about a developing obsession with *charismata* in his community, notably "signs and wonders," accompanying a truncated gospel proclaimed by false prophets. These ecstatics exulted in immediate revelation attributed to the Risen Christ/Holy Spirit and neglected the teaching and deeds of the earthly Jesus. Evidently these self-styled prophets were gaining recognition and a following in the community. Mark believed that their deficient gospel and theology constituted a vital danger to the church, its unity and its survival. The saving act of God in Jesus Christ, climaxed in the cross-resurrection, and the accompanying call to obedient, sacrificial discipleship were being virtually ignored by these false prophets. Mark recognized that the suffering, reconciling mission of the historical Jesus was integral to the Gospel and its continuing power and relevance for the church. The mediation of the Spirit for the survival of the community was contingent upon its acceptance of the whole Gospel, not an abridged version. Hence, he composed a work that included the motifs of suffering and discipleship without negating the miraculous and revelatory aspects. By utilizing the traditions derived from and attributed to the historical Jesus, Mark shifted the locus and norm of authority for the church's belief and practice from current prophetic leaders to the Gospel empowered by Jesus/Risen Christ/Holy Spirit.

Apparently the theological and relational tensions between Mark and the "false prophets" had not yet resulted in hostile conflict and open schism. Mark still regarded these persons as part of the community who needed instruction in the fullness of the Gospel. Thereby, he sought to overcome a potentially divisive element and to restore and to preserve unity within the church. A unified church, instructed and strengthened by the Spirit of Christ through a quickened Gospel which served as a norm and basis for the faith and hope of the community, provided a strong defense against the assaults of external foes, both Jews and Romans. The ingenious way in which Mark structured traditions and motifs into a unified Gospel was vital to the accomplishment of his purpose. As we have shown, his explicit and indirect redactional references to the Holy Spirit demonstrate that Mark regarded the Spirit to be inseparably related to the Gospel for the empowerment and survival of the church.

ROME—A BRIDGE BETWEEN PAUL AND MARK

Our lines of investigation converge in support of the conclusion that Rome was the provenance for the composition of Mark's Gospel in the late 60s.

(1) The external evidence provided by Papias and the church fathers affords a valid, unbroken testimony to Rome, in spite of recent attempts to negate or to minimize the witness.

(2) The association of a non-apostolic Gospel with Rome, an influential church center, offers the most plausible explanation for the undisputed inclusion of the Gospel in the canon.

The internal evidence in the Gospel, e.g., Latinisms, the prominence of Peter, the persecution motif and the apocalyptic discourse, accords with a Roman context more closely than with any alternative site suggested by current scholars (e.g., Galilee, Syria, Jerusalem).

(3) Paul's letters, especially Romans, reflects a church *Sitz* that corresponds remarkably to the socio-theological context portrayed

in Mark's Gospel. Both writers establish the Gospel (εὐαγγέλιον) as the authoritative norm for the church's belief, practice, and existence against all adversaries—internal faction occasioned by the preaching of ecstatic false prophets and external oppression from the synagogue and the state. Both authors appeal to the unity of Jesus/Christ/Spirit as the empowerer of Gospel to fortify and to guide the church in facing persecution and heresy.

These lines of convergence via the bridge of Rome further buttress the motif of "Spirit and Gospel" as a permeating theological theme in the Gospel of Mark. Mark wrote with intentionality to a church beset with the same challenges and problems addressed earlier by Paul. Their mutually supportive witness affords new insight into the substantiation of the sociological and theological context of the church at Rome in the 50s and 60s. Each author approached his literary task with the distinctive form demanded by the situation. Each in his own way proclaimed "Gospel and Spirit" as the ultimate authority for the survival and triumph of the church. Hence, the linkage via the bridge of Rome of Pauline and Markan theological motifs and sociological contexts lends support to our conclusion: "Spirit and Gospel" constitutes a central motif in Mark's theology and unique composition.

—EPILOGUE—

MARK'S GOSPEL AND
THE CONTEMPORARY CHURCH

By virtue of its form or genre and its content and intent, Mark's Gospel remains relevant to the contemporary church. Mark artfully ordered traditions stemming from the Jesus of history into a new, dual presentation of Gospel. Through the authoritative Jesus-traditions, the Risen Jesus, now present in the Spirit, continued to address the church, affording instruction and encouragement. Receptive readers still experienced the power and guidance of Jesus as the Risen Christ in the reading and preaching of the Gospel.

Time has not altered the efficacy of the Gospel. From and through it, the church continues to hear the correcting and assuring Word of Jesus Christ. Although the church no longer suffers from persecution and oppression by the Roman State and the Jewish Synagogue, religious oppression and political persecution have not vanished from the earth. Characteristic of the Greek god Zeus, they have only changed in form and have returned in new guises to afflict the community of faith. To oppressed disciples in every age and area the Gospel speaks with divine authority: This is my beloved Son; hear ye him! . . . He is going before you to Galilee; there you will see him . . . (Mk 1:11; 9:7; 16:8). Thereby, the church receives courage and aid to persevere in hope against every adversary in anticipation of eventual triumph. For almost two thousand years the church has met every challenge and survived every crisis. Today she continues to proclaim and to model her mission of discipleship through the empowerment of Spirit and Gospel.

Consistent with Mark's original purpose, his work remains relevant for the Christian community by serving as a norm for the complete, correct formulation of Gospel. In this age of religious pluralism with a multiplicity of beliefs and emphases, Mark's Gospel stands as a standard for central truths and practices that should characterize the church. In many congregations attention is focused on a narrow range of religious beliefs and practices that are proclaimed repeatedly. The result is that the congregation hears and adheres only to a truncated Gospel and tends to ignore and to lose the fullness of Gospel that is needed to sustain the community for the totality of life's experiences, including hardships, suffering, and death.

The danger of relying upon an abridged Gospel and unbalanced theology is illustrated by the deficiencies in worship and/or ethics in both traditional denominational churches and independent charismatic churches. Often the former allow little opportunity for the Spirit to move with power in the worship and lives of the people. The emphasis is upon structure and order, frequently resulting in rigidity. Often the latter know little of a discipleship of suffering in faithfulness to Christ and in service to humanity. The emphasis is upon praise in worship, frequently resulting in subjectivism. To each extreme Mark's Gospel offers a corrective and an alternative theological perspective. The Gospel contains in paradoxical union both the divinity and the humanity of Jesus, his glory and his suffering, his bestowal of authority and power and his command to obedience and service, his promise of eternal reward and his assumption of earthly evil, culminating in his acceptance of the cross and his assurance of the resurrection. Preaching, worship, and ethics based on anything less are not truly Gospel but a perversion that may lead to heresy and endanger the very life and future of the community. Thus, Mark's Gospel constitutes a valid norm for the church's belief and practice and guards against aberration and disunity. Through it the Risen Christ addresses the divided church and says, "Repent and believe in the Gospel. . . . come, follow me" (Mk 1:15, 17).

Although examples of the contemporary relevance of Mark's Gospel could be multiplied manifold, one additional instance will suffice: Mark's contribution to the controversial issue of the coming of the Eschaton. In many churches (and among churches) a polarization has developed between members who adhere fervently to imminent apocalyptic expectations and those who reject such views as outmoded. Does not Mark's Gospel offer a viable, mediating alternative perspective? Mark included in his work an apocalyptic discourse (ch. 13) attributed to Jesus, thereby affirming that belief in this future event was a valid aspect of Gospel. Though commentators and church laity may disagree about the nature and function of the language—literal or symbolic—the account expresses a firm hope in the coming of the Eschaton and the final decisive victory of

God. However, it is equally clear that Mark was disturbed by the insistence of some persons in the community that this climactic event was imminent and soon would be manifested. Quite likely this view was accompanied by the declaration that the Eschaton would come in its fullness before the Roman church was subjected to direct persecution.

Against this erroneous teaching Mark proclaimed that amid wars and rumors of wars, "the end is not yet" (13:7), that the upheavals to be experienced are "but the beginning of the sufferings" (13:8), that "the gospel must first be preached to all nations" (13:10), that no one knows the day or hour of the end, "not even the Son, but only the Father" (13:32). Hence, the community is enjoined to watch in faithful discipleship in adherence to the true, complete Gospel until the End comes. The Gospel does not promise the disciple or church escape from calamity and persecution, but rather the presence and power of the Risen Christ/Holy Spirit to cope and to endure until the Eschaton comes. This is the triumphant realism of the Gospel that deserves to be heard anew in many churches today.

BIBLIOGRAPHY

Achtemeier, Paul J. "He Taught Them Many Things: Reflections on Marcan Christology." *CBQ* 42 (1980): 465–481.
———. "Mark as Interpreter of the Jesus Traditions." *Int* 32 (1978): 339–352.
———. "Towards the Isolation of Pre-Marcan Miracle Catenae." *JBL* 89 (1970): 265–291.
Allen, W. C. *The Gospel According to St. Mark.* New York: Macmillan Co., 1915.
Anderson, Hugh. "The Easter Witness of the Evangelists," *The New Testament in Historical and Contemporary Perspective.* Eds. H. Anderson and W. Barclay. Oxford: Basil Blackwell, 1965.
———. *New Century Bible Commentary: The Gospel of Mark.* Grand Rapids: Eerdmans, 1976.
Aune, David E. "The Problem of the Messianic Secret," *NovT* 11 (1969): 1–31.
———. *Prophecy in Early Christianity and the Ancient Mediterranean World.* Grand Rapids: Eerdmans, 1983.
Bacon, B. W. *Is Mark a Roman Gospel?* Cambridge: Harvard University Press, 1919.
Barrett, C. K. *The Holy Spirit and the Gospel Tradition.* London: S.P.C.K., 1966.
———. "The Background of Mark 10:45," *New Testament Essays: Studies in Memory of T. W. Manson.* Ed. A. J. B. Higgins. Manchester: University Press, 1959.
Bartlet, J. V. *St. Mark.* New York: H. Frowde, Oxford University Press, 1922.
Bauer, W. *A Greek-English Lexicon of the New Testament and Other Early Christian Literature.* Ed. and transl. by W. F. Arndt, F. W. Gingrich and F. W. Danker. Chicago: University of Chicago Press, 2nd revised edition, 1979.
———. "The 'Colt' of Palm Sunday." *JBL* 72 (1953): 220–229.
———. *Orthodoxy and Heresy in Earliest Christianity,* Philadelphia: Fortress Press, 1971.
Beare, F. W. *The Earliest Records of Jesus.* Nashville: Abingdon Press, 1962.
———. "Sayings of the Risen Jesus in the Synoptic Tradition." *Christian*

History and Interpretation: Studies Presented to John Knox. Eds. W. R. Farmer, C. F. D. Moule and R. R. Niebuhr. Cambridge: University Press, 1967.

Beasley-Murray, G. R. *Commentary on Mark 13.* London: Macmillan, 1957.

————. *Jesus and the Future.* London: Macmillan, 1954.

————. "Jesus and the Spirit." *Mélanges Bibliques.* Ed. A. Descamps. Gembloux: Duculot, 1970.

————. "Second Thoughts on the Composition of Mark 13." *NTS* 29 (1983): 414–420.

Behm, J. "διαθήκη." *TDNT* (1964) 2:124–134.

Best, Ernest. *Following Jesus: Discipleship in the Gospel of Mark.* Sheffield: JSOT Press, 1981.

————. *Mark: The Gospel as Story.* Edinburgh: T. & T. Clark, 1983.

————. "Spirit-Baptism." *NovT* 4 (1960): 236–243.

————. *The Temptation and the Passion: The Marcan Soteriology.* Cambridge: Cambridge University Press, 1965.

Betz, H. D. "Jesus as Divine Man." *Jesus and the Historian.* Ed. T. Trotter. Philadelphia: Westminster Press, 1968.

Betz, Otto. "The So-Called 'Divine Man' in Mark's Christology." *Studies in New Testament and Early Christian Literature.* Ed. D. E. Aune. Leiden: E. J. Brill, 1972.

Bilezikian, G. G. *The Liberated Gospel: A Comparison of the Gospel of Mark and Greek Tragedy.* Grand Rapids: Baker, 1977.

Bird, C. H. "Some γάρ Clauses in St. Mark's Gospel." *JTS* 4 (1953): 171–187.

Birdsall, J. N. "Critique of W. R. Farmer, The Last Twelve Verses of Mark." Miracle Material." *JBL* 87 (1968): 409–417.

————. *Mysterious Revelation: An Examination of the Philosophy of St. Mark's Gospel.* Ithaca: Cornell University Press, 1963.

————. "Strain on the Secret: An Examination of Mark 11:1–13:37." *ZNW* 51 (1960): 31–46.

————. "The Notion of Miracle With Special Reference to St. Mark's Gospel." *ZNW* 50 (1959): 33–48.

Butler, B. C. *The Originality of St. Matthew.* Cambridge: University Press, 1951.

Carlston, C. E. "Transfiguration and Resurrection." *JBL* 80 (1961): 233–240.

Carrington, Philip. *The Primitive Christian Calendar: A Study in the Making of the Marcan Gospel.* London: Cambridge University Press, 1952.

Carroll, William D. "The Jesus of Mark's Gospel." *Bible Today* 103 (1979): 2105–2112.

Conzelmann, H. "Gegenwart und Zukunft in der Synoptischen Tradition." *ZTK* 54 (1957): 277–296.

Crossan, J. D. "Mark and the Relatives of Jesus." *NovT* 15 (1974): 81–113.

Cullmann, Oscar. *Christology of the New Testament.* Philadelphia: Westminster Press, 1963.

Dahl, Nils A. "Eschatology and History in the Light of the Dead Sea Scrolls." *The Future of Our Religious Past.* Ed. J. M. Robinson. New York: Harper & Row, 1971.

Danker, F. W. The Demonic Secret in Mark 15:34." *ZNW* 61–62 (1970–71): 48–69.

Delling, G. "βαπτισμα βαπτισθηναι." *NovT* 2 (1957): 92–115.

Dewey, Joanna. *Marcan Public Debate*. SBL Dissertation Series 48. Chico: Scholar's Press, 1980.

Dibelius, Martin. *Die urchristliche Überlieferung von Johannes dem Täufer.* Göttingen: Vandenhoeck & Ruprecht, 1911.

———. *From Tradition to Gospel*. New York: Charles Scribner's Sons, 1934.

Dinkler, E. "Petrusbekenntnis und Satanswort-Das Problem der Messianität Jesu." *Signum Crucis*. Ed. E. Dinkler. Tübingen: J. C. B. Mohr, 1967.

Dodd, C. H. "The Appearances of the Risen Christ: An Essay in Form-Criticism of the Gospels." *Studies in the Gospels*. Ed. D. E. Nineham. Oxford: Basil Blackwell, 1955.

———. "The Framework of the Gospel Narrative." *ET* 43 (June, 1932): 396–406; reprinted in *New Testament Studies*. Manchester: University Press, 1954.

Donahue, J. R. "Jesus as the Parable of God in the Gospel of Mark." *Int* 32 (1978): 369–386.

———. "Temple, Trial, and Royal Christology (Mark 14:53–65)." *The Passion in Mark: Studies on Mark 14–16*. Ed. W. H. Kelber. Philadelphia: Fortress, 1976.

Donfried, Karl P., ed. *The Romans Debate*. Minneapolis: Augsburg Publishing House, 1977.

Drane, John W. "Why Did Paul Write Romans?" Essay supplied privately by the author, Stirling University, 1984.

Dunn, J. D. G. *Baptism in the Holy Spirit*. Philadelphia: Westminster Press, 1970.

———. *Jesus and the Spirit*. London: SCM Press, 1975.

———. "Mark 2.1–3.6: A Bridge Between Jesus and Paul on the Question of the Law." *NTS* 30 (1984): 395–415.

———. "Spirit and Fire Baptism." *NovT* 14 (1972): 81–92.

Elliott-Binns, L. E. *Galilean Christianity*. Chicago: Alec R. Allenson, Inc., 1956.

Ellis, E. Earle. "Christ and Spirit in I Corinthians." *Christ and the Spirit in the New Testament*. Eds. B. Lindars and S. S. Smalley. Cambridge: University Press, 1973.

———. *Prophecy and Hermeneutic in Early Christianity*. Tübingen: J. C. B. Mohr, 1978.

Evans, C. A. "On the Vineyard Parables (Jes. 5; Mk. 12)." *Biblische Zeitschrift* 28 (1984): 82–86.

———. "The Function of Isaiah 6:9–10 in Mark and John." *NovT* 24 (1982): 124–138.

Evans, C. F. "I Will Go Before You Into Galilee." *JTS* 5 (1954): 3–18.

Farmer, William. *The Synoptic Problem: A Critical Analysis*. New York: Macmillan Co., 1964.

———. *Jesus and the Gospel*. Philadelphia: Fortress Press, 1982.

Farrar, Austin. *St. Matthew and St. Mark*. Westminster: Dacre Press, 1954.

———. *A Study in St. Mark*. Philadelphia: Westminster Press, 1951.

Fisher, Kathleen M., and Wahlde, Urban C. von. "The Miracles of Mark 4:35–5:43: Their Meaning and Function in the Gospel Framework." *Biblical Theology Bulletin* 2 (1981): 13–16.

Fitzmyer, J. A. "The Contribution of Qumran Aramaic to the Study of the

New Testament." *NTS* 20 (1973–74): 382–407.

―――. *To Advance the Gospel: New Testament Studies.* New York: Crossroad, 1981.

France, R. T. "Mark and the Teaching of Jesus." *Gospel Perspectives* I. Ed. R. T. France and D. Wenham. Sheffield: JSOT Press, 1980.

Freyne, S. *The Twelve: Disciples and Apostles.* London: Sheed and Ward, 1968.

Friedrich, Gerhard. "εὐαγγελίζομαι, εὐαγγέλιον, κτλ." *TDNT* (1964) 2:707–738.

Globe, A. "The Caesarean Omission of the Phrase 'Son of God' in Mark 1:1." *HTR* 75 (1982): 209–218.

Georgi, Dieter. *Die Gegner des Paulus im 2. Korintherbrief.* Neukirchen-Vluyn: Neukirchener Verlag, 1964.

Gould, E. P. *A Critical and Exegetical Commentary on the Gospel According to St. Mark, ICC.* New York: Scribners, 1905.

Goulder, M. D. *The Evangelist's Calendar.* London: S.P.C.K., 1978.

Grant, F. C. *The Gospels: The Origin and Their Growth.* New York: Harper and Brothers, 1957.

―――. *The Interpreter's Bible: The Gospel According to St. Mark,* 12 Vols. Nashville: Abingdon Press, 1951.

Grässer, E. *Das Problem der Parusieverzögerung in den synoptischen Evangelien und in der Apostelgeschichte,* Beihefte zur *ZNW* 22. Berlin: Alfred Töpelmann, 1960.

―――. "Jesus in Nazareth (Mark v:1–6a)." *NTS* 16 (1969): 1–23.

Guelich, Robert A. "The Beginning of the Gospel, Mark 1:1–15." *Biblical Research* 27 (1982): 5–15.

Hadas, M. L. and Smith, M. *Heroes and Gods: Spiritual Biographies in Antiquity.* New York: Harper & Row, 1965.

Hahn, Ferdinand. *Christologische Hoheitstitel: Ihre Geschichte im frühen Christentum.* Göttingen: Vandenhoeck & Ruprecht, 1963.

―――. *Mission in the New Testament.* Naperville: Alec R. Allenson, Inc., 1965.

Hamilton, N. Q. "Resurrection Tradition and the Composition of Mark." *JBL* 84 (1965): 415–421.

Hartmann, Lars. *Prophecy Interpreted.* Lund: CWK Gleerup, 1966.

Hauck, F. *Das Evangelium des Markus.* THNT. Leipzig: Deichert Verlag, 1931.

Hawthorne, G. F. "Christian Prophets and the Sayings of Jesus: Evidence and Criteria for." *SBL Seminar Papers,* Vol. 2. Missoula: Scholar's Press, 1975.

Hay, Lewis S. "The Son of God Christology in Mark." *JBR* 32 (1964): 106–114.

Hebert, G. "The Resurrection-Narrative in St. Mark's Gospel." *SJT* 15 (1962): 66–73.

Hengel, Martin. *The Charismatic Leader and His Followers.* Edinburgh: T. & T. Clark, 1981.

―――. *Studies in the Gospel of Mark.* Philadelphia: Fortress Press, 1985.

Hiers, Richard H. "Not the Season for Figs." *JBL* 87 (1968): 394–400.

Higgins, A. J. B. *Jesus and the Son of Man.* London: Lutterworth Press, 1964.

―――. "Son of Man—*Forschung* since 'The Teaching of Jesus.'" *New*

Testament Essays: Studies in Memory of T. W. Manson. Ed. A. J. B. Higgins. Manchester: University Press, 1959.

————. *The Son of Man in the Teaching of Jesus.* Cambridge: University Press, 1980.

Hill, David. *New Testament Prophecy.* London: Marshall, Morgan, and Scott, 1979.

Holladay, C. R. *Theios Aner in Hellenistic Judaism: A Critique of the Use of This Category in New Testament Christology.* SBL Dissertation Series 40. Missoula: Scholar's Press, 1977.

Holst, Robert. "Reexamining Mk. 3.28f. and Its Parallels." *ZNW* 63–64 (1972–73): 122–124.

Hooker, Morna D. *The Message of Mark.* London: Epworth Press, 1983.

————. *The Son of Man in Mark.* Montreal: McGill University Press, 1967.

Hughes, J. H. "John the Baptist: The Forerunner of God Himself." *NovT* 14 (1972): 191–218.

Iersel, B. M. F. van. *'Der Sohn' in den synoptischen Jesusworten.* Leiden: E. J. Brill, 1961.

————, and Linmans, A. J. M. "The Storm on the Lake, Mk. 4:35–41 and Mt. 8:18–27 in the Light of Form-Criticism, 'Redaktionsgeschichte' and Structural Analysis." *Miscellanea Neotestamentica.* Ed. T. Baarda, A. F. J. Klijn, and W. C. van Unnik. Leiden: E. J. Brill, 1978.

Jeremias, J. "Αδαμ." *TDNT* (1964) 1:141–143.

————. *Servant of God.* Naperville: Alec R. Allenson, 1957.

Johnson, E. S. "Mark viii. 22–26: The Blind Man from Bethesda." *NTS* 25 (1978–79): 370–383.

Johnson, Sherman. *The Gospel According to St. Mark.* New York: Harper and Brothers, 1960.

Juel, Donald. *Messiah and Temple: The Trial of Jesus in the Gospel of Mark.* SBL Dissertation Series 31. Missoula: Scholar's Press, 1977.

Kähler, Martin. *The So-Called Historical Jesus and the Historic, Biblical Christ.* Philadelphia: Fortress Press, 1964.

Käsemann, E. *Essays on New Testament Themes.* London: SCM Press, 1964.

Kazmierski, Carl R. *Jesus, the Son of God: A Study of the Markan Tradition and its Redaction by the Evangelist.* Forschung zur Bibel, Band No. 33. Wurzburg: Echter Verlag, 1979.

Keck, L. E. "Jesus in New Testament Christology." *Australian Biblical Review* 28 (1980): 2–21.

————. "Major Book Reviews: Mark and the Passion." *Int* 31 (1977): 332–334.

————. "Mark 3:7–12 and Mark's Christology." *JBL* 84 (1965): 341–358.

————. "The Introduction to Mark's Gospel." *NTS* 12 (1966): 352–370.

Kee, Howard C. *Community of the New Age: Studies in Mark's Gospel.* Philadelphia: Westminster Press, 1977.

————. *Jesus in History: An Approach to the Study of the Gospels.* New York: Harcourt Brace Jovanovich, 1977.

————. "Mark's Gospel in Recent Research." *Int* 32 (1978): 353–368.

Kelber, W. H. "Mark and Oral Tradition." *Semeia* 16 (1979): 7–56.

————. "Mark 14:32–42: Gethsemane." *ZNW* 63–64 (1972–73): 166–187.

————. *The Kingdom in Mark.* Philadelphia: Fortress Press, 1974.

————. *The Oral and the Written Gospel.* Philadelphia: Fortress Press, 1983.

————, ed. *The Passion in Mark: Studies on Mark 14–16.* Philadelphia: Fortress Press, 1976.

Kingsbury, Jack D. *Proclamation Commentaries: Jesus Christ in Matthew, Mark, and Luke.* Philadelphia: Fortress Press, 1981.

————. "The Divine Man as the Key to Mark's Christology—The End of an Era?" *Int* 35 (1981): 243–257.

Knigge, H. D. "The Meaning of Mark." *Int* 22 (1968): 53–70.

Knox, W. L. *Some Hellenistic Elements in Primitive Christianity.* London: H. Milford, 1944.

Koester, Helmut. "One Jesus and Four Primitive Gospels," *Trajectories Through Early Christianity.* Eds. James Robinson and Helmut Koester. Philadelphia: Fortress Press, 1971.

Kuby, Alfred. "Zur Konzeption des Markus-Evangeliums." *ZNW* 49 (1958): 52–64.

Kümmel, W. G. *Promise and Fulfillment.* Naperville: Alec R. Allenson, Inc., 1957.

Kysar, Robert. *John, the Maverick Gospel.* Atlanta: John Knox Press, 1976.

Lambrecht, J. *Die Redaktion der Markus-Apokalypse.* Rome: Päpstliches Bibelinstitut, 1967.

————. "The Christology of Mark." *Biblical Theology Bulletin* 3–4 (1973–74): 256–273.

————. "The Relatives of Jesus in Mark." *NovT* 16 (1974): 241–258.

Lampe, G. W. H. "The Holy Spirit in the Writings of St. Luke." *Studies in the Gospels.* Ed. D. E. Nineham. Oxford: Basil Blackwell, 1955.

Leder, H-G. "Sündenfallerzählung und Versuchungsgeschichte." *ZNW* 54 (1963): 182–216.

Leivestad, R. "Exit the Apocalyptic Son of Man." *NTS* 18 (1972): 243–267.

Lightfoot, R. H. *History and Interpretation in the Gospels.* New York: Harper and Brothers, 1934.

————. *The Gospel Message of St. Mark.* Oxford: University Press, 1950.

Lindeskog, G. "Das Rätsel des Menschensohnes." *Studia Theologica* 22 (1968): 149–175.

————. "The Veil of the Temple." *Coniectanea Neotestamentica* 11 (1947): 132–137.

Linnemann, Eta. *Gleichnisse Jesu: Einführung und Auslegung.* Göttingen: Vandenhoeck & Ruprecht, 1966.

————. *Studien zur Passionsgeschichte.* Göttingen: Vandenhoeck & Ruprecht, 1970.

Lohmeyer, E. *Das Evangelium des Markus.* Göttingen: Vandenhoeck & Ruprecht, 1959.

Manson, W. *Jesus and the Christian.* London: James Clarke & Co., 1967.

Marshall, I. H. *Luke: Historian and Theologian.* Grand Rapids: Zondervan, 1971.

————. "Son of God or Servant of Yahweh." *NTS* 15 (1968–69): 326–336.

Martin, R. P. *Mark: Evangelist and Theologian.* Grand Rapids: Zondervan, 1972.

Martitz, W. von. "υἱός, υἱοθεσία." *TDNT* (1972) 8:334–340.

Marxsen, Willi. *Mark the Evangelist.* Nashville: Abingdon Press, 1969.

————. *Introduction to the New Testament.* Philadelphia: Fortress Press, 1970.

Maurer, C. "Knecht Gottes und Sohn Gottes im Passionsbericht des Markusevangeliums." *ZTK* 50 (1953): 1–38.

Mauser, U. W. *Christ in the Wilderness.* Naperville: Alec R. Allenson, Inc., 1963.

Mead, Richard T. "The Healing of the Paralytic—A Unit?" *JBL* 80 (1961): 348–354.

Metzger, B. M. *A Textual Commentary on the Greek New Testament.* New York: United Bible Societies, 1971.

Meye, R. P. *Jesus and the Twelve.* Grand Rapids: Eerdmans, 1968.

————. "Messianic Secret and Messianic Didache in Mark's Gospel." *Oikonomia.* Ed. Felix Christ. Hamburg: Herbert Reich, 1967.

Montefiore, C. G. *The Synoptic Gospels.* London: Macmillan, 1927.

Moore, A. L. *The Parousia in the New Testament.* Leiden: E. J. Brill, 1966.

Moulder, W. J. "The O.T. Background and the Interpretation of Mark x.45." *NTS* 24 (1977): 120–127.

Müller, U. B. "Die christologische Absicht des Markusevangelium und die Verklärungsgeschichte." *ZNW* 64 (1973): 159–193.

Neirynck, F. *Duality in Mark: Contributions to the Study of the Marcan Redaction.* Leuven: University Press, 1972.

————. *Evangelica.* Betl 60, 1982.

Nineham, D. E. *The Gospel of St. Mark.* Baltimore: Penguin Books, 1963.

————. "The Order of Events in St. Mark's Gospel—An Examination of Dr. Dodd's Hypothesis." *Studies in the Gospels.* Ed. D. E. Nineham. Oxford: Basil Blackwell, 1955.

Oepke, A. "βάπτω, κτλ." *TDNT* (1964) 1:529–546.

Parker, Pierson. "A Second Look at *The Gospel Before Mark.*" *JBL* 100 (1981): 389–413.

————. *The Gospel Before Mark.* Chicago: University Press, 1953.

Perrin, Norman. "Mark XIV.62: The Product of a Christian Pesher Tradition?" *NTS* 12 (1966): 150–155.

————. "The Christology of Mark." *JR* 51 (1971): 173–187.

————. "The Creative Use of the Son of Man Traditions by Mark." *A Modern Pilgrimage in New Testament Christology.* Ed. N. Perrin. Philadelphia: Fortress Press, 1974.

Pesch, Rudolf. *Naherwartungen: Tradition und Redaktion in Mk. 13.* KBANT. Düsseldorf: Patmos-Verlag, 1968.

————. *Das Markusevangelium.* HTKNT. Band I, II. Freiburg: Herder, 1976–77.

Petersen, Norman. *Literary Criticism for New Testament Critics.* Philadelphia: Fortress Press, 1978.

————. "Point of View in Mark's Narrative." *Semeia* 12 (1978): 97–121.

Popkes, Wiard. *Christus Traditus.* Zurich: Zwingli Verlag, 1967.

Porter, J. R. "The Messiah in the Testament of Levi XVIII." *ET* 61 (1949): 90–91.

Räisänen, H. *Das "Messiasgeheimnis" im Markusevangeliums.* Helsinki: Länsi-Suomi, 1976.

Rawlinson, A. E. J. *St. Mark.* London: Methuen & Co., 1936.

Reploh, Karl-Georg. *Markus-Lehrer der Gemeinde.* Stuttgart: Verlag Katholisches Bibelwerk, 1969.

Reumann, John. "Mark 1:14–20." *Int* 32 (1978): 405–410.

Rhoads, D. and Michie D. *Mark as Story: An Introduction to the Narrative of a Gospel*. Philadelphia: Fortress Press, 1982.

Robbins, Vernon K. *Jesus the Teacher: A Socio-Rhetorical Interpretation of Mark*. Philadelphia: Fortress Press, 1984.

———. "Last Meal: Preparation, Betrayal, and Absence." *The Passion in Mark*. Ed. W. H. Kelber. Philadelphia: Fortress Press, 1976.

Robinson, J. A. T. "The Temptations." *Twelve New Testament Studies*. London: SCM Press, 1962.

Robinson, J. M. *The Problem of History in Mark*. London: SCM Press, 1957.

Robinson, W. H. *The Christian Experience of the Holy Spirit*. London: Nisbet and Co., 1928.

Rohde, Joachim. *Rediscovering the Teaching of the Evangelists*. London: SCM Press, 1968.

Schenke, L. *Der gekreuzigte Christus*. Stuttgarter Bibelstudien 69. Stuttgart: Katholisches Bibelwerk, 1974.

Schille, G. "Bemerkungen zur Formgeschichte des Evangeliums. Rahmen und Aufbau des Markus-Evangeliums." *NTS* 4 (1957–58): 1–24.

Schniewind, J. *Das Evangelium nach Markus*. NTD. Göttingen: Vandenhoeck & Ruprecht, 1960.

Schreiber, J. "Die Christologie des Markusevangeliums." *ZTK* 58 (1961): 154–183.

———. *Theologie des Vertrauens*. Hamburg: Furche-Verlag, 1967.

Schulz, S. *Die Stunde der Botschaft*. Hamburg: Furche-Verlag, 1967.

Schulze, A. W. "Der Heilige und die wilden Tiere." *ZNW* 46 (1955): 280–283.

Schweizer, Eduard. "Anmerkungen zur Theologie des Markus." *Neotestamentica et Patristica*. Supplement to NovT, Vol. 6. Stuttgart: Zwingli Verlag, 1963.

———. "υἱός." *TDNT* (1972) 8:354–357.

———. "Mark's Contribution to the Quest for the Historical Jesus." *NTS* 10 (1964): 421–432.

———. "πνεῦμα, κτλ." *TDNT* (1968) 6:389–455.

———. *The Good News According to Mark*. Atlanta: John Knox Press, 1970.

———. *The Holy Spirit*. Philadelphia: Fortress Press, 1980.

———. "The Portrayal of the Life of Faith in the Gospel of Mark." *Int* 32 (1978): 387–399.

Scott, E. F. *The Spirit in the New Testament*. London: Hodder and Stoughton, 1923.

Scroggs, R. "The Exaltation of the Spirit by Some Early Christians." *JBL* 84 (1965): 359–373.

Seitz, O. J. F. "Gospel Prologues: A Common Pattern." *JBL* 83 (1964): 262–268.

Shae, G. S. "The Question on the Authority of Jesus." *NovT* 16 (1974): 1–29.

Stein, R. H. "A Marcan Seam in Mc 1:21f." *ZNW* 61–62 (1970–71): 70–94.

———. "A Short Note on Mark XIV.28 and XVI.7." *NTS* 20 (1973–74): 445–452.

Stoldt, H. H. *History and Criticism of the Marcan Hypothesis*. Macon: Mercer University Press; Edinburgh: T. & T. Clark, 1980.

Streeter, B. H. *The Four Gospels: A Study of Origins.* London: Macmillan & Co., 1956.

Stuhlmacher, Peter. *Das paulinische Evangelium. I. Vorgeschichte.* Göttingen: Vandenhoeck & Ruprecht, 1968.

Swete, H. B. *The Holy Spirit in the New Testament.* London: Macmillan, 1909.

Talbert, C. H. *What is a Gospel? The Genre of the Canonical Gospels.* Philadelphia: Fortress Press, 1970.

Tannehill, R. C. "The Disciples in Mark: The Function of a Narrative Role." *JR* 57 (1977): 386–405.

————. "The Gospel of Mark as Narrative Christology." *Semeia* 16 (1979): 57–95.

Taylor, V. *Jesus and His Sacrifice.* London: Macmillan & Co., 1951.

————. *The Gospel According to Mark.* London: Macmillan & Co., 1959.

————. *The Names of Jesus.* London: Macmillan & Co., 1954.

————. "The Origin of the Marcan Passion Sayings." *NTS* 1 (1955): 159–167.

Theissen, Gerd. *The First Followers of Jesus: A Sociological Analysis of the Earliest Christianity.* London: SCM Press, 1978.

Tiede, D. L. *The Charismatic Figure as Miracle Worker.* SBL Dissertation Series 1. Missoula: Scholar's Press, 1972.

Tödt, H. E. *The Son of Man in the Synoptic Tradition.* Philadelphia: Westminster Press, 1965.

Torrey, C. C. *Documents of the Primitive Church.* New York: Harper and Brothers, 1941.

Trocmé, É. "Is There a Marcan Christology?" *Christ and the Spirit in the New Testament.* Ed. B. Lindars. Cambridge: University Press, 1973.

————. *The Formation of the Gospel According to Mark.* Philadelphia: Westminster Press, 1963.

Tuckett, C. *The Messianic Secret.* Philadelphia: Fortress Press, 1983.

Turner, C. H. "A Textual Commentary on Mark i." *JTS* 28 (1927): 145–158.

Tyson, J. B. "The Blindness of the Disciples in Mark." *JBL* 80 (1961): 261–268.

Vaganay, Léon. *Le problème synoptique: une hypothèse de travail.* Tournai: Desclée, 1954.

Vermes, G. *Jesus and the World of Judaism.* London: SCM Press, 1983.

Via, D. O. *Kerygma and Comedy in the New Testament: A Structuralist Approach to Hermeneutics.* Philadelphia: Fortress Press, 1975.

Vielhauer, Philipp. "Erwägungen zur Christologie des Markusevangeliums." *Zeit und Geschichte.* Ed. E. Dinkler. Tübingen: J. C. B. Mohr, 1964.

————. "Jesus und der Menschensohn." *Aufsätze zum Neuen Testament.* Ed. P. Vielhauer. Münschen: Chr. Kaiser Verlag, 1965.

Votaw, C. W. *The Gospels and Contemporary Biographies in the Graeco-Roman World.* Philadelphia: Fortress Press, 1970.

Weeden, T. J. *Mark—Traditions in Conflict.* Philadelphia: Fortress Press, 1971.

————. "The Heresy that Necessitated Mark's Gospel." *ZNW* 59 (1968): 145–158.

Weiss, Johannes. *Das älteste Evangelium.* Göttingen: Vandenhoeck & Ruprecht, 1903.

Wellhausen, Julius. *Einleitung in die drei ersten Evangelien.* Berlin: Georg Reimer, 1911.

Werner, Martin. *Der Einfluss paulinischer Theologie im Markusevangelium.* Giessen: Alfred Töpelmann, 1923.

Williams, J. G. "A Note on the 'Unforgiveable Sin' Logion." *NTS* 12 (1965): 75–77.

Williamson, Lamar (Jr.). *Interpretation: Mark.* Atlanta: John Knox Press, 1983.

————. "Mark 1:1–8." *Int* 32 (1978): 400–404.

Wilson, R. McL. *Gnosis and the New Testament.* Philadelphia: Fortress Press, 1968.

Winstanley, E. W. *Spirit in the New Testament.* Cambridge: University Press, 1908.

Wrede, W. *Das Messiasgeheimnis in den Evangelien.* Göttingen: Vandenhoeck & Ruprecht, 1963.

Yates, J. E. *The Spirit and the Kingdom.* London: S.P.C.K., 1963.

Zahn, Theodor. *Einleitung in das Neue Testament.* Leipzig: Deichert'sche Verlagsbuchh. Nachf., 1899.

Zimmerli, W., and Jeremias, J. *The Servant of God.* Naperville: Alec R. Allenson, Inc., 1957.

INDEX OF SCRIPTURE REFERENCES

OLD TESTAMENT

ANCIENT AUTHORS
AND SOURCES

INDEX OF AUTHORS